THE
TECHNIQUES OF LANGUAGE
TEACHING

The
Techniques of Language Teaching

F. L. BILLOWS

*Head of Department of Language Methods
Faculty of Education, Makere College,
University of East Africa*

LONGMAN

LONGMAN GROUP LIMITED
London

*Associated companies, branches and representatives
throughout the world*

© F. L. Billows 1961

*First published 1961
New impressions *1964; *1967; *1968; *1970;
February 1971

ISBN 0 582 52505 5

*Printed in Hong Kong by
Dai Nippon Printing Co (International) Ltd*

CONTENTS

projector; the epidiascope; maps, plans and charts
—Three-dimensional representation; dramatization, mime, etc.; puppetry; the sand-table; the
classroom window—Miscellaneous visual aids

ACKNOWLEDGMENT

WE are indebted to Professor J. B. Carroll for permission to quote material from *The Study of Language*, published by the Harvard University Press.

INTRODUCTION

THIS is the book of a practising teacher who has had opportunity to see the work of a great many other teachers and has been engaged in training teachers for some years. It is not written from the point of view of the linguist nor of the psychologist, though as many of the findings of the psychologist and the linguist as can come within the reach of a busy adviser of teachers have been taken into account. Nothing here is based on theoretical considerations alone; everything has been tried, and most of it has been evolved in the classroom. I hope that my interpretation of what I have found in the books is correct, but I have used them primarily to explain phenomena encountered in the classroom, not to initiate policy.

Some teachers concern themselves a great deal with the arrangement of the material which they wish to teach, and this is certainly important, but of limited value if they do not also concern themselves with the minds that are to receive the material. I have preferred to combine concern with material and mind by working, always experimentally, on the material in its human context, judging the merit of any arrangement of language material, not on theoretical or logical grounds, but on the grounds of practical success in stimulating expression in the pupils. It is very important to grade the language material which we teach to our pupils, both structure and vocabulary, but we must bear in mind that the needs of a situation can overrule any theoretical presuppositions about when it may be appropriate to introduce particular words or language structures. Once we have arranged our material for teaching, we have to apply it to a human mind in a particular context.

The teacher may never make up his mind that he has found a formula for success in teaching; he must always be on the boundary of his experience, forcing his way on to the next stage of enlightenment which he sees always ahead but never quite reaches. For this reason it would be a mistake for anyone to regard what is written in this book as in any sense final, but I do hope that it will help others to greater success by showing the way.

On some points I am disposed to be dogmatic. I believe that to teach successfully we must take into account the social, as well as the psychological, situation of the pupil, remember that we are teaching language to be put to use for social purposes, for the expression, communication and reception of ideas, for establishing and maintaining contacts between people on the emotional as well as the intellectual level. I believe that we have to abandon the onlooker attitude to language when we are teaching or learning it, sink ourselves in it and use it for every purpose, and not begin to scrutinize or analyse it until we know it well. I believe that we are only helped by grammatical or other rules if they come to us as a handy summary of what we already half know. It is an advantage if we have ourselves worked hard to achieve the clarification they give.

The book is, of course, in some ways, a compendium of what other people have written and said about teaching. If I have not acknowledged all the ideas I have received from others, it is either because I believe them to be too generally accepted to require justification by reference to a particular statement on the subject, or because I am not sure where I read or heard them. A great deal more I have learnt from particular teachers whom I have watched. It is impossible to acknowledge my debt to them except in general terms. My practice has been to observe success in learning, whether in my own classes or those of others, and try to abstract the cause of the success from the complex of what was done. From this I tried to establish a rule which can be generally applied. I believe that we can only perceive generality, or abstractions such as rules for teaching or behaviour in the classroom, in terms of numerous particulars.

This is the account of an active skill, a form of athletics practised in relation to human beings. Thought, based on reading and reflection, may inform and guide the skill, but the skill has to be acquired and exercised in the classroom; it has to be compared with the skill of other practitioners, discussed and modified. The teacher must learn ultimately by submitting himself to the judgment of success or failure in the classroom. If I have been able to show the way to do this, rather than by any actual technique suggested, this book will have been worth writing.

I

Situational Language Teaching

1. THE CHILD'S FIRST LANGUAGE

The child learns its first language by getting used to hearing certain patterns of speech in relation to certain situations. We say to the child: "Let me look in your eye," and draw him towards us, hold his head in our hands and open his eye. He has long been used to his mother repeating in words what she is doing to him, washing, dressing, cutting his nails. Words have formed clusters and patterns in his mind. He has begun to find some of them come unbidden to his mind. The language teacher can learn a good deal about language teaching and the kind of repetition needed for learning language if he listens to a mother washing her baby or to a child of four or five speaking to himself when he thinks he is not observed. The mother's speech is largely unconscious and is designed rather to wrap the child in her love, in a cocoon of words that will cover him and hold him in the family and the community, and make him feel accepted there; the child's speech is also partly unconscious; he brings out the teeming sentences to look at and put back, as he brings out his favourite marbles, enjoying the grain and the colour of them, but not worrying much about their relevance to one another or their meaning. The details of the language may change—the nouns, the verbs and the adjectives—but the structural elements are relatively few and constant. He learns them and certain nouns that are necessary to his life and well-being before he is conscious of learning language. He makes a good many mistakes at first, but the nearest grown-up patiently repeats the correct form and does what is expected. The child learns a great deal by using scraps of language before he understands more than the fringe of the meaning of what he says. The situation and his needs are understood well enough by the grown-ups round him for language to be hardly necessary; they fill in the gaps for him. But we seldom realize how little the child understands or means what he says; the grown-up uses language as usual as if everything were plain, he is so used to language as an accompaniment to what he does that he could never do otherwise; but he reinforces what he says with gesture and pushing.

2. SPEECH PATTERNS FORM IN THE MIND

Speech is not at first understood or regarded for itself but as an accompaniment to action and situation. Who would associate a white line across the water with the passing of a ship unless he had seen ships leaving wakes, and perhaps leant over the stern and watched the wake of his own ship receding? Just as Pavlov's dogs got used to the ringing of the bell when they were fed, so we get used to hearing certain words with certain events or situations. The dogs salivated at the ringing of the bell even when no food was given; so we recognize, in time, the action spoken about from the words alone. The sounds and patterns of sounds have been heard often enough, in connection with certain actions or situations, to become associated with them so that the sounds alone can bring the actions or situations to mind without support from the situation. But before this happens the association of sound and situation must have been prolonged and close, the variations of the non-essentials on the essential theme must have been profuse enough for the essential pattern to emerge.

A dog barks; that dog is barking now; can you bark like a dog? Bark, then. (Pupil imitates teacher's imitation of barking.) Can you bark like a dog too? (Second pupil barks.) Yes, two of you can bark like a dog. Who else can bark like a dog? What does a dog do?   It barks.

Do you bark?—No, we don't; but we can bark like a dog.
Can this dog bark?—No, it can't, it's only a picture.

The same with *mew like a cat, cackle like a hen, crow like a cock, bleat like a lamb, bray like a donkey, neigh like a horse, growl like a bear*, and the essential patterns of language, the simple (or general) present tense, with its "s" in the third person contrasted with *can*, begin to establish themselves, and the words *bark, mew, cackle*, etc., can be abandoned and forgotten as having done their work of building up general language patterns and associations in the mind. Or they can be remembered by the whole exercise being repeated from time to time, members of the class taking over the role of questioner; gradually pictures of animals and imitations of their sounds can be dropped and the words take over alone.

3. A TEACHER'S MAIN TASK IS TO GIVE EXPERIENCE OF WORDS

When teaching a language we should spend very little of our time in giving the meanings of words, and whenever we have done so we should ask ourselves if it was really necessary. The teacher's first and most urgent task is to give his pupils the opportunity to hear words used, to hear them used often and significantly enough for the sounds and the patterns of sounds to form in their minds and make durable impressions there, impressions that stand for something when they are repeated. As soon as he sees that this is beginning to happen, the teacher should give his pupils the opportunity to use the sounds themselves to explore the situation they are in with these new tools of perception. They must experience language, live in it, not merely understand it; every movement, every process, every wish, every need must be introduced by words, accompanied by words, commented on in words, followed by words and dismissed by words. But action should always come before expression. The words themselves, beginning as an accompaniment of action like the tail of a comet or a cock, may end by being the most significant and memorable characteristic of the action in the classroom.

> This is a glass; I'm pouring water into it. Now there's water in the glass, it's full. I'm going to drink some water from the glass. I'm drinking. I'm drinking water from the glass. Now the glass is not full; it's half-full. I have drunk half the water. The glass is half-full (indicating the bottom half with the fingers) and half-empty (indicating the top half). Now I'm going to drink the rest of the water.
>
> Now the glass is empty; I have drunk the water. What have I been drinking?—You've been drinking water. How much have I drunk?—You have drunk a glassful, etc.

Then:

> This is a cup; I'm pouring tea into it. Now there's tea in the cup, it's full, etc.

Gradually the pupils begin to take part in the use of language:

> This is a glass. What's this?—It's a glass.
> What am I pouring into it?—Water.
> Is it full or empty?—Empty.

As they take over more and more of the speaking, we can expect longer answers, and either one or two pupils can take over the demonstrating and questioning roles.

> What's this? It's a glass.
> or What's that? It's a glass.
> What am I pouring into it? You're pouring water into it.
> or What's he pouring into it? He's pouring water into it.
> Who's pouring water into it? You are (or He is) (or John is).
> Is the glass full or empty? It's full.

This can then be expanded and varied, written on the board and copied down, and pairs of pupils can practise it together, varying it with coffee, milk, soup, etc., in mugs, bowls, etc., until the patterns are quite at home in their minds. Throughout the whole process the teacher may have explained not a single word except to say at the beginning "This is a glass," and to demonstrate *full* and *empty*. The repetition of the words and word patterns in situations that are perfectly clear brings the language into the mind without any effort of comprehension or memory being called for, even if no single word is understood at first.

4. THE BASIS OF SPEECH IN LISTENING

To speak a language with confidence learners must have the opportunity of hearing it spoken correctly and fluently in this significant way, so that their minds can move rapidly in the language without reflection on the individual words or their positions in the sentence. They must therefore never be expected to speak before they are quite ready to do so. If the teacher uses language naturally and significantly, asking questions and answering them himself until the pattern of question and answer has begun to establish itself in the learners' minds, they will begin to join in with the answers quite spontaneously without prompting, when they are ready. If the teacher tries to hurry the process, the learners may be uncertain of what to say, make mistakes and lose confidence. For this reason the first answers expected should be simple short responses that show little more than recognition. *Is this a book? Yes, it is. Is that a table? Yes, it is. Is this a table? No, it's not.* Probably a great many tongue-tied language learners have been frustrated and discouraged by the teacher expecting too much from them too soon.

There is a period, which we may call the incubation period, for a word or sentence pattern to settle in the mind; it may be different for each word or pattern according to the nature of the word or pattern or the circumstances of learning. The skill of the teacher is seen in his ability to judge the time required to absorb a word before the pupil can be expected to use it. He

B

may encourage the pupil to use it before this if he thinks the use of it is clear, but he should never expect it or pause for a moment—giving the answers himself—if the pupil has any difficulty in producing it. Very often, however, the pupil can quickly be given a formula that he can use as his part of the dialogue; his use of it then helps him to learn the whole pattern. He should not be discouraged from using a word, or participating in a dialogue, as soon as he shows signs of wanting to. He need not wait until he understands the essential words or knows the pattern independently.

> We are all here now. I have come here, you have come here, he has come here, she has come too. We have all come here today.
> Have you come here, Dillip?—Yes, I have (the teacher whispering the answer into his ear).
> Has Chicku come too?—Yes, he has (again the teacher whispers him the answer conspiratorially).

With these pattern answers and a return to Dillip and Chicku, or more whispering if someone misses his cue and the flow is checked, the teacher goes on:

> Have you sat down, Balu?—Yes, I have. Has Dillip sat down?—Yes, he has. Have I sat down?—No, you haven't. Have I written anything on the blackboard?—No, you haven't. Have you written anything in your book?—Yes, I have.

Then, when they are ready for the next stage:

> What have you written?—I have written these sentences (helped by whispering and pointing). Where have you written them?—I have written them in my book.

5. LANGUAGE TEACHING MUST BE SITUATIONAL

It follows from all this that effective use of language, economical and telling language teaching, in which no time is wasted in explanations, translation or reflection on patterns of usage not yet learnt, must be situational. The need for expression in language must arise from the need to realize and deal with the situation we are in; the fascination of bringing new language tools to bear on the familiar circumstances we live among must be exploited to the full. The mind must be passed to and fro over the well-known landscape dressed in the disguise of a new language, as a gardener sprays the familiar garden with new chemicals, or a ghost might revisit his home after death.

If the need for the language we use is urgently felt it is learnt quickly. We are making a village with cardboard houses and paper trees in the first few weeks of learning the language; a boy wants more sticky paper to stick the walls of his house together. He hesitates and looks at the sticky paper in the teacher's hand: "May I have some sticky paper, please?" whispers the teacher in his ear. "May I have some sticky paper, please?" he repeats urgently, reaching for the roll, and in no time the rest of the class are repeating the formula, varying it with: "May I have some green paper?" "May I have some more cardboard?" "May I have some more glue?" etc. Or a boy in his first few lessons in writing has come without his pencil; again the whisper, "May I have a pencil, please?" followed by "Thank you" after borrowing it and again on returning it. These are used as a sailor might hoist a signal laid ready for him by the officer but might learn to recognize and use it at the right moment by continually hoisting it in similar circumstances.

But the circumstances must be perfectly clear and unmistakable. The story is told of a teacher of French who used to come into class every morning in a great rush, saying: "Bonjour, mes élèves, comment allez-vous?" and require from them the answer: "Bonjour, monsieur." After a time he asked them what they thought his opening words meant, and they answered: "Good morning, boys, I'm sorry I'm late," and their answer: "Oh, that's quite all right, sir." The boys who say "May I have a pencil, please?" for the first time know the word *pencil*, and either already know the word *have* or learn it soon after, in the sense of *to have by one* or *to possess*. By using such expressions as soon as they are needed, we save ourselves the trouble of teaching them by demonstration and prepared repetition; by the time we reach the place in the book where they are nominally to be taught, they have become thoroughly familiar through having been used so often.

Teachers who give all the incidental orders, instructions and explanation in the home language of the pupil, on the grounds that they may not be understood in the language being learnt, not only miss a great many opportunities of teaching useful expressions, without trouble or noticeable expenditure of time, but also help to build up an attitude that the language cannot be used for ordinary practical purposes. If the circumstances in which the words are used are perfectly clear it is quite unimportant whether the words are exactly understood or not. It is enough for them to be understood by being often used in the right place at the right time. Teachers impose unnecessary strain on their pupils by being impatient for everything they introduce into their lessons to be learnt at once, completely. Zeigarnick's[1] researches into the memorability of completed and uncompleted tasks—cited by Koffka —show that uncompleted tasks are remembered nearly twice as well as completed tasks, presumably because the mind remains in a state of tension as long as a task is uncompleted, but relaxes as soon as the task is completed. The giving of meanings in the mother tongue or equivalents in the language being learnt, or rounding off the learning process prematurely, causes this relaxation in tension which makes remembering more difficult. This is not to deny the importance of a relaxed, easy atmosphere in the classroom as a background for language learning.

[1] B. Zeigarnick (1927), "Über das Behalten von erledigten und unerledigten Handlungen", *Psych. Forsch*, ix, 1–85, cited by Koffka in his *Principles of Gestalt Psychology*, p. 334.

6. THE SITUATION OF THE PUPIL

It is a natural question to ask at this point: "What, then, is this situation of the pupil, which has been placed at the centre of the language-learning process? How can we make use of it for language teaching? Are we to teach only what we can see and touch?" It seems convenient to divide the situation of the learner into four concentric spheres with the learner at the centre.

(i) The first or inner sphere consists of what the pupil can see, hear and touch directly. In practice, this is the classroom situation, including all that can be seen and heard through the classroom window. It also includes any expeditions or sorties which the teacher is able to make from the classroom with his class, repeating classroom lessons, learnt with classroom vocabulary, in the playground or the street with playground or street vocabulary but with the same structural elements. As an example of the use that can be made of the first or inner sphere of the learner's situation, we may take his shirt and its colour.

> My shirt is white, your shirt is blue, his shirt is green.
> What colour is your shirt? It's blue.
> What colour is my shirt? It's white.

At a later stage we may make use of the same circumstances to teach the verb *to have*:

> You have a blue shirt, he has a green shirt, I have a white shirt.
> Have you a blue shirt? Yes, I have.
> Has he a green shirt? Yes, he has.

From this we may pass on to the Continuous Present Tense:

> I am wearing a white shirt, you are wearing a blue one, etc.
> Who is wearing a white shirt? You are.
> And who is wearing a blue one? I am, etc.

Once, with a class of little girls squatting on the floor without the usual pencils, books, paper and other paraphernalia of the classroom, I taught the verb *to have* with the various coloured marks on their foreheads.

> You have a black mark on your forehead.
> She has a red mark on her forehead.
> This girl has a black exclamation mark on her forehead, etc.

It was immaterial that they did not know the words *forehead* or *mark* or *exclamation mark*. They soon learnt them from the situation and my use of them, and their attention was agreeably distracted from the verb *have* that I was insinuating into their heads so subtly.

Although the situation should be memorable and unmistakable, there is no need for a newly introduced word to be specially brought to the attention of the class. It should certainly not be written on the blackboard until it has been learnt, nor should it be printed at the top of the lesson in the book. A word may often be introduced and made familiar without its being noticed until it has been nearly learnt.

(ii) The second sphere, which should always be approached through the first, consists of what the pupil knows from his own experience, his daily life, his family circle, what he has seen and heard directly but cannot see or hear at the moment. The teacher has to remember that, although the actions, objects and situations in this sphere are familiar, a slight effort is required to call them to mind, because they are not in sight. For this reason they should always be approached through what can be directly experienced in the classroom. For instance, when the time comes to introduce the General Present Tense we say:

> I wear shirts and you wear shirts. We all wear shirts, but today I'm wearing a white shirt, yesterday I was wearing a green one.
> Do you wear a shirt every day? Yes, I do, etc.

As soon as we begin to speak of what is generally true, or of the past, we enter the second sphere.

(iii) The third sphere consists of what the pupil has not yet experienced directly, but what he can call to mind with an effort of the imagination, with the help of pictures, dramatization, charts and plans, the sand-table and other visual aids. All work in this sphere must be based on work in the first and second spheres, because through the imagination we can only grasp the unknown in terms of the known. The teacher should try to make all stories or descriptions which the pupil is to study easier to grasp by simple spontaneous dramatization or drawing on the blackboard. Blank faces in a class when a text is being introduced or read usually mean that the teacher has failed to bring it near through stimulating the imaginations of his pupils. For instance, I once saw a teacher teaching a class the story of an elderly Chinese man who had just been celebrating his birthday with a feast. As he was clearing away the food and drink he saw the shadow of a man's head on the floor. Looking up he saw a man concealed in the rafters. He apologized for clearing away while a guest was still in the room, and invited him to come down and eat. The man came down and ate as much as he wanted, served by the host who finally, with scrupulous tact, offered him a beautiful coat from among the presents he had received. The story concluded with the reformation of the burglar. I was surprised that the class showed so little interest in such a charming story, but it was evident that it had remained in China for them. The teacher had not even noticed that the shadow of his own head could be seen on the floor. He had not pointed towards the ceiling as he had said that the burglar was concealed in the rafters, he had not gone through the motions of clearing away the feast. It is easier even for people who understand the language very well if the speaker helps their attention in this way; an anecdote is all the better for a little mimicry and gesture from the teller.

(iv) The fourth sphere of the pupil's situation consists of what is brought into his mind through the spoken, written or printed word alone, without help through audio-visual aids.

Ultimately most of what the pupil reads or hears in the language will come to him in this sphere; but he should not be brought straight to it until he has a fairly good command of the language. While learning the language he must first hear and use in the inner spheres the language which he will need in order to understand what he is to read or hear in the fourth.

7. WORKING FROM THE CENTRE OUTWARDS

All new language material must be made familiar in the inner sphere before it is brought to bear on action or situation in the second or third spheres. We can never expect it to do reliable work in the fourth or outer sphere until it has become a reliable tool in the inner spheres. This leads us to introduce all textual material by using as much of the structural language and the vocabulary as possible within the first and second spheres; that is, we begin by speaking about what is familiar to the pupil at first hand in the vocabulary needed. It also leads us on to exploit other elements in the learner's situation; it leads us to make use of language in a way that compels his attention and satisfies his social instincts within the two inner spheres, in speaking and writing to others out of his own experience and what he has seen, to tell them what they want to know. This theme will be further developed later.

8. ALL NEW LANGUAGE TAUGHT IN CLASSROOM SITUATION

All actual teaching of new language material must be done in relation to the situations of the classroom and the familiar home surroundings. We should never attempt to speak about what is not familiar until we are confident that the words we need have been exercised enough and have proved themselves reliable tools in the familiar spheres of the pupil's situation. Especially structural material, which is universally valid, can early be introduced and practised in the classroom before it is taken into the sphere into which it is introduced in a particular textbook lesson.

Suppose, for example, we have to teach a lesson in which the main structural item is relative clauses, and the subject of the lesson is archaeology and the ancient cities of Mesopotamia, we shall start:

The boys with blue shirts stand up.
Which boys are standing? The boys with blue shirts are standing.
What are they wearing? They are wearing blue shirts.
The boys who are wearing blue shirts are standing.
Which boys are standing? The boys who are wearing blue shirts are standing.
Which boys are sitting? The boys who are not wearing blue shirts are sitting.

After some practice on variations of this theme we begin to ask if any boys have seen any of the ancient cities in the neighbourhood. Then we speak of the boys who have seen this or that ancient city, of the people who have looked for other ancient cities, of archaeologists who have excavated ancient sites, etc. The vocabulary of a prose text is usually special to the piece or the subject; the structural material is general, so we begin with the structures and lead them gradually into the subject of the piece, introducing more general vocabulary first and slowly adding more specialized vocabulary.

9. SUCCESS SHOULD LEAD TO FURTHER SUCCESS

Success in language learning, as in the learning of any skill, depends on the learner quickly achieving a limited success. As the pupil feels that he has hit the mark, that he has been able to answer a question correctly, that someone has received and acted on his message, that he has asked a question which has been recognized and replied to, he feels good; he likes this sensation and pushes ahead after more. A limited success brings a thirst for more success, and a succession of successes leads to mastery of the skill and a feeling of having a stake in it. Those methods of teaching a language which emphasize the strangeness and the difference from the mother tongue, by continually comparing one with the other and translating or escaping from the foreign to the home language, and by pestering pupils with too much correction, or demanding long complicated answers before the simple ones have been mastered, have the effect of shutting the pupil out of the language with gates too high for him to climb. He becomes discouraged, he begins to dislike the language and reject it in his mind, he never gets the feeling that he has a stake in the language. One of the quickest ways to overcome this feeling of defeat, in initiating a campaign of remedial work, is to pass over what has been learnt wrong and concentrate the pupil's attention on the stake he has in the language, what he has, after all, learnt in spite of a general sense of failure.

A boy likes cricket and goes on playing it if he finds he is able to hit the ball smartly or catch it neatly or bowl accurately. He aims for constantly increasing skill. The boy who, like myself at school, seldom hits the ball, fumbles his catches and bowls mostly wides, soon comes to dislike the game and disowns it with indignation, saying it is the most tedious waste of time ever devised to plague poor schoolboys. Success is therefore the only valid incentive for prolonged application to language learning, and the teacher is successful who helps his pupils win minor victories and overcome obstacles to understanding and expression continually. This kind of reward goes with the pupil when he leaves school, for it is part of the process of successful learning, unlike marks, punishments, prizes and threatening scowls, which are the peculiar and irrelevant creation of the school.

10. THE SITUATION OF THE LEARNER IN SOCIETY

An aspect of the learner's situation which has not yet been considered, though referred to above, is the situation of the learner in relation to others. One of the legacies of Newtonian physics is that we have learnt to atomize and analyse, but not so well to relate and synthesize. Whitehead has said: "Newtonian physics is based upon the independent individuality of each bit of matter," but goes on to say, "Modern science has abandoned the doctrine of Simple Location,"[1] and that an important part of the qualities of any object depends on its position, velocity, and relationship to other objects and its development. He considered that thinking and behaviour based on the Newtonian conception of the universe still predominated in society although scientists have moved on to a new conception.

The teacher who teaches his pupils as unrelated individuals, as if he were giving fifty private lessons simultaneously, or cutting a lesson into fifty individual fragments, and who makes no use in his teaching of the inescapable fact of their situation in a social group, is guiding himself by Newtonian conceptions of unrelated particles of matter and individual organisms, which no longer hold good. Frustration follows from ignoring this essential element of the pupil's situation. We can only teach a language effectively if it is the basis for a genuine personal relationship between teacher and pupil; the relationship may not be able to develop very far or go deep, but there should be no artificial barrier, either the mask which some teachers prefer to put on in the presence of their pupils, or the simplification, or silhouette, of their pupils, which they prefer to see rather than the rounded whole which calls for more effort to perceive. This relationship can be developed gradually into a complex network of relationships between pupil and pupil, based on co-operative work and the normal social interplay of language.

Language depends on society and society is built up on relationships supported and realized through language: no learner can be expected to take seriously a language which fails to do what his own language does for him: namely, set up and carry genuine contacts with others, even if the contacts are different from those carried by his own language. He needs to

---

[1] *Adventures of Ideas*, pp. 200–1. Quoted, Ivor Leclerc, *Whitehead's Metaphysics*, Allen and Unwin, London, 1958.

see his skill mirrored in others and realize it in relation to others. Methods of dealing with this element in the learner's situation will be discussed in detail in Chapter 6 and in subsequent chapters.

As soon as possible all spoken and written composition should be functional and be directed towards the needs of the community, the class and the school. Speaking in class may be co-operative and provide information or amusement for those who want it, writing should develop out of this co-operative team-work in speech, and along the same lines. Several short talks of one, two or five minutes, planned together and supporting one another, can make a short lecture; when written down they may become a short illustrated brochure. The higher classes may write readers for the lower classes. Most of the writing which is done may be done for the reading of other members of the class. Team-work gives satisfactions rooted in the gregarious nature of mankind and builds, out of skills harmoniously and effectively applied, high morale. Where morale is high teaching is efficient and learning is quick, agreeable and successful.

CONCLUSION

The teacher, whether he is aware of holding certain metaphysical beliefs or not, has an attitude to his pupils and to the material which he teaches, based on definite first principles. If these first principles are assumptions which he seldom questions, they are largely beyond his scrutiny and control and may be quite unconscious. If he teaches his pupils as though they had no bodies and no individual characteristics, he will also assume that they have no relevant social relationships on which classroom language work can be based. He may go further and assume that the flesh is evil and a clog on the spirit; he will make his pupils sit still with folded arms and answer only after putting up their hands. He will give immaterial rewards (marks) to their spirits and concrete punishment to their bodies. He will try to stifle whatever is unwelcome. He will try to atomize and analyse, to estimate and judge, each individual as though he were alone in the universe and incapable of development or growth, as if he were only a receptacle capable of containing more and more. He will teach from an unchanging, unassailable text in a book.

If on the other hand, with Schiller,[1] he welcomes the association of the soul and the body as the essential condition of our human situation, and glories in the ability of the body to serve and nourish the mind and expects both together to be related to others in work and friendship, he will assume that the body and social relationships are capable of contributing to the development of the mind if they are patiently accepted and their qualities are made use of. If the mind is worked with the body, and language harmonizes and links the two, relating them to their situation, the mind is alert and fully engaged and language makes effective marks on the mind. If this is so, language is learnt quickly and not easily forgotten; above all, language learnt in the situation that calls for it, language which the body and fully engaged mind require and respond to, moves the mind easily afterwards and is not used emptily without relation to the circumstances of the speaker.

The material of the language lesson is not language, but life itself; the language is the instrument we use to deal with the material, slices of experience.

[1] *Zusammenhang des Tierischens mit dem Menschlichen.*

2

Language through Speech

If we decide that language must be taught situationally, there is no alternative to teaching it through speech; only in speech can we exploit and probe the immediate situation of the pupil, catching it as it changes and develops, turning its oddities and delights into language, recording, investigating, commenting and interpreting. The book can be used to take us to a distance in the newly acquired equipages of language, once we have got them to run smoothly up and down the home streets. The problem of basing oral language teaching on the texts of a book has been referred to in the previous chapter, section 8; it will be dealt with in detail in Chapter 4. The advantages of teaching a language through speech can be grouped under twelve heads. Dealing with each head in turn gives an opportunity to explore the techniques of teaching through speech.

1. LANGUAGE IS PRIMARILY SPEECH

For thousands of years man has been combining for work and social life through speech; speech is still the chief vehicle in industry, politics and religion for ideas to pass and relationships to be expressed. Speech affects us more closely than what is written, especially if it is applied to the situation we are actually in at the moment of speaking. The written word is one remove further away from us if only in that it deals with some other situation beyond our immediate view. But writing is a recently acquired characteristic still beyond the reach of millions, and only the normal equipment of man in society for the last eighty or ninety years. During the last fifty years gramophone, telephone, radio, television and sound films have increased the potency and scope of speech enormously. Factories and commercial organizations, once limited in size to the range of the human legs and voice, have been able to increase greatly in size and complexity with the improvement of telephone and speech-recording devices. Armies which once had to be organized and set in motion through visible signals and a few officers on horseback can now be controlled at speed through wireless. This has brought about far-reaching changes in military organization and discipline. The motto of the Crimean War was correctly voiced by Tennyson: "Theirs not to reason why, theirs not to make reply, theirs but to do and die." The introduction of compulsory education and radio telephony made a different attitude and motto possible. In the second world war great initiative could be given to small commanders because of the greater reach of speech and better training in its use. Armies which had learnt this lesson won the most surprising victories over those which had not.

Political life and industrial organization call for effective and economical speech; international trade and political organization depend on the efficient use of a world, or internationally understood, language. Foreign language teaching must therefore, with all the urgency of a rescue operation, concentrate on producing a large number of responsible, adaptable people who are able to build up and maintain international organizations in a second language. Because of the need for the best to be chosen, and to allow for a rapid turnover of experts, who may not wish to be away from their home countries throughout their working lives, a very large number of people need to have the readiness in speech to maintain a relatively small body of international officials and experts.

Besides this, a training in speaking and understanding a foreign language can in itself be a training in civilized attitudes towards strange people and customs. This is much more likely to be so than a training in understanding a written language. A reader identifies himself less with what he reads than a speaker with what he speaks and hears; so to him the language tends to remain distant and strange. Discussion in the second language can immediately follow the learning of social studies, science and mathematics in the home language; this leads on to effective reading.

Good manners, fluency and an ability to discuss concrete problems in a foreign language are desirable for every educated man in the world of today, and may be essential in the near future. Language is a social bond as well as a medium of communication; international co-operation must depend on real understanding in a background of common knowledge and calls for habits of tolerance and patience. These attitudes and habits can be cultivated most effectively in speech.

2. THE FIRST LANGUAGE IS LEARNT THROUGH SPEECH

We learnt our first language through speech; anyone who learns a second language through speech finds that he has much of the experience and skill, and the same quality of mind, to help him learn a second language in the same way. It is true that the mind loses the resilience or plasticity which makes the learning of the essentials of a language child's play before the age of ten, but the mind does not change its character entirely, and even an adult finds that he learns a second language in a foreign country, through speech arising out of his daily life and work, almost without noticing how he learns it. All the children in school have been successful in learning at least one language in this way; they are still fresh from the process and have not yet become too slavishly dependent on books. It is difficult to achieve the atmosphere of a foreign country in a classroom; there may be fifty pupils to one teacher, whereas at home, learning the first language, there were perhaps fifty teachers—all the family and neighbours, passers-by and people in shops—to one learner; but in practice in the classroom the teacher can achieve a very intensive use of language; he can supplement his own speech by radio, tape-recorder, and gramophone to achieve even greater intensity, and to compensate for any inadequacies in his pronunciation or fluency. The teacher must use the language for every purpose and tolerate no lapses into the home language; he must teach it through activity, and allow no use of the language to become unreal, remote from his pupils' interests, or vague.

The best time for the essentials of a foreign language to be learnt is before the age of ten or eleven. Dr. Wilder Penfield, of the Neurological Institute, Montreal, has shown the theoretical and practical justification for this. The child must be taught entirely through activity, the language being used as if it were the mother tongue of the child, regardless of whether it is understood or not. I have seen a Froebel-trained English girl, in the English Girls' High School, Istanbul, working as if she were with a class of English children. She was able to teach English to children speaking several different languages by simply using it to direct their activities and in nursery rhymes and games. At the end of two years they were able to take their places in English medium classes on a par with children whose mother tongue was English.

3. SPEECH IS A HANDIER INSTRUMENT FOR PRACTICE
   THAN WRITING

Speech is also a handier instrument than writing for quick practice and repetition. To learn our multiplication tables most of us found it easier to say them over aloud than to stare at the printed figures. An additional advantage was that in this condition they could be checked by any chance listener. We can repeat many more sentences in a shorter time in speech than in writing, and others can overhear us and criticize, point out mistakes or learn themselves from our repetition of the sentences which they also want to learn. The learner is saved time and effort if he can let a large number of meaningful sentences pass through his mind. This establishes a pattern

C

quickly. After this, written exercises are likely to be relatively free of mistakes and rapidly written. The practice of others provides him with plenty of correct sentences to hear.

4. GOOD WRITING FOLLOWS FROM CORRECT SPEAKING

Good writing can be based on fluent, correct speaking, because a correct speaker depends on his ability to improvise correct sentences, without reflection, out of the store of patterns which he has collected in his mind in prolonged and attentive listening. They must be near enough to the surface of his consciousness to be immediately available for expression the moment his situation or activity calls for them. When a fluent speaker writes, he simply imagines himself into the situation called for by his writing, and sentences come to him complete without his having to reflect on them; he is free to concentrate on the subject matter which he is holding in front of his mind's eye. On the other hand, writing is seldom a proper preparation for speech, because an ability to write correctly which is not based on speech must be built up by the painstaking assembly of numerous sentences from their separate component parts according to elaborate rules, rather than from stereotypes which can be quickly modified. Speech based on writing remains slow and hesitant because the speaker has to reflect constantly on the correct or most elegant mode of expression, rather than on what has to be said.

Although I had long known this theoretically, it was exemplified rather strikingly in my own learning of Turkish. In Ankara, where most of my Turkish friends and acquaintances spoke either English, French or German, I had hardly any contact with the spoken language. My teacher was unable to teach me, except through grammar rule, and talking in English about Turkish sentence construction. I wrote my own sentences and relieved the boredom by making them fantastic. When I was transferred to a provincial town where very few people spoke or understood anything but Turkish, I was able to write fairly ambitious sentences in a decidedly literary—or at least bookish—style. But I soon found myself tongue-tied when people spoke and expected a quick answer; while they waited I was arguing with myself over the most elegant manner of expression and the most suitable word order; possibilities crowded my mind, but there was no external evidence of this. After waiting politely for some time, the people I was trying to impress with the elegance and scope of my mastery of the language would turn wearily to my wife, who had picked up what seemed to me a few words while shopping, or talking to the cook, and seemed to have no grasp of the tense system. "What a pity," they said, "that your husband has learnt no Turkish; you speak so well and fluently."

5. THE TEACHER CAN BE PRESENT DURING LEARNING

If the teacher is always present during the learning process, he can control what happens. He can see immediately that this is easy or that is difficult; and he can modify or develop what he is teaching accordingly. He can ensure that correct forms are learnt; he can help with difficulties; he can give more practice on something that his pupils seem unable to learn within the exercises provided in the book; he can overcome shortcomings in the book; and he can give his pupils enough repetition for all essential language patterns to become instinctive, so that all the class can use them correctly without reflection. If the actual teaching of new language patterns and essential vocabulary is always carried out in speech before the whole class, and then practised with smaller groups, the greater part of the process of learning takes place in the open, for all to see and hear. The teacher needs to do very little testing to know how his pupils are progressing; as time spent on testing is largely wasted, from the point of view of learning, this is a great advantage. When I was at school, I was frequently face to face in the evening preparation period with new material not yet explained in class. I was often puzzled and dismayed, or else the unfamiliar material made no impression at all; very often I learnt something quite wrong which required effort to forget and relearn later. We were tested in what we had been given to learn, next morning, and I often found myself in detention, to learn over again what I had failed to grasp, but the question whether this was a fruitful way of teaching by proxy did not seem to be asked. A similar comfortable avoidance of thought, or counting of cost, led eventually, by slow attrition, to the winning of the Crimean War. I passed my School Certificate by laying long and tedious siege to sternly defended fortresses, with inadequate organization, commissariat and weapons. The signal was raised; the struggle might as well cease. I became eligible to enter a university.

6. IMMEDIATE CORRECTION OF MISTAKES

The techer can keep control over the learning process if he initiates it and develops it in speech. He can see that mistakes, if learnt, are immediately corrected. He can follow the correction of them by enough examples of the correct form to expunge the memory of the incorrect form from the minds of his pupils. Mistakes made in written work may not be seen by the teacher for days; allt he time they are lying uncorrected in the pupil's mind, sinking deeper into his recording brain cells.

My mother speak Tamil, says a boy.

Your mother speaks Tamil, does she? says the teacher. My mother speaks English. What does Ramaswamy's mother speak, Balasubramaniam?—She speaks Tamil. And what does *your* mother speak?—She speaks Tamil. What does your father speak?—He speaks Tamil.

There is no need to point out the mistake, it is just rolled flat by the correct form repeated over and over again. To have looked up the point in a grammar, and then written some unrelated sentences to learn it on, would have been more laborious, much less certainly successful, and would have all depended on the teacher's noticing the mistake and pointing it out quickly; it would also have been dependent on the pupil's co-operating willingly and intelligently. More effort, time and thought would have been required.

7. AVOIDING STRAIN

An active teacher can save his pupils effort and strain by giving them the opportunity of hearing the language used in relation to their experience; he can match his use of the language exactly to what they are going through or seeing. If he repeats what he is teaching often enough and makes the repetition interesting and clear enough, they can relax and allow the language to flow in without having to strain after meaning, or trying to unravel what seems always just beyond them. He can drill or practise correct pattern sentences, sometimes in the form of rhymes and songs, in chorus. A sentence which proves especially difficult he can develop spontaneously into a rhythmic choral chant. By his fluent use of the language he draws them into the heart of it, so that they need not be constantly forcing their way with an effort of will into impenetrable thickets or dry deserts of language. If he can then record the most important sentences in the form of a simple, easily followed dialogue on the blackboard, the class can practise it among themselves quietly until it is learnt. No one need have the feeling that essentials are flying by unnoticed. If the teacher can also record these type sentences on the tape-recorder for the learner to play over to himself as often as he needs it, strain is removed altogether and close, patient concentration can be cultivated. In work with others, and in a growing sense of mastery, based on such frequent listening to the correct sounds and intonation that they all fall into place quite naturally in the mind, the pupil builds up his confidence and his feeling of well-being in the language.

8. LANGUAGE IN DAILY WORK

Sailors, waiters and engineers, doing their daily work amongst people who speak another language, live their way unconsciously into the language. They have to understand and carry out orders, they have to respond to what is said, and speak, when they speak, about their daily work. No mental effort is required to link words to what they stand for; action is always being commented on, explained, referred to and called to mind in words. This close linking of language to action can only be done, in the first place, through speech.

Joseph Conrad, the novelist from Poland, who wrote in English, is a case in point. He came to England after he had passed the age of twenty, without knowing any English. He went to work in English ships sailing up and down the coast. All that he heard was in reference to his work and went with practical instruction in seamanship; his daily work was followed by a wake of words which arose from everything he did. When he began to speak, he was supported by the framework of his employment. When he began to read, he read simple text-books on seamanship which developed out of everything he did and every word he spoke. When he began to listen to stories, they were stories about the sea, many of them illustrating points in seamanship. When he began to tell stories they were about life and adventures at sea. The English he learnt was sound and compelling because it was based at every point on completely felt experience. For some months he hardly ever heard an unintegrated word.

9. VERBAL EQUIVALENTS UNNECESSARY

No child that has learnt:

> "Hickory, dickory dock
> The mouse ran up the clock"

has had any more difficulty in learning the words:

> "Hickory, dickory dock"

than in learning the words:

> "The mouse ran up the clock."

Yet many teachers seem to believe that giving the equivalent of a word in the home language, or explaining what it means, is to teach it. A child beginning to play for the first time with children who speak a different language begins to make the sounds which they make, as he learns to hide himself or run when chased, without waiting to learn why, or what the words mean. In a very short time he has learnt the meanings of the words by using them in the right place at the right moment. Yet many teachers seem to think that a child can use no sentence in a foreign language which has not been carefully explained and accounted for. If we learn a language as part of behaviour, as dependent on it and as much a part of it as the foam is of the wave, and as inconceivable as the flower is inconceivable without the plant, we can learn words and expressions, and work them into our knowledge of the language, without necessarily understanding exactly what they mean. Our suddenly realizing, one day, that we know what they mean is a sign that we know them.

On the other hand, to learn a language from a book, by deciphering texts and interpreting rules, is to be involved in a constant search for and preoccupation with meaning; there is nothing else to concern oneself with. A concern with interpretation and exact verbal equivalents in the mother tongue diverts our attention away from the language we are trying to learn, to concentrate on something else, a possibly not very satisfactory substitute, that is all the duller for being in familiar language. The pupil can seldom in the early stages do this interpretation for himself, and later cannot do it well; so he sits passively and watches it being done for him. When it has been done he has even less reason to read the original than before. He believes he has learnt the piece, whereas the work has hardly begun; the essential work of learning the new slice of language has been passed over. He has been trained never to trust himself in the new language, but to turn his back on it and bolt for his own language as soon as a difficulty appears.

10. GIVING EQUIVALENTS WEAKENS THE IMPRESSION OF NEW WORDS

If we give the meaning of a new word, either by translation into the home language or by an equivalent in the same language, as soon as we introduce it, we weaken the impression which the word makes on the mind. The pupil's curiosity is dissipated, the tension is relaxed before his interest even begins to be stretched. The familiar word, beside the unfamiliar one, makes a stronger impression and tends to blot out or outshine the impression of the new word. It is wiser to let the word stand by itself without a stronger rival beside it; the curiosity to unravel the unknown, to solve the puzzle, to hunt the stranger, helps to concentrate our attention on the word intensely, so that it is easily remembered. We cannot afford to weaken or waste the force of this tension. Most learners who have been trained to listen intently to what their teacher says, while concentrating on what he is doing, enjoy the game of trying to understand what unfamiliar words mean. We spoil the game if we give the solution to a puzzle before it has been really worked at, before our pupils have had a chance to try their wits and the quickness of their ears on it. Words should only be written on the blackboard after they have been learnt, as trophies showing that they have been learnt, as a man might hang up a tiger skin or the antlers of a stag after, but not before, he has shot it.

When learning Turkish I often used to notice a feeling of relief as I wrote a word, with its English equivalent, into my notebook. I analysed this feeling as relief that the struggle was over; I had caught the elusive word in my notebook; I no longer needed to strain after it to remember it. After a short interval of time I usually found that I had remembered the English equivalents of a list of words, but not the Turkish words I wanted to remember. To remember them I found it was best to read and reread the piece I had first met them in, not worrying too consciously about their meaning until they had settled into my mind fairly strongly. By this time I had an instinct for their use and a half-conscious knowledge of their meaning. If I then looked them up in the dictionary they were already familiar and were not to be driven out by the equivalent in English. Since then I have made it a rule to give equivalents in the home language only of those unimportant words which need to be understood for their part in a piece of prose or poetry to be clear, but which need not be learnt for their own sake. This is really a way of not learning them. Laborious attempts to explain words without translation are very little better than translation, and, if they are difficult to follow, even worse. The teacher is not a dictionary, and seldom does the work of explaining words so well. On the other hand, he is a living, interesting person and he can make use of the new word in all kinds of contexts and situations; he can relate it to the experience of the pupil as no dictionary can.

Suppose we want to teach the word *hardly*.

We can hardly see that tree because it is behind the house.
I can hardly see Satyanarayanamurti because he is behind Balakrishna.
Can you see Mahalakshmi, Balasubramanian?
No, I can hardly see her, because Meenakshi is between us.
Can you lift this desk, Chandran?
No, I can hardly lift it. It's very heavy.

After intensive use of the new word on these lines, an attempt at a definition may be made, and lastly the dictionary may be consulted as the final judge.

11. SAFETY DEVICE AGAINST GOING TOO QUICKLY

If we teach a language through speech we are prevented from going too quickly by the simple inability of the pupils to follow what we are saying, if we try to include too much in one lesson. We can crowd forty new words on to a page, if there is room to print them, but if we are making a serious attempt to teach words by using them significantly in the pupil's situation, basing everything we say on what he knows, we must repeat them until they form a firm enough foothold for us to make the next step. In speech, the pupil is unable to hold in his head, for use or reference, words which he has not fully learnt. If he cannot remember what they mean, the teacher has to remind him of them by repeating them in significant contexts until he can. If he can remind his pupils of the word's identity in the home language whenever he likes, he is likely to give too little significant repetition. In practice, only ten or twelve new words can usefully be presented in a lesson of forty-five or fifty minutes, though, at the beginning of the course, we may give up to twenty to get the language well launched, with varied enough material to sustain interest. All words have to be repeated in every lesson for some time if they are to be fully absorbed; this is especially true if an unusually large number has been introduced into any lesson.

We can go on to a new word or language pattern before the one preceding it has been completely learnt. If the material has been well arranged, the learning of the new pattern helps us to practise and consolidate the previous one; but there is a curve in learning energy. It is steepest at the beginning, while the novelty of the new word still attracts us, but it gradually becomes flatter as our minds begin to grow tired. When the teacher sees that the rate of learning has slowed down to such a degree that answers begin to be made at random, without concentration, he must switch to something quite different, either new or old.   Zeigarnik's researches cited in Chapter 1 show us that uncompleted tasks are remembered better than completed ones, and the incubation period must be allowed for.

12. ADAPTABILITY OF LANGUAGE TO AGE AND
CAPABILITY

Teaching a language through speech makes it possible for the teacher to adapt all that he teaches to the needs, interests, experience, age and capabilities of whatever class faces him.

The lesson can be whatever the teacher likes to make it. He lives amongst his pupils, he knows them and knows their limitations; he knows every detail of their background; he can measure the language which he uses, and the manner of its presentation, to their capacity and interests. He prepares the ground of language carefully and skilfully for the reading of the book, and then fits the material of the book into it. He brings it within their reach linguistically and connects it with their knowledge and belief systems.

We must teach language through speech, to give each individual a personally fitted instrument which he can use and develop as part of himself. Our awareness of each pupil as an individual entity, our concern for him as a person, can only be developed through personal speech. Any attempt at greater uniformity or economy which withholds responsibility from the teacher or denies him his position as an individual with a duty to have direct, personal, unique and unrehearsed relations with individuals through spoken language produces results that are less than human, that stultify instead of enlightening, that close the mind instead of opening it.

3

Ear Training

I. SELECTIVE LISTENING

An educated man, a civilized, cultivated person, we think of as someone who is sensitive on many wave lengths, who is receptive and open-minded, attentive, tolerant and sympathetic, a person who has learnt to reserve judgment. Yet this sensitivity or tolerance seems to have to be cultivated. Bartlett cites[1] the case of a boy who appeared to be deaf and dumb, except that he was noticed to be able to imitate the sounds of certain animals very accurately. By getting his confidence and encouraging him in his imitations of animal cries a patient psychologist was able to bring him to imitate certain human sounds and ultimately lead him along the way to speech. He had suffered from shock after a severe operation as a small child, and this seemed to have had the effect of destroying his confidence in human beings; he was no more attentive to the sounds of human beings than we usually are to the sounds of animals or birds.

The child learns in self-defence to shut out what he is not able to absorb usefully. In a modern town we all have to build up a kind of mental defence or deafness against obtrusive sound. Unfortunately this very necessary mental habit of isolating ourselves against unwanted sound comes to be practised assiduously in school, to cut out the indigestible or the unwelcome. Too many of us are bad listeners, preferring to give our own opinions; conversations consist of two people each waiting impatiently for the other to stop talking.

[1] Bartlett, *Remembering*, Cambridge, 1954 ed., pp. 188–9.

32

The end of our education should not be, after all, that a man can attend to nothing. Apart from the loss of influences and information, there is a loss of energy in keeping this mental sound barrier up. Teachers who find ways to train their pupils to listen attentively and concentrate on what they hear are well rewarded, for a good listener is always an agreeable person and is likely to be more open to new ideas than a bad listener.

2. PRACTICE IN FACING STRANGENESS

In teaching a language we have an opportunity to give our pupils small and adjustable samples of strangeness. They learn to accept strange sounds, modes of expression, and through them, ideas and customs, as natural phenomena and not something to be shut out of consciousness as unwanted or disturbing. In the wider world outside the school this may lead to success in meeting all kinds of strangeness.

The pupil who is to make effective use of a language must learn to listen and absorb, to accept and perceive what is strange to him. He needs practice in listening carefully, if he is to catch the drift of what is being said, even when he does not understand every word; he finds himself learning to hold unfamiliar words in his memory for future reference, reserving judgment about their meaning. So he learns to concentrate absolutely, to follow the thread of what is being said tenaciously in spite of difficulties.

3. LANGUAGE LEARNING AS TRAINING IN INTERNATIONAL UNDERSTANDING

The study of a foreign language does not necessarily promote a sympathetic interest in the people who speak it and write it. If the language course is virtually no preparation for being plunged in strangeness, if the sounds of the language are approximated to the familiar home sounds, and if the differences in outlook and culture embodied in the language are not squarely faced, strangeness may be too startling when it is met; there may not be enough toughness or experience to deal with the difficulties when they come. To train our pupils in attentive listening, we may have swamped their ears in apparently trackless floods of sound through which they are ultimately able to find a thread to follow, and so build up techniques and skills in fastening on this apparent chaos and reducing it to order. We may have taught them to welcome variety as new opportunities for understanding. If so, we can hope to have helped them towards habits of sympathy and forbearance for strange people and strange ways of thinking and behaving as well as to useful attitudes to language.

The learning of languages alone does not develop more patience and insight in the individual, nor greater harmony in the world community; these essential bases for a world civilization can be consciously sought after and cultivated through right attitudes practised on the sounds and steadily built up in years of systematic training.

4. THE VALUE OF PASSIVE LISTENING—I

There may be more value than we realize even in passively listening to a flow of speech that seems beyond our grasp. In certain circumstances, we can learn from what we only hear and hardly listen to at all. I have, myself, had experience of this. I have learnt German without taking any lessons; I went to Germany on a cycling tour, with a friend who had learnt German for two years at school. We supposed that he would be the interpreter, but his two years' learning had so inhibited him that he never opened his mouth in German except to help me to pronounce a word or sentence in our phrase book. His teacher must have built up in him such a fear of making mistakes that he could never risk an independent sentence. I had no such inhibitions and plunged into the language in attempts to find the way, buy food, discuss the surfaces of roads, get repairs done to my bicycle and change money. Besides this, I listened as intently as I could to people speaking round me in the streets, in youth hostels and in restaurants, and consequently left Germany able to express myself on simple matters rather cumbersomely, understanding more than I could consciously label.

A few years later I spent seven weeks with a German-speaking family in the Tyrol to practise the English of two German boys. When I was not on duty, and at meal-times, I heard a flood of German that I could not follow at all. One of the boys, one day, said that I was getting a wonderful opportunity to learn German. I replied that I could learn nothing from conversations that were outside my reach. "That doesn't matter," he said. "You are filling your ears with the sounds." At the time I found it difficult to credit this, but at the end of seven weeks, on my way home in the train, I noticed how much more I could understand—without necessarily being able to identify all the words—and I found ready-made sentences slipping out of my mouth to strangers. A year or two later, when I went to live in Germany, I noticed this even more: sentences that I was not conscious of having learnt flowed out of me and seemed to hit the mark; sometimes I found myself looking over my shoulder to see who had spoken them; I wondered whether they really meant what I thought they meant, until I was reassured by the answer.

Since then I have always kept my expression in German well within the bounds of my knowledge and kept the frontiers of my knowledge well up in the realm of listening. This is what we all do in our own languages, we always wait for a new technical or specialized word or a smart new slang expression to become familiar to our listening ear before we venture to use it ourselves.

5. THE VALUE OF PASSIVE LISTENING—II

My second example of the value of listening fulfilled remarkably closely the specifications which I once read for learning a language; to arrange to live for five years in the country where the language is spoken, but to be careful not to speak during the first two years. An Austrian musician working in Ankara seemed to speak Turkish exactly like a

Turk. I admired his ease in the language and his use of idiomatic expressions quite unlike their German counterparts; I asked him how long he had been in Turkey and how he had learnt Turkish. He said he had been five years in Turkey, but was not at all clear how he had learnt Turkish; he had been amongst Turks a great deal from the beginning, but had spoken only to those who understood German, until one day he was in a grocer's shop and noticed himself asking for cheese in Turkish. At that time he had been in the country about two years; since then he had only spoken Turkish to Turks—at first, of course, within very narrow limits—except to those Turks with whom he already had built up habits of relationship in German.

Quite evidently this musician had built up large stores of impressions—helped, perhaps, by his highly developed musician's capacity for attentive listening—which suddenly began to flow out in the form of speech, when they had matured sufficiently or had acquired enough strength through constant renewal of the impressions in daily listening. He was fond of playing with words and was quick to seize on any unusual expression and carry it around—repeating it in his mind—until he had an occasion to ask a friend about it or use it to astonish the unwary. There should not be any cause for surprise in this if we remember how long a child listens and stores up impressions before it begins to speak and how miraculously ready-made expressions tumble out without having been built up piecemeal, or apparently learnt and practised in speech in embryo beforehand. Yet adults seldom see the need for the patience, or the habit of listening, that a trained musician and a child have; so the capacity, if it is there, passes unnoticed. This is particularly so because the process of absorbing words and speech forms is largely unconscious.

6. THE IMPORTANCE OF THE INCUBATION PERIOD

A new word or expression needs to sink into the mind and remain maturing there for a definite period, like a seed in the earth or an egg in the nest, until it emerges as an independent and living unit of speech. Plugging away at a new word or expression during this incubation period may produce only exasperation or staleness. I have noticed again and again that a class which seems slow to respond in speech to what I say, but waits and listens to my prolonged use of a new expression until the pressure becomes too great for silence, achieves fluency with accuracy in a shorter time than the class that begins to speak before the heard impressions have matured in the mind. I have learnt therefore to wait for the moment when a class has reached that degree of ripeness which produces a spontaneous bursting of the skins of reserve.

"Wenn die Zeit gekommen ist, platzen auch die Pfirsiche im Schatten."

("When the time has come even the peaches in the shade burst.")

I see to it, however, that my pupils hear enough repetition of the speech forms they are learning, or revising, for this piling up of impressions to be possible.

7. EAR TRAINING FOR ALIGNING THE MIND

The explanation of why one person learns a language without any very decided intention to do so, while another does not, seems to be that the set of the mind of the one was favourable, or towards the language, while the set of the mind of the other was unfavourable, or away from the language. That is to say, the efficacy, or penetrating power, of what is presented to the ear for learning does not depend exclusively on the material itself, or on what we would normally recognize as overt listening; it seems to depend at least as much on an inner—and often even unconscious—alignment of the mind that may be determined by emotional states, by prejudice, by personal affections or preferences, or by purely transient preoccupations; it often seems to depend too on an attitude of respect. Moses was told to take off his shoes—assume an attitude of respect—

D

before he could listen to what God had to tell him from the burning bush.

Conquering races have seldom learnt the languages of the races they have conquered: the ancient Britons who lived on in England after the Anglo-Saxon invasions learned English; the native races of South America learned Spanish. They were not forced to; it was not purely self-interest. The conquerors were not able to learn the language of the conquered—their minds were not adjusted to do so—unless they deliberately abandoned their attitude of superiority, or picked up the language as children. Boys and girls in school throughout the ages have seldom been able to learn a subject they could not—as we say—take seriously. Opinionated, over-confident people have not the flexibility of mind to learn languages easily.

A part is played in the process of learning by the conception or *Gestalt* we have of the finished product we hope to be; this is Adler's "final goal," seen by him as the mainspring of human effort. This image or goal may be largely unconscious, but is, to some extent, based on the expert and mature figure of the teacher, far ahead, executing his graceful arabesques on the icy surface that we only slide and tumble on. He comes back and leads us on, giving us his voice to hold on to; we hang on tightly, with teeth clenched, and wonder at the sureness we get in shadowing his movements in our minds. This is one reason why teacherless learning is difficult.

8. THE VALUE OF SIGNIFICANT REPETITION

The nearest I ever got to liking French during my schooldays was when our French master gave us the same piece of dictation twelve times over within a few weeks. I adored the swing of it, the murmur of the whispering breezes in it, the pictures so clearly perceived through countless repetitions, the clarity of it, the sparkle of each familiar dewdrop. I waited eagerly for each echo. If I were to hear it now in that well-remembered, rather rasping, voice I should stand up with a tear in the corner of each eye. In learning a language, repetition can be prolonged for the learner to the point at which a native speaker would dash, unhinged, from the room; an even quite modest piece of literature presented and familiarized with countless repetitions to the foreign learner comes to be loved more tenderly the more it is repeated, as each well-loved promontory comes into sight. Few teachers realize how often they may repeat a piece, either dictating it or reading it aloud to their pupils, if it has a melodious and picturesque character, without their getting tired of it. The sentence patterns will sink into their minds and be added to the general store of language patterns for active use.

9. THE TRAINING OF THE EAR—PREPARATORY WORK

The teacher who wants to give his pupils systematic ear training sees to it that when he is reading to them aloud, they are not allowed to rely on the eye for a rival impression either to corroborate or cancel the first impressions of the ear. That is, he gives them as much experience as he can in listening to the spoken word, or to the "read" word with books shut. Only when a piece is familiar should they be allowed to follow with the eye what is being read aloud. At first, all his teaching consists of speaking in relation to the situation he and they are in. He speaks about what he is doing and repeats the actions and sentences clearly enough for them to become related and familiar; he expects no response until his pupils spontaneously begin to form the sounds. This will be the procedure for the teaching of any new material right through to the end of the course.

As soon as possible he will give orders in the imperative for the pupil or pupils to carry out silently. When the class can answer simple questions and obey orders within the vocabulary they have learnt, the teacher will show them how to ask one another questions, and give one another orders, in pairs or groups. Ear training has started.

As time goes by he will give verbal instructions of a more complex kind for actions to be carried out. Because they are more complex, such instructions will have to be repeated and then written down before they are carried out. This may be done on the spot, or for homework; examples of this sort of work have been given in the chapter on homework. Another example might be: "After you have finished your supper this evening go out into the street and watch what is going on; then come back into the house and write down what you have seen." After several repetitions the pupil will write this down and change it to: "After I have finished my supper this evening I am to go out into the street for five minutes and watch what is going on; then I am to go back into the house and write down what I have seen." In time he may be able to write down his version direct from the teacher's orders.

Obviously the teacher never neglects opportunities to train the ears of his pupils, but he must remember that they will try to relax if they can, and depend on their eyes to make good the inattention of their ears. By allowing them no resort but attentive listening, by grading the difficulty of the demands he makes on their ears, by giving them the satisfaction of exercising a skill in listening, by making the exercises amusing, lively and worth while, by building up and developing a co-operative and workmanlike attitude towards ear training, by giving them at every stage the feeling that they are acquiring a useful, practical skill, he will bring them to enjoy and even glory in this sort of work. In time, they will neither need nor want help, just as a soldier who can shoot accurately would scorn to use a rest for his rifle.

10. CULTIVATED LISTENING ENSURES CONCENTRATION AND EFFICIENCY

I have found, in learning several languages, that what I need most urgently is the ability to listen attentively to representative samples of language, in such a way that I can hold them in my mind complete and see them whole. If I can do this I am well on my way to understanding the spoken language. If I can hold enough of them in my mind for long enough, and if

I can practise modifying them to varying conditions and uses, I have a store of readily accessible language units that can be applied to my own needs for expression, and this is the basis for a fluent spoken or written knowledge of the language. I have rendered my mind sensitive to the language and I have assembled the essential tools of expression for speaking and writing. If I have learnt to cling on to a new word or expression with all the tentacles of my conscious mind because there will be no entry in a notebook to hold it for me and save me the trouble, I am keying up my mind to that state of tension that makes the learning of language easy. In short, systematic and thorough training of the ear is the shortest and most concentrated way of applying the mind totally and unreservedly to the perception and absorption of language.

II. TECHNIQUES OF EAR TRAINING

A. *Dictation*—(i) *Preliminary Work*

When the pupil has been given some practice in attentive listening and in holding what he has heard in his head for long enough to respond to it or repeat it, we can start written dictations. The first will be very simple and only a few lines long; but there is no point in our reading abnormally slowly. We are primarily training the ear of the pupil to hear and understand normal speech uttered in normal speech rhythms, at normal speed in real conversations. The usual method of dictating practises nothing but the skill of doing dictations; it is not a skill that is immediately applicable to everyday life and its needs. In giving dictation I always read complete sentences and read them at nearly normal conversation speed; I grade the difficulty of the dictation to the ability of the class by choosing short, simple sentences for the beginners and increasing progressively the length and complexity of sentences to suit the class. An example of a dictation which might be the first given is: "We come to school at ten o'clock; we come here on foot; we stay at school until 4 o'clock. We read and write and speak English at school. We go home at four o'clock." These are all sentences which will be well-known and will often have been written before, copied or adapted from similar sentences. After I have read each sentence I walk round the class to see who is writing it correctly; I may whisper a word to someone who is held up for a word, or I may send a boy who has written it correctly to help one who has written it wrong, or who is finding the sentence difficult to finish. I then repeat the sentence after getting those who have written it right to read it out. In this way a sentence may be read five or six times. A class which is trained in this way can grasp and write down extremely long and complex sentences.

(ii) *The Second Stage*

But we shall not only dictate sentences; as the class increases in skill and acuity in listening, we can dictate even nonsense syllables to give our pupils training in hearing the sounds of the language accurately. In dictating sounds alone, we begin by dictating the sounds and having them repeated before they are written down; as soon as we can count on good recognition and reproduction we may let the class write these sounds straight down, from our dictation. Another way is to call up in turn a member of each group of a class which is organized in groups and say the sound to him. He then has to run back to his group and repeat the sound. Everyone must recognize it and write it down before the next boy may run up to the teacher for the new sound. The boy may have to say it to each other member of his group separately. Quite boisterous games may be enjoyed in this way, as interludes to more sober work. The dictation of unrelated sounds should not be attempted until the class has become interested in the sounds of the language as such; this may not be till the third or fourth year of work, or it may be later or earlier according to the keenness of the class. Not more than a few minutes of such dictation should be attempted in any one lesson. A little often is of far more value than long periods less frequently.

Those who are good at pronouncing the sounds may be set up to dictate lists of sounds either to the whole class or to delegates from groups, as just described, or to groups only. They can also be asked to dictate orders to the class or groups; the orders can be just carried out, or repeated before being carried out, or they can be repeated and written down, or else repeated to others who must write them down and pass on the written instructions to still others to carry out.

This sort of work supports and prepares for the more familiar forms of ear training. It can be carried out by one or more groups of a class only indirectly supervised. Any useful sentences can be handled in this way; they may be taken from earlier lessons which we want to keep in mind, but which hardly require any further active revision. Connected narratives from earlier lessons that are so well known that they can almost be written by heart can be dictated. There are so many possibilities that we need never be short of material to train the ear and keep it constantly alert.

(iii) *Third Stage—Dictation of Connected Narratives*

During the first two or three years only familiar material should be dictated, either pieces of earlier lessons, or material made up for the purpose out of the language and structures of the lessons. The same piece may be given several times, but the speed may be increased each time progressively to the speed of normal speech. The walking round to see how the individual pupils are getting on, and the repetition of the sentences, may be dropped at the third or fourth repetition of a dictation. A piece that is well known may be read by one of the members of the class, or by several, each reading a sentence or saying it from memory. In the third or fourth year, according to how they do these simple dictations, we may begin to give pieces which the class have not seen before, including some words and structures which they have met, but which are perhaps not yet quite familiar to the whole class.

The procedure then is developed as follows: the teacher

reads out the sentence at normal speaking speed and goes round the class to see how they write it. He may be able to see from a third to a half of the exercise books after each sentence; that is, each book after every two or three sentences.

If he sees that a pupil is held up he may ask him to give the gist of the sentence; he knows from this whether he has understood it, at least. He may then give him the sentence again in an undertone and pass on to another, or he may give him one word and leave him to try and remember the rest.

If there is a word which he knows is relatively unfamiliar he may speak about it before he begins the dictation, and write it on the blackboard; on the other hand, he may prefer to concentrate the attention of the class on it by bringing them up against it, so that when he gives it he is supplying a strongly felt need; or he may find a boy who knows it, and get him to write it on the blackboard and spell it out clearly several times over. All such words should be brought to full consciousness by being talked about and used before going on with the next sentence.

If the teacher finds that a boy has written the sentence correctly, he may make use of him by sending him round to see if the others near him have written it right. In this way the teacher can help and supervise many more pupils than he alone can see, and he can at the same time build up a spirit of mutual help: it is not always the same boy who writes the sentence first correctly. If a boy has written one word wrong the teacher may say to the whole class: "Did I say 'are' or 'were' after the words 'the older women'?" and the answer comes from all round: "were"—"the older women were all at home." The teacher may get a difficult phrase repeated in this way several times, to ensure fluency and to help understanding.

One of the boys may be told to write his dictation on the blackboard, where all can see it if they want to, instead of in his exercise book. This practice has several advantages: the boy who is completely stuck, and would not be able to write anything, is helped to write the sentence correctly, or as correctly as the sentence gets written on the blackboard; the boy who might rely on copying from another sees that he may do this if he likes, but it is allowed—and even encouraged for the weaker ones—so his self-esteem challenges him to write it without help; sometimes he may also find that he copies mistakes if he is not alert. The whole class soon learn to look for mistakes on the blackboard and draw attention to them, sometimes with delight; in this way they learn to look critically at what they see written, and get experience in correcting mistakes.

The whole process contributes to building up a co-operative atmosphere and a sense of personal responsibility in each boy for his own work; the boy soon begins to notice improvement in his skill and comprehension, if we grade the difficulty of the pieces carefully. Boys are helped at once if they need help, but they are encouraged to manage as far as possible without help. Each sentence is corrected on the blackboard before we go on to the next sentence so that mistakes can be corrected immediately in each exercise book; if we notice that a boy is failing to correct his mistakes, we put him beside a boy who will correct them for him, until he can learn to correct them for himself. The teacher may paraphrase a difficult sentence in some of his repetitions but always return to the original version before he goes on to the next sentence.

When the whole piece has been written on the blackboard, and corrected carefully, it may be read through by the members of the class sentence by sentence. In the first reading each boy may read a sentence; in the second and third readings each boy may read two or three sentences. When the teacher finds that the piece has become familiar to the class, he may rub out every fifth word and ask them to read it again. When they have read it successfully, filling in the missing words, he rubs out every fourth word and gets them to read it once more; now they must fill in each pair of missing words. So he goes on, rubbing out words until the class can repeat the whole piece from beginning to end, although there is nothing left on the blackboard.

When this point has been reached the dictation can be considered to have done its work of familiarizing the patterns contained in it, of co-ordinating hand, eye and ear, of relating the written to the spoken word, and of drawing the attention of the pupils to spelling and punctuation. In this type of dictation those who can spell and punctuate fairly correctly are given practice, so that they become better and surer; those who spell and punctuate badly are helped by being able to copy, if necessary, and by having the words which they find difficult spelt and respelt for them. They have their attention drawn to the correct punctuation often enough for them to become aware of the rules. If a boy is seen to make the same mistake in spelling fairly frequently, he is asked to say how many times he thinks he needs to copy it, to learn the correct spelling; if this is found not to be enough, and he still makes the mistake, he is asked to name a further number, and so on, until he learns it, supervised, perhaps, by another member of his group.

B. *Mechanical Aids*

In recent years there has been a very great increase in the use of mechanical aids for language learning. The most important are the gramophone and the tape-recorder, though in some countries, where there is a shortage of properly trained teachers, great and successful use has been made of the radio. Radio lessons supplemented, where possible, with exercises, have been supervised by quickly trained instructors. This has been the basis of a campaign to teach English on a nation-wide scale in Sweden, and the campaigns to teach English to new immigrants into Australia have been supplemented with carefully co-ordinated radio programmes.

(i) *Gramophone*

The gramophone is, and will remain for many years, the most convenient, portable and cheap mechanical device for bringing the authentic sounds of a native speaker of the language into the most remote classroom.

A gramophone which is to be heard by a large class must be electrically amplified, but where there is only a portable or other mechanically operated gramophone very good use can be made of it in small groups. In some schools there is a central gramophone with amplifiers in every classroom. If one side of a twelve-inch or two sides of a ten-inch record can be played every day, with a short introduction or commentary, the pupils are helped very much to build up a store of pattern sentences; they absorb pronunciation and intonation, and their ears are trained. The same record may be repeated several times. It is not essential that very close attention should be paid to it, though its effectiveness is increased if it is. A natural way of securing repetition is for the record to be played to the whole school, say, at 9 o'clock, when the school assembles, then once in each class during the day. It may then be available for groups of those interested, for further listening, after school is over. It is often possible for one group, when a class is working in groups, to be listening to gramophone records; where a classroom has a small room attached or a large vestibule or—as in India—a wide verandah, such work can be done there. A machine with earphones makes this listening possible in a classroom without the other groups being disturbed.

Records such as those that accompany Palmer and Blandford's "Everyday Sentences in Spoken English", or the various series produced by the Linguaphone Institute and the B.B.C. are suitable; but for variety, stories can be recorded that will be listened to again and again, and poetry and songs are likely to be repeated still more. With a tape-recorder a school can and should produce most of its own material. Just as sounds only and invented words—for their sounds only—can be dictated by the teacher, so they can be played on the gramophone and repeated several times, one or two of the repetitions being used as dictation. We can give a place to the spoken language in external examinations, which are conducted on too wide a scale for visiting examiners to be able to get round to all the schools, if a dictation and some questions are recorded on gramophone records or tapes. These can be sent out with the question papers to the schools to form part of the examination.

In normal classroom practice the gramophone record will only supplement the teacher's work. It can hardly be so effective as a teacher, because there can be no reciprocal response or any play of personality, and a gramophone record cannot adapt itself to a particular set of pupils, or develop its lesson out of contact with them as people with needs and abilities. The stereotyped lesson which the teacher has prepared at home and brings into the classroom determined to carry right through in spite of all difficulties, is not so insensitive and inflexible as the lesson dictated on to a gramophone record and played over in the teeth of inattention and even blank incomprehension. We cannot expect from gramophone records what they are not fitted to give, a teaching lesson which only a living person can usefully give. They are especially valuable where the pronunciation of the teacher is not to be relied upon. Unfortunately it is just those teachers who are reluctant to let gramophone records show up their pronunciation. By convincing them that their prestige does not rest on their maintaining a myth of perfection, but on their skill in helping their pupils to attain a good standard, we may help them to lose their fear of the perfection of gramophone records and show them how to improve their own pronunciation from careful and repeated listening to them.

(ii) *Tape Sound Recorder*

Some of the most modern techniques of language teaching are based on the use of the tape-recorder. The voice of the teacher is recorded and the learner records his voice beside it; the comparison helps the learner to correct his mistakes.

During the second world war soldiers were trained to understand foreign languages and to interpret, in far shorter periods of time than had ever been thought possible before. They were taught very intensively by the Direct Method; only normal, conversational rapid speech in natural situation was used, and when the lessons were over the students sat for hours with headphones on, listening to the same patterns endlessly repeated, in typical situations. In time the rhythms and intonation began to work on their subconscious minds and build up patterns that began to develop into active speech; and, through that, the meaning—wherever it had not been clear—gradually crystallized out. This kind of course may not be suitable, as it stands, for normal school use. The groups were, firstly, selected with carefully worked-out aptitude tests; secondly, the motives which the trainees had for applying themselves to the work intensively were unusually strong; thirdly, a fair proportion of them had to stop after a few weeks' work because of the nervous strain, and, fourthly, the trainees were adults who had learnt to concentrate. We can, however, recognize the value of voluminous listening, with and without response in speech.

We can make use of the tape-recorder to record our own speech and that of our pupils and compare them with that of native speakers. We can do individual and group work with it, and we can encourage the keener students to put in extra work on it out of school. One can preserve or wipe out sound impressions at will; one can record and keep, for reference, talks of visiting lecturers or specimens of their speech for intensive study; one can record radio talks and play them over again to study them in detail, and one can wipe out a student's unsuccessful speech and record an improved version that he would prefer to be represented by.

(iii) *Radio—Supplementary to a School Teaching Programme*

The great disadvantage of radio is that the speaker is invisible; the human mind has not yet had many years to adapt itself to disembodied voices. We still require something to watch while we are concentrating on a speaker's voice; a box with a latticed hole in it, or a silent, motionless teacher, is not a satisfying substitute for the speaker himself and his actions. Another disadvantage is that the voice comes to each single listener separately. A good radio lesson should therefore provide a suitable picture or a chart for the pupil to look at while he is listening. It should also take care of his gregarious instincts by relating him to his teacher, by giving the voices of an invisible class or conversation group that he can identify himself with, and by giving him something to join in with, a song, or an exercise that he has received a copy of beforehand. There must be some concrete evidence that he himself has a place, not only in the class, but in the system. If the radio lesson is kept short and placed in the middle of the school period, the teacher has time to do some preliminary work based on the notes sent out in advance, and then some follow-up work in the last ten minutes of the lesson. This gives the broadcast a good chance of making an effective contribution to the work on the language.

There is still the problem of the broadcast that fails because it is not listened to. In Sweden, the radio broadcast is made the kernel of a system of teaching where semi-trained instructors simply direct the practice work, according to printed instructions, after the broadcast is over, and they lead the class in responses to the questions of the radio voice. Elsewhere there is no very strong incentive to the teacher to tune in regularly. With no bell to ring in the classroom to announce it, he can easily forget it. Those who listen regularly do so because they are, on the whole, satisfied, and those who never listen are not interested and have nothing to base an opinion on.

(a) *Independent Radio Lessons.* There has been a good deal of success in independent language learning from radio programmes intended for the adult listener, with explanation in the mother tongue of the listener in the early stages. Their success presupposes a considerable desire in the listener to learn the language, however, and a good deal of tenacity in application. Many who start such a course soon give up. The organization of learners in listening groups gives a greater likelihood of success.

(b) *Radio Talks and Plays*. Other types of radio programmes than prepared lessons are helpful in building up experience in a language, and especially in maintaining skill in listening at a high standard once it has been developed, or in keeping touch with a language one might otherwise lose touch with. Talks, especially the more intimate and practical ones on gardening, household work and travel, are good for keeping a language alive and giving experience of following a description or a simple line of thought in the language, but radio plays are the best training in participation in real-life situations. The speech is mostly conversational in form in modern plays, and the action, with sound effects, makes listening easy. If the story is gripping enough the pupil will not notice the language, and then he will absorb the language patterns most effectively.

If a class is to listen to a play together, the teacher should either arrange to listen to it twice or he should prepare for the listening by getting the text beforehand. He can then make the story, or at least the setting of the story, and the most important of the words and language patterns familiar to the class before the broadcast begins. All radio listening should be strengthened, either by preparation and follow-up work in class, or by the isolated pupil trying to find a partner to practise aloud the speech forms which he has heard on the radio. If this is really out of the question he should read the script aloud, or half-aloud, to himself.

12. PHONETICS

All ear training involves training in phonetics whether conscious or systematic or neither. Yet a language teacher who has no systematic knowledge of the sounds of the language which he is teaching, nor of how they are made, and who has no accurate idea of how they differ from the comparable sounds of the home language, can hardly be regarded as a professional teacher. His pupils must pay in effort and waste of time for his lack. On the other hand, I have seen classes in which all interest in the language was extinguished before the course had really started, where the teacher spent a month or two in practising the sounds before introducing any real sentences. A class of adults who are really keenly interested in learning the language and are accustomed to systematic study may survive, but not children, who need activity, human traffic and response, as long as they have not yet been won for the language by the sense of mastery that comes with the ability to use genuine language intelligibly. It is also not necessary. Ninety per cent of pupils in the average class can imitate pronunciation quite adequately if they have enough representative samples to hear. If there are gramophone records of the sounds of the language the teacher can play them regularly; if he is not sure of his own pronunciation he should never be ashamed of learning to pronounce the sounds more and more accurately with his pupils.

In the first few years it will be enough if the teacher gives a few hints for the correct positioning of lips and tongue whenever he hears sounds wrongly pronounced, putting the point of a pencil to his lips to help the rounding for the English "w" sound, emphasizing the vibration of the lower lip against the top teeth to help towards a correct "v" sound, showing the difference in the opening of the mouth in the sounds in the English words "hot", "ought", "heart" and "hurt".

I usually introduce a class to the phonetic symbols early in the fourth year of work, or some time towards the end of the third year, in a good class. I make the pupils consciously aware of the twelve pure vowel sounds and the diphthongs, and show them how to distinguish between the voiced and unvoiced consonants. This may well be enough if pronunciation has been consistently checked and if the ear has been trained systematically; the pupil, by this time, has got used to normal spelling, which he must in any case depend on for his usual reading. Now he will gradually learn the symbols well enough to consult the dictionary, but he need not be expected to read continuous passages in phonetic script. A good class may, however, be expected to study patterns of conversation and intonation with the help of the script; there is no other way of showing—on paper—the unemphatic forms of words such as "have", "can", "shall", etc., so that they can be distinguished from the emphatic forms. This sort of work is best done with the help of gramophone or tape-recorder.

CONCLUSION

As we realize more and more clearly the value of attentive, concentrated listening as a basis of language learning, we can help ourselves to a readier and easier contact with languages that are beyond our immediate reach by gramophone and radio listening. As the learning of foreign languages becomes more urgent, with the diminution of barriers of space and the necessity for an increase in international co-operation, we are lucky to have a vast increase in the availability of specimens of language, spoken by the best native speakers of them, and dealing with current affairs, scientific and cultural topics, and simple domestic situations, at a standard of intelligibility that puts them within the reach of the common man.

Courses—whether radio, gramophone or taped—specially designed for home learning, and supplemented with attractively prepared printed material, worked over, where possible, in groups, give the best chances of success for adults who are unable to attend regular classes. They make a valuable supplementary source of language experience for all those—whether children or adults—who are having regular instruction from competent teachers. Where not enough competent teachers are available, a state system of education can make a short-cut to economy and success in language learning by working out a full programme of instruction in which radio lessons play a predominant role. These may provide material broadcast by experts for practice in groups and individually, under the

E

supervision of partially trained instructors. The knowledge and skill of the instructors may be expected to increase rapidly with regular listening and systematic repetition of the speech patterns with their classes. There is no longer any reason why a state should resign itself to poor and uneconomic results from a language teaching programme on account of shortage of trained teachers for the beginners. Where competent teachers are available, systematic training of the ear, supplemented by gramophone, tape-recorder and radio, can reduce the amount of work for the teacher to a manageable quantity; he can delegate some of the supervision to group leaders, and gradually train all the pupils to supervise one another. This can lead to better results over a wider area than was ever before possible.

4

Teacher and Textbook

1. THE ROLE OF THE TEXTBOOK

One of the chief purposes of learning a foreign language is to bring near what is distant, to get information which is inaccessible in the home language; we seldom read a book to find out about what we already know, to read stories already long familiar. It is true that an adult learner with a strong interest in learning a language can sometimes learn a good deal by reading and rereading a familiar passage or story in the foreign language, but this is a person who is able to concentrate on the language for its own sake, who can ignore the tedium of repeating an oft-told story. Children in school are seldom able to suspend their interest in the subject-matter in favour of the language. The role of the textbook is to stand for the distant and hardly accessible delights that lie behind the forbidding barriers of strangeness of language, the imaginative life of the child as well as its craving for knowledge. It is to represent, and give a foretaste of, all those books which the learner aspires to read and master. The role of the teacher is to bring the pupil to this strange territory, but with language tools prepared at home, in familiar situations.

2. THE PREPARATION FOR READING

All new language material should be used first so that it is thoroughly familiar to the ear and is almost a piece of habitual behaviour, before it is ever read in a book. A language is a habit to be copied, an activity to be developed, a skill to be practised. It is a referential skill: just as the saw, the chisel and the plane have no significance or use without the wood they are made for, so language has no life in itself. It must live in the mouth of the teacher in relation to the activity and situations of the classroom. It is a social skill: unless it sets up a personal relationship between teacher and pupil and later, a community relationship between learner and learner in the class, it cannot really live, or do significant work, in the minds of the pupils. In other words, the teacher must really be himself and give himself, talking to real people about real things and then training his pupils to talk to one another about real things, if at first in formulae, at least true formulae that can be modified to become spontaneous speech, so that there is real communication and social contact, however limited at first.

> How many books have you?
> I have three; how many have you?
> I have three too, but Subramanian has more than that.
> Ask him how many he has.
> Subramanian, how many books have you?
> I have five. How many have you?
> I have three. Please lend me one. Now I have four and you have four, too. Subramanian and I have each four books.

In this way we prepare the pupil's mind to understand the structural material, and then add the vocabulary to these patterns to make it possible for him to read a passage in a book and understand it in the way he understands a paragraph in a book in his own language when he reads it for the first time. It is a joint enterprise of teacher and pupil and the group to win their way into this tract of language by helping one another to realize the words and the structures in use, and apply them to the book. Any attempt to use language which has not been brought to life in some way such as this, to approach and study texts in a book, is bound to be wasteful and inefficient.

3. TEACHER, IN RELATION TO NOTEBOOK AND TEXTBOOK

The teacher should not confuse his role with the role of the textbook by identifying himself with the textbook, teaching everything from the unchanging texts, acting solely as an interpreter of them. He may help himself to avoid this error by setting up two poles to move between, the pupil's personal notebook to represent the near, and the textbook to represent the far. The notebook can contain sample sentences of all that the pupil has learnt in his own setting, all the preparation work for reading a text, all the sentences which he has copied from the blackboard and practised with his neighbours in the class, all the sentences which he has adapted to his own personal situation from the more general ones given by the teacher. It becomes the pupil's private textbook, reminding him of many situations which he has himself experienced, repeating the language patterns as he remembers them.

The textbook, on the other hand, brings into the classroom what is otherwise beyond it. It can contain further uses, in an unfamiliar setting, of words and sentence patterns which have been learnt and practised in the familiar setting; it can bring into the classroom what otherwise would remain outside. The subject-matter of the lessons in the textbook need not be familiar, because the learning of the language needed to understand them has been done in the familiar world of every day: now is the time to go out in search of exotic sights and experiences. The child delights to reach out into the unknown, into the unknown world of the imagination and into the world of strange peoples and customs. But there might not be much justification for our helping him to this in our language lessons if we did not, after reading a passage in a book, return to apply what we have learnt to our own experience.

We must train our pupils to reflect on what they read, look at their own life and circumstances with new eyes, come down to earth again the right way up. Their reading should stimulate new expression, first in speech and then in writing. This will be a developed form of the expression begun, perhaps very haltingly and with a great deal of help from the teacher, before the piece was read. The comparative freedom now possible will stimulate to further effort.

4. THE NEED FOR A TEXTBOOK

We can teach without a textbook; we learnt our first language without one, and many people learn others later, but, to make the best use of time in the classroom and to avoid unintended repetition or the neglect of essential language patterns, the teacher is wise to have a textbook, at least in the background of his mind. The pupil who has passed the age of nine or ten, and has got used to having textbooks in his own language for other subjects, likes to have something in his hand which stands for the language and measures the rate of his progress. It gives him convenient passages to practise reading on. If it is attractively printed and illustrated, and the stories are interesting, he will often turn over the pages he has finished and enjoy the feeling of mastery which they give him. Each lesson in the textbook should stand for a set of skills, a set of language patterns, and associated vocabulary first learnt in speech and then tested and exercised in the reading of a text and in the attached exercises. Both teacher and pupil, realizing that the language-learning process does not begin and end in the textbook, may yet base their work on it. Provided they neither of them see their chief duty in the interpreting and reading of the material in the textbook, but regard the fluent reading and understanding of it as a sign that the language contained in it has been learnt, the book can be a welcome support and guide.

Very few teachers are so fully aware of what has to be taught, and of what gives the most trouble in the learning, that they can afford to do without such help. The writer of a good textbook is an experienced teacher who has put the best of his knowledge and skill at the disposal of whoever uses his book. He has graded his material so that each structural point follows naturally and easily on the one before it, adds to it, and ensures opportunities for significant repetition. He has given exercises for practising language taught for the lesson, and supplementary exercises for points which his experience tells him give special difficulty.

But the writer of the textbook has to condense; he cannot print everything in his book which the teacher should teach, it would become too thick and unmanageable; and, in any case, he can never forecast what will happen in this or that class, or what the circumstances of a particular lesson will be. The most he can do is to give—preferably in a separate teacher's handbook—suggestions of probable classroom situations and activities which may be made use of to introduce and teach the language needed for the lessons in the book. The teacher must still make the language digestible and prepare his pupils to absorb it by using it to talk about their experience and circumstances, before he allows them to see what is laid out for them in the book.

5. THE PUPIL'S NOTEBOOK

The pupil is able to lavish a great deal of affection and care on his notebook if the teacher knows how to stimulate him to create something which is really his own and which stands for his own personal growth in the language. Nothing should be dictated into the notebook, though dictations, once they have been gone over and corrected, may be copied into it. As soon as the pupil has acquired the habit of compiling a personal notebook, and has begun to take pride in its appearance, the test of what goes in should be his own private preference and interest. But those with no special interests may be helped to cultivate interests and, in the meantime, copy in their own modifications of the material written on the blackboard for the class to copy and modify.

Copying of this kind is not mechanical, because the pupil has to concentrate on the meaning to be sure that he is adapting the sentences to suit his own different circumstances, or to record the teacher's circumstances afresh from his own point of view. The words are nearly all provided, but the sentences, and sometimes the punctuation, have to be modified. An example of such an exercise is given in the chapter on unsupervised work.

We should allow our pupils to illustrate their notebooks as lavishly as they like. This is not to say that we should stimulate language learners to over-elaboration in drawing and neatness by competitions that involve spending hours in work that is not a spontaneous expression of delight in skill and craftsmanship. The teacher should try to select as many of the notebooks as possible in turn, for display, always for some particular excellence or marked improvement. It is usually possible to find something worth display in any notebook which is carefully kept. Illustrations may be cut out of newspapers or magazines and pasted in, with captions and titles complete, or specially rewritten.

The pupil should learn to look on his notebook as a supply of material for exercises to strengthen any weakness which he has, as a reminder of what he has actually learnt in class, and as a source of sentences and sentence patterns to draw on for composition. When he has done an exercise which he has personally found to be particularly useful, he should make up a new one for himself, with new sentences but the same instructions at the top, and record it in the notebook, ready for revision at some later date. All language which is learnt, all language which is met in the textbook, should be found in the notebook in sentences which deal with the familiar situation, with the first two spheres of the pupil's situation. The notebook is then the real textbook, the textbook which means most to the pupil, and the printed textbook takes its proper place, at one remove from him, in the third and fourth spheres of his consciousness.

6. THE TEXTBOOK AS A GENERALIZATION

The textbook is a generalization which cannot meet the

needs of every class. The teacher must apply what he finds there to the needs of his class. He must learn to control his vocabulary and reduce it to the point his pupils have reached. He must know exactly which words they have learnt and introduce no others unless he intends to teach them or prepare the class for learning them fully later. If he knows that he will need them so often in future lessons that they will be really learnt without elaborate demonstration or formal teaching being necessary, he may use them when he wants them, without drawing attention to them or expecting them to be learnt quickly. The compulsion of the moment and the situation where the word is really needed will make it easy to teach any word or structure economically, even though it may be printed later in the book. The place where a word is printed may be regarded as the place where the word is given formal recognition as having been introduced and fully learnt, but most of the learning process may have gone on unobtrusively before this, and even, perhaps, for a long time.

Although the skilled teacher may introduce any word or structure wherever he needs it, a beginner in teaching, or a teacher who is learning to apply structural grading, should try to keep to the grading that has been worked out in the textbook. This has been worked out on the basis of the experience of the writer of the book, who tries to imagine himself in any classroom—usually a composite conception of all the classrooms he has known—and imagine the general characteristics of most classrooms, ignoring or extracting the peculiarities. It is the business of the individual teacher to put back the peculiarities, but also to prepare his pupils for the generalization, demonstrating that language is neutral, and can be applied to anything, to the classroom situation or to the situation in the book.

If language is to be generally applicable it must be applied in class to more than the circumstances it was learnt in, otherwise the pupil may be inhibited all his life from applying it to other circumstances because the words are too closely linked with particular experiences. The textbook has an important part to play here; it applies the language to distant, second-hand experience in the third and fourth spheres of the pupil's consciousness; it permits the generalization which makes it possible for the teacher to link and fuse the near and the far, to go out to the far, equipped with language learnt on the near, and finally return with the harvest gathered there to absorb and digest the strange impressions once more at home.

7. MAKING USE OF A TEXTBOOK LESSON

If the textbook has been carefully written, and if each lesson introduces structural material suitably graded to the standard of the class, developing out of previously learnt material and leading on to what has to be learnt afterwards, there is no difficulty in identifying the most important structural material; but it is a great help to the teacher if the new structural material and the vocabulary intended to be taught in the lesson are shown separately, preferably in a teacher's handbook. The oral introduction to the lesson can be sketched in a series of sentences, and question and answer, based on a probable classroom situation. These can be modified to suit the conditions of the actual classroom. The structural material, because it is universally applicable, is introduced first.

Supposing Conditions are the structural item to be presented in the lesson; wishes have been introduced, but must be practised.

> I am not eating ice-cream now: I wish I were.
> If I were eating ice-cream, my tongue would be cold.
> Balasundaram, are you eating ice-cream just now?
> No, I'm not (helped, perhaps, with whispered prompting); I wish I were.
> If you were eating ice-cream, would your tongue be warm or cold?
> It would be cold.
> Have you a big car, Chandrasekhara?

No, we haven't; I wish we had.
Would you often go out in it, if you had a big car?
Yes, I should.
Would you ever drive it?
No, I shouldn't; I'd be too young.

After a good deal of practice of this kind, the teacher can begin to introduce the vocabulary necessary for understanding the piece. As the piece is about the four seasons in Europe, we can begin, in a tropical country, by saying:

Do we have a cold winter here, Sundaram?
No, we don't.
Quite right; if we did we should have ice and snow on the ground.
Are we in Europe now?
No, we aren't; if we were we should have ice and snow now.

"If we were in Europe we should have a cold winter; we should see no leaves on the trees in winter, we should see them come out"—making use of pictures, or drawing on the blackboard—"in the spring, and the trees would be covered with leaves in the summer."

If we were going to Europe, how should we go?
We should go by sea or by air, etc.

By the time the subject of the seasons in Europe has been sufficiently discussed for all the important words in the piece to have been used, or at least mentioned several times, the formation of a conditional sentence will have become familiar. Then a set of sentences can be written on the blackboard to act as a pattern and be copied down by the class. Personal modifications of them or the original sentences can be copied into the notebooks, the dialogues can be composed in the class and copied down for practice by the pupils in groups or pairs. These can be repeated at home for homework.

By this time the pattern of the conditional sentence has

become really familiar, and the most important words used in the piece have begun to settle permanently in the mind. At this point the book may be opened and the teacher may begin to read; but it is really better to read the piece over once or twice, not too fast, but without any long, artificial pauses, before the pupils open their books; then their full attention is concentrated on the reading of the teacher. The next stage is to read the piece line by line, slowly, paraphrasing where necessary, perhaps explaining, but preferring, where possible, to explain action and situation rather than words. We may ask the class to listen to a passage carefully to catch the answer to a question; we read and reread it until they catch it. When the piece has been read through in this way slowly, once or twice, a few new words being left to be brought out in each reading, the class can read it through three or four times silently. Finally, the teacher reads it again. Now is the time to look up any new words in a dictionary. This is merely to confirm that they have been understood correctly. There is nothing to be gained by looking up the words in a dictionary beforehand, as a kind of preparation for reading the piece.

8. EXPLANATIONS

No time should be lost in explanations of usage. If the teacher catches himself explaining anything he ought always to ask himself if his explanation was really necessary. It may have been necessary, but many explanations given in the class-room could have been avoided. Even when explanation seems necessary, an explanation in words alone may be hard to follow. An explanation which is not understood is not worth giving. While teaching language, explanations of usage are almost always a waste of time. They are necessarily abstract, and are difficult to follow if we have not learnt the usage which is being described; they often call for vocabulary and expressions which the pupil has not yet learnt, or is not sure enough of to rely on. Explanations which appeal to the intelligence seldom help the formation of language habits. It is a strain to remember the explanation and the justification while trying to use the form of words to talk about something else. We save the learner the worry and strain of trying to think about or juggle with two quite different ways of thinking at once if we guide him and help him to use the language forms needed until he can move confidently without help.

Explanations, on the other hand, in clear simple language, of natural occurrences, such as how rain falls or dew forms, or how a volcano erupts, as in any geography or physics lesson, need never be a waste of time. If based on simple diagrams drawn on the blackboard, which can almost be understood alone without any words being used, the words themselves may not be understood, but they will have been heard being used in a way that makes their meaning clear; this helps the pupil to learn them. A few repetitions of the explanation, with the same words, is enough to ease the words into the mind.

A story is told in a book on the teaching of English in India of an inspector who came into a class while the author of the book was teaching, and, after watching him for a time, asked him if he never taught by the direct method. Hearing that he never did, the inspector took over the class and began to demonstrate what he took to be the direct method. It happened that the class had reached the middle of a prose piece, and the next word to be taught was "dew". The inspector asked what the boys saw on the grass when they went out in the early morning. They answered, "Snakes." Slightly dismayed, he asked what they thought when they saw that the grass was wet. "We think that the gardener has been watering it," they answered with uncanny unanimity. At this the inspector gave up, leaving the teacher to give the meaning of the word "dew" in the home language, triumphant at the loyalty of his class and the discrediting of the direct method.

This little story is instructive. The inspector allowed himself to be challenged on his opponent's ground; he seems not to have understood the need for all direct method teaching to arise from the pupil's situation; he allowed himself to be baffled by two wilfully—it seems to me—obtuse answers. Why did he stop at these two questions? What became of his patience and his tolerance for an enterprising joke? Was there no further question to be asked? He could have agreed that one might see snakes on the grass in the early morning, that one might also see water—perhaps more often—and that if one saw water there were various possible explanations, rain, gardener, an overflowing cistern or irrigation ditch, hundreds of boys spitting on the grass, and possibly dew. It might be DEW, dew; yes, dew. Rain can be discussed, how and why it falls; it falls from clouds when the temperature or pressure drops; when a cloud rises, drops of water form, grow larger and begin to fall. If we pour out a glass of very cold water in warm weather, or take a bottle from the refrigerator, drops form on the outside; these drops are dew. If there is water in the air in the evening some of it forms drops on the grass, as the air gets cooler; this is dew. We walk through the grass at night or in the early morning, our feet or shoes get wet with dew, if it is a fine night and it has not been raining. Some people say dew is good for prickly heat. We begin to talk about dew, not worrying very much if everyone understands the word at first. The language is being used; the class is being drawn in and the word dew ceases to matter much. It is learnt, but tossed on one side as we discuss matters of greater interest to us, temperature, pressure, cloud formation, the shape of falling drops, etc.

An experienced teacher of language never lets himself be caught by a word such as "dew" in the middle of a piece of prose. If it is important to the understanding of the piece, he sees that he introduces it, with the words and ideas that go with it and group round the subject of the piece, before ever allowing anybody to open a book. If it is not, he may pass over it with hardly a reference—"water, the water we find on grass and leaves in the early morning, or on the side of a glass of very cold water, or iced water"—and go on with the main material of the piece. In writing a piece for a textbook it is wiser to exclude words which do not contribute anything to the main material of the piece, which distract the attention from the theme and the vocabulary in which it is expressed, which are not integral to the particular segment of language being presented. If we have to make use of an ungraded or carelessly arranged textbook it is wiser to disregard such words or give their meaning briefly and pass on. Time need never be spent on a word alone; it is only worth spending time in the way just shown on the word "dew" if this gives us an excuse and opportunity to use the language in an interesting way to talk about what interests the class.

In the same book the question is asked, how we are to teach the word or the idea of Christmas Pudding to Indian children who have never seen such a thing, except by an elaborate explanation and description in the mother tongue. It seems to me to be exaggerating the power of language very greatly to suppose that any language, native or foreign, can give any but a very rough approximation of the taste of anything which we have never tasted. The Indian child with no prospect of eating Christmas Pudding can understand enough about it if he knows that it is roundish and brown, sweet and spiced, and eaten as part of the rejoicings on Christmas Day in England. The rest may come when he goes to spend Christmas Day with an English family. The problem is not one of language, but of experience. There is no point in spending time in trying to describe the sort of idea which they can make no use of, nor deal with at their stage of development; there are some matters which are beyond the grasp of children or adolescents, as there are some matters which are beyond their physical reach. It is better to leave these matters untouched, or merely glanced at, as long as there are more accessible topics to deal with.

9. THE PLANNING OF A LESSON

Every lesson must have its roots in the preceding lesson and its branches and flowers in the succeeding lessons. No lesson should be an isolated entity for itself alone; yet every lesson should be complete in itself, introduced, brought to its climax and concluded, all as if the class were to have no other lessons. Just as there are no individual people with no relationships to others, so there are no unrelated lessons; to ignore the relationship is to deceive oneself. The good teacher avoids waste and confusion by making the relationships clear; the language is a seamless robe which never comes to an end once we take up one end of it; to call one lesson Grammar, another Composition, another Prose and another Poetry and isolate them from one another is to atomize the language and cut up the mind into unrelated segments. Education should produce minds capable of finding and establishing relationships.

Two or more teachers should not teach the same language to the same class unless they can keep very full and exact records and continually discuss what each of them does with the class. Where this is not done, even if the lessons of one are called Grammar and the lessons of the other Poetry, there will be harmful division and also wasteful overlapping and disagreement at some points.

To switch back to a previous lesson on what seems to be a different topic, for a few minutes, may preserve continuity; it will avoid monotony in a strenuous lesson. In a grammar lesson I sometimes repeat a poem just learnt, perhaps at the beginning, and in the middle again, with another one at the end. In a poetry lesson I may include five minutes on the essentials of a preceding grammar lesson. The cinema technique of constantly changing the angle of the shots and occasional quick switches to earlier scenes is my guide here.

Composition and textual study are interrelated, in that textual study should lead naturally into renewed expression, and that the preparation of texts calls for speaking and writing about the subject. Composition exercises lead out of grammar exercises and poetry can form the subject of discussion and written composition. There need be nothing which hangs unrelated and unintegrated in the air.

A busy teacher has very little time for the planning of his lessons; fortunately detailed planning is not necessary, even for the oral lessons in which he introduces and practises new patterns, when once he has learnt the technique of developing the use of language out of the circumstances of his pupils in the class. Too detailed a plan may deprive a lesson of its spontaneity. The course needs some planning, but this is usually done by the writer of the textbook. Once the course is well launched the most effective planning of an oral lesson is to run over the main structural material and vocabulary taught in the previous lesson and enter it up in a notebook. A loose-leaf notebook or file is suitable, so that the record of key-sentences can be kept on a sheet of paper by one of the best members of the class who can write quickly and accurately; such a pupil is usually glad to demonstrate his ability, and so save the teacher's time for work in helping the weaker members of the class. Another member of the class can write the key-sentences on the blackboard for copying, or several members can write a sentence each. As much of the writing on the blackboard as possible, once their handwriting is good enough, should be done by the members of the class. With the responsibility of keeping class records, and of other work for the class, this helps to develop the atmosphere of a co-operative workshop in which everyone's work is significant and the neglect of any work by an individual is seen as a loss to the community.

The teacher can go over these sentences, which summarize the work of the lesson, at home. Then he turns to the new lesson in the book and analyses it. He looks first for the main structural point. This has to be taught first, so he prepares a few new sentences, which are likely to arise from the situation of the class and which can be made to lead naturally into the material of the textbook lesson. After this he thinks out some ways of introducing the vocabulary; perhaps he will think out some likely sentences round a unifying theme, which will lead into the theme of the textbook lesson. He may note them

F

on paper, but he will probably not look at them during the lesson; it will be enough for him to have thought them out and prepared his mind for working to this pattern. The rest of the lesson should come from the class and the situation.

The teacher helps the backward and those who have missed a few lessons—there may always be a few—if he introduces new structural material in sentences which repeat the work of previous lessons in quite unmistakable situations. A useful rule is to introduce new structure in familiar vocabulary, and new vocabulary in structure which has, at least, been introduced. It is best to revise structural· material on new situations, with some new vocabulary. Those who have learnt the patterns best may become his accomplices or demonstrators; they answer his questions first, then they lead groups in dialogue, and finally they take charge of those who find the new language material difficult, to give them further practice. In this way the teacher is able to ensure that the weaker members of the class are not overlooked or neglected, but at the same time the stronger are given opportunities to feel and enjoy their ability in a useful, sociable way. Their helping others to learn helps them to learn too; above all they need not feel frustrated by feeling that the teacher grudges them recognition or passes them over as not requiring his attention.

10. THE PLACE OF THE TEXTBOOK

The place of the textbook in a normal school language course may be summarized as follows. It is:

(a) A guide for the teacher.

(b) A memory aid for the pupil.

(c) A permanent record or measure of what has been learnt.

(d) A generalization or canalization, a uniting factor in the language learning of a wide area.

(e) A means of extending linguistic experience beyond the local scene and the limited experience of the pupil.

(f) An exercise-ground for reading.

CONCLUSION

The textbook is one—perhaps the most important—of many visual aids. We should never allow it, or any picture or sentence in it, to stand between our pupils and the concrete world which they ought to look at and experience directly and without prejudice. No paper tree or paper person should take the place of the real trees and real people around them; the language must not be allowed to stay imprisoned between the pages of a book. It is the teacher's part to relate the pupil to the book by taking up his experience of the world around him and developing it in speech until it can include the world of the book. By his illumination of the textbook he should light up his pupils' local and personal experience. In opening up the textbook he opens windows on the world, which both show the world and let light into the home.

5

Unsupervised Work

Up to now the emphasis has been on the teacher's part, on how he should marshal and deploy his language to deal with the situation he and his pupils are in, and—if he is teaching according to a textbook—how he may adapt the language of the textbook for these needs. This chapter will be devoted to the work that may be left to the pupil to do at times when the teacher is not at hand to help him.

I. LARGE CLASSES AND PERSONAL SUPERVISION

However carefully and economically the teacher apportions his time, he cannot give every pupil in a large class much personal attention. To overcome this difficulty he divides the class into groups for further practice of what he has taught; but even then there is a great deal of practice in the use of language, and a great deal of working of it to and fro in the mind, which the pupil will have to do for himself if his grasp of the language is to be more than superficial. The interior monologue of thought has to be based on the practice of the exterior dialogue of discussion, so group-work should always be followed by reflection and the absorptive study alone of what has been apprehended in class. As language pupils gain in experience and skill in the use of the language, more and more of the necessary practice in its use will take place in groups and pairs, either under the indirect supervision of the teacher, or altogether beyond his reach.

How learners may help one another will be shown in the next chapter; in the meantime, what a teacher may expect to happen when he sets his pupils homework or unsupervised work, and what he ought not to expect, needs careful and detailed examination.

2. A CLASS THAT LEARNED NO MISTAKES

My attention first came to be focused critically on the problem of the pupil's private work when I was attempting to account to myself for what I observed with a particular group of adult students which I was teaching without a textbook during the last war. This group consisted mostly of university teachers, who had had at least part of their training in France and Germany. They had a lesson of fifty minutes, only twice a week, for seven or eight months in the year. Most of them completed two years, though some were often absent through pressure of work, and others only attended one year of the course.

I left the town and saw none of them for a period of five years after I had finished teaching them. When I met them again there were two aspects of their knowledge of the English language that I found puzzling. First of all, they were not at all reluctant to speak and had no apparent shyness; secondly, they made few or no mistakes, either in grammar or in pronunciation. Both these qualities of their mastery seemed to me unusual enough to ponder over. Most language students who have been at work for only one or two years are afraid to open their mouths in the language; if they do so they often make mistakes. These students of mine all spoke slowly; some knew more than others; some could express themselves more accurately and more fluently than others, but all spoke correctly; if they found difficulty in communicating some idea, they were always able to find a way round the difficulty, expressing themselves in simple language, perhaps, but still quite adequately. I asked them about the use they had made of their knowledge of the English language in the intervening period; they had read more and more widely in scientific literature in their subjects, helped often by a synopsis in French or German, and they had had opportunities of talking English from time to time with visiting English and American scientists. Their use of the language had been based on, and closely bound up with, their daily work and interests. This certainly gave point and concentration to their learning, and a healthy outlet for their knowledge and skill when they had it, but it did not explain their confidence, nor their freedom from error. The fact that they had already learnt one foreign language might have given them confidence in learning another, and would certainly have given them experience in absorbing language material in general. They could be expected to have a trained ear and perhaps a facility in learning to make new sounds, but fluency and correctness in one language are not transferable to another, though a care for these things may be.

In thinking back over the peculiarities of that course, accidental or planned, one comes to my mind first. I was the only source of their English; they heard every word and sentence from me first; they were never able to prepare a lesson in advance and give a new word their own interpretation, pronunciation or intonation, because they had no textbook. If ever they read a word, it was a word they had often used and knew how to pronounce without having to puzzle over the spelling for clues. They read it, too, when they read it alone, in their own handwriting; the sound of it had been ringing in their ears as they wrote it, and only later did they meet it in print.

Another peculiarity of that course was that they never did any homework. I frequently scolded them for not doing what I had set them to do, but they were too busy. Most of them found, however, that if they left the pattern sentences they had copied from the blackboard for too long, without looking at them in their rough notebooks, they were unable to read their handwriting or remember what they had written. If they copied their rough notes into a fair-copy notebook the same evening, they found it went down easily; they still had the lesson in their minds. One of them used to teach his wife the day's lesson that same evening, and during the following days they would repeat odd sentences or scraps of dialogue for fun, until the next lesson provided a new crop. Others used to tell their wives of the jokes we had had in class, and in this way pass their minds cursorily over the material of the lesson. When they met one another during their work in the college, day by day, they would repeat phrases and expressions that were still ringing in their minds from the last lesson, as if they were passwords to the membership of a kind of club. The humour and comradeship of our association together in the common effort to swim about in the small bath of language we had brought into existence in the classroom seemed to be an important element in the effectiveness of this very informal sort of homework. And this is what I have now come to see that it was. At the time, I did not take it seriously.

I began thinking afresh, however, about the value of what I had hitherto been setting for home study, and what I had myself been trying to do when working on my own at a foreign language. Should we be wiser to abandon unsupervised study altogether? Could we leave to the normal working of the brain the turning over in the mind of language material that had, somehow, to take place between classes of active instruction? I did even give up for a time the setting of regular homework, convinced that most homework was the learning and driving home of error and misconceptions. The observation of other teachers' practice, the evident popularity with learners and the undoubted usefulness of certain types of homework then set me thinking more constructively about the problems involved. I turned to the experience of that group of learners and asked myself whether they did stumble unawares on something valuable. What I seemed to find I began to apply to classes of children in school.

3. THE TEACHER'S HELP

First of all, which types of work need to be done with the teacher, and which can safely be left to the pupil to do alone, without supervision? Obviously, work difficult to do without occasional advice or help cannot be done successfully out of school. For instance, help is needed for original composition, until certainty and skill have been acquired.

A good many of the mistakes that trouble the mature language user have been made and then learnt as he sat at home, beyond reach of help, and tried to spin out of his poor head ideas thought out in his own language that he had not the linguistic equipment to build up in the foreign one. He has had to hunt with dictionary and grammar for means of expression which he could not yet call up naturally; he has strained his limited powers and wasted time; or he has sat in front of a piece of paper, his mind a blank or a confusion of conflicting scraps of language and ideas. In the chapter on composition the theme will be dealt with in greater detail, that a pupil who has to sit and search his brains for what is not there, either in ideas or language, has been set a task which is beyond him, and which can only lead to discouragement and frustration. He has been set work which ought not to be done out of sight of the teacher.

4. USE OF LANGUAGE SHOULD COME BEFORE GRAMMAR

The second type of work which should not be attempted alone is the learning of grammar. Looking at other people's systematizations of language in advance is not so valuable as making one's own systematization of the language one has learnt, as a means of completing or rounding off the learning process. This is especially valuable if the work is done in group or class discussion. Grammar learnt in advance of the experience of using the language remains dead and unassimilable in the mind, as if the baby were to have swallowed the bottle instead of the milk, out of impatience, because the milk was not ready. Learnt alone, without help from the teacher, grammar is often misunderstood or learnt inaccurately, and tends to postpone actual experience of the language itself, by taking up time needed for essential practice.

5. PREPARING TEXTS

A third type of work, which also cannot usefully be done without help from the teacher, is the preparation of lessons in the textbook, or prose passages, for reading. Even if a class is told to read a prose piece for the first time silently, the teacher should see that the vocabulary has first been made familiar in discussion, and the subject, too, if it is likely to be at all strange to the class. The reading should then be done in class, so that the teacher is within reach to give help when it is needed. This help may take the form of simply reading aloud a passage that is giving difficulty, to make sure that the correct pronunciation and intonation are heard; this alone will often make the meaning clearer. Until near the end of the course, pieces for reading will be better read aloud for the first time by the teacher, with books closed, so that the pupils can concentrate on the sound and general meaning of the piece without being distracted by details. But this subject will be developed further in a later chapter.

6. PRACTICE OF CORRECT LANGUAGE

Most of the early work on a language requires supervision. Speaking, reading, and—in the very early stages—even copying, must be under the control of the teacher. The teacher must decide when his pupils are likely to be able to copy accurately if they are out of his sight; some, of course, will be able to do so earlier than others; those who are not yet ready to copy without supervision may, however, be able to copy usefully and avoid mistakes with the help of one of those who are ready. The aim of getting pupils, by whatever method and under whatever pretext, to repeat correct sentences, orally or in writing, with the minimum risk of error, should take precedence over any desire which the teacher may have to classify or test his pupils. For this reason, it is always better for a learner to write a sentence right with help than wrong without. Only by the repetition of countless correct sentences can we learn to speak or write a language correctly.

The correction of mistakes after they have been made can never be so effective a training in correct speaking or writing as the experience of speaking or writing them the first time without mistake. This may seem to clash with the equally important principle that fluency should always be preferred to accuracy, because an undue preoccupation with accuracy may dam up fluency for ever, while the sense of mastery that comes from fluency leads on to a wish to cultivate accuracy. But there is, in fact, no contradiction; if all the independent writing of the pupil in the early stages consists of the copying, or the slight modification, of sentences he knows well and has often spoken, sentences that can be written rapidly and in great quantity because they are easy, he will become a fluent writer and an accurate one at the same time. Writing which demands thought and improvisation, which may need careful rewriting and revision, should be done under the eye of the teacher, so that serious mistakes and hold-ups may be noticed quickly and dealt with.

7. WRITING PRACTICE OUT OF SCHOOL

A beginner whose mother tongue is not written in the Roman script, before he is able to copy the sentences he is learning through speech may begin to practise—as a kind of handwork unrelated to his language work—the shapes of the letters of the Roman alphabet. For the foreign learner of English, some system that begins with the primary shapes of the capital letters and uses them decoratively, as in Marion Richardson's *Writing and Writing Patterns*,[1] seems to me the best. The satisfaction of achieving pleasant shapes on the page, and an attractive appearance of the page as a whole, is usually adequate inducement to a child, or even an adult, to practise drawing the letters until they can be drawn skilfully; this prepares the mind and concentrates the interest on the language, although it may not seem, at first, to be very directly related to the oral skill that is being acquired at the same time. In draw-

[1] University of London Press, Books I to V and Teacher's Book.

ing rows of letters, V's and W's, and then A's, first without, then with, their cross-bar, and of the letters B and P and D, the pupil has no difficulties of understanding or of imagining to overcome; he has only to practise certain simple movements of the hand. These movements may be strange at first, but they can as well be repeated to develop skill when he is alone as when he is under the eye of the teacher.

8. THE IMPORTANCE OF COPYING

Some teachers regret any time spent on copying sentences from the blackboard; they consider it a waste of time for their pupils and try to avoid asking them to do it. They duplicate sheets of questions for them, or else they keep closely to the book. Everything written is slowed down by its having to be puzzled over. They give rules for spelling, and worry and despair over the impossibility of teaching English spelling. Yet those pupils of mine mentioned above, who had to make their own textbook by copying sentences which I wrote for them on the blackboard, had no difficulty with spelling or punctuation. They copied so many correct sentences with correct punctuation from the blackboard, and recopied them so regularly into their tidy notebooks at home, that the correct spelling, queer though it might have seemed at first, came to be second nature to them. This was an unintentional by-product of my method of teaching, but I have now come to see it as a very important ingredient in a language course. Indeed, I now rather look for excuses for requiring copying from my pupils than try to avoid it.

Fortunately, there are many compelling reasons to do plenty of copying. First of all, the learner writes most things twice; once when he writes an exercise or a dictation, or copies sentences quickly from the blackboard on pieces of paper or in a rough notebook; secondly, when he makes up his notebook carefully afterwards. At first he copies the sentences which the teacher has written on the blackboard, but gradually he will learn to make adaptations to suit his own situation.

9. COPYING WITH MINOR MODIFICATIONS

An example of this might be as follows:

The teacher might write on the blackboard:

"I woke, this morning, at six o'clock, and got up about ten minutes later. I washed myself with hot water and shaved with a safety razor. I dressed quickly and had a cup of tea soon after half-past six, and worked for nearly an hour afterwards. At about half-past seven I had my breakfast; I ate some bread and butter and an egg; I drank two cups of coffee. I left home for school at about half-past eight and got here just before nine."

The boys might perhaps copy this in class, but their homework would be to adapt it so that it would be true for them. For example:

"I woke, this morning, at half-past five and got up about two minutes later. I washed myself in cold water and didn't shave at all. I dressed slowly, and had a glass of water soon after a quarter past six, and worked at my homework for nearly an hour afterwards. At about a quarter to eight I had my breakfast; I ate some iddlies and chutney; I drank a mug of milk. I left home for school at about twenty past eight and got here just before ten to nine."

A few days later he might write the following:

"My teacher, Mr. Sundaram, woke, last Wednesday morning, he tells me, at six o'clock, and got up about ten minutes later. He washed with hot water; I washed with cold; he shaved, but I didn't. He dressed quickly, he says, but I dressed slowly. He had a cup of tea soon after half-past six, and I had a glass of water soon after a quarter-past six, etc."

This is the sort of exercise in which the non-essentials change, but the essentials, the past tense forms of the verbs, remain the same throughout, except for "I shaved" becoming "I didn't shave at all". The changes required force the attention of the pupil on to what he is writing, so that it really passes through his consciousness and the words do their full work in his mind; at the same time there is no opportunity of making mistakes in the verb forms which are being taught at this stage; the other forms, the adverbial expressions of time and the nouns, will have been learnt before, and can be played about with.

10. SUBSTITUTION TABLES

A more mechanical form of this kind of exercise is the substitution table, in which a large number of sentences can be made up by interchanging the words in each column. I am rather suspicious of these and seldom use them because of the difficulty of keeping them real and meaningful. They need not be dead, but unless the teacher is careful they almost inevitably are. Only real sentences related to the learner's own situation and experience should be worked out, at least until the pattern is fairly well established. When only practice is required to bring the language form to complete fluency there may be no danger, but then they are no longer necessary. The substitution table in the book should first be adapted by the teacher to the circumstances of his class. Only when the teacher's adaptation can be done easily should the table in the book be attempted.

Examples of substitution tables:

No. 1. Introducing a noun clause with or without *that*.

I think know hope am afraid am sure	(that)	he is right they are wrong the Browns live in London my headache is no better we shall hear before next week he has finished his work

Read these sentences off, first with *that* and then, a second time, without it.

No. 2. A polite form of request.

1. Do you mind	handing me your book?
2. Could you oblige my by	lending me your tennis racket?
	speaking more quietly?
3. Would you object to	keeping this for me?
	showing me the way?
4. Would you have any objection to	shutting the door?
	holding this while I light my pipe?

The reply to Nos. 1, 3 and 4 is "No, not at all," to No. 2, "Certainly."

The same substitution table can be done again and again with different nouns and verbs suggested by the pupils. The pupils can later be given the work of devising their own substitution tables in class for working out sentences at home. This should ultimately be the aim of all such work, as otherwise the substitution table tempts pupil and teacher to mechanical, half-conscious work.

II. PERSONAL STATEMENTS

Another fruitful basis for homework may be the personal statement. A typical one can be worked out in class and copied down, each boy or girl can then be expected to work out his or her own version of it. An example might be: "My name is Shanmugam; I am twelve years old; I am a boy; my father's name is Gopalakrishna; my mother's name is Suseela." This is enough to begin with, but the statement should be progressively added to, so that it can contain in simple form all the information which any teacher or stranger might be expected to ask. For example: "My name is Shanmugam; I am a boy and I have three brothers and two sisters; there are eight in our family; my mother and father have six children.

I am an Indian boy. I am not a Turkish boy or an English boy. My father's name is Gopalakrishna and he works as a salesman in a shop. My mother's name is Suseela and she works at home."

The adding to it may be done in class to begin with, but as their knowledge of the language develops the individual learners should be encouraged to work out their own additions on slips of paper, hand them in for correction and then write them into their fair-copy notebooks. The personal statements can be learnt by heart at home and recited to the class at the next opportunity. The teacher should leave everyone free to produce what he likes and not probe too far in search of more information, otherwise the class may be embarrassed and tongue-tied, and the exercise will fail in its purpose.

12. DRAWING TO DICTATED INSTRUCTIONS

Another type of homework for the early stages that can be followed up and developed amusingly later, is the instruction for a drawing. This may be practised in class before being given for homework. Before the pupils can write independent sentences themselves they may be given the following instructions: "Draw a picture of a man sitting in the shade of a tree, eating his dinner." After this has been done, they may be given the instruction: "Draw a picture of a man sitting in the shade of a tree, eating his dinner, and saying something." Remarks can be suggested, if necessary, and they can be shown how to write them on a balloon, as in a comic strip. A few days later still, they may be given the instruction: "Draw a picture of a man sitting in the shade of a tree, eating his dinner and saying something to a woman who is coming towards him." The instruction and the drawing may develop indefinitely in complexity and fantasy; each new instruction will be simple because there will only be a minor addition to something already basically familiar. In this way the pattern of complex sentences can become familiar and comprehensible before the pupil could be expected to grasp sentences of similar complexity in a prose passage.

Some teachers may ask themselves what the value is of drawing a picture to illustrate a sentence in this way. First of all, the pupil hears the sentence several times, spoken by the teacher; he then writes the sentence once or twice, and, in order to illustrate it, has to comprehend it. The drawing is a test of his comprehension, but, more important than that, the drawing of the picture helps the pupil to visualize the scene outlined in the sentence, and then, as he draws it, to keep his visualization in his mind. He is forced to repeat the sentence over and over again in his mind all the time he is drawing it. It is better to learn one useful pattern sentence as thoroughly as this than twenty sentences so superficially that they will soon be forgotten, or to write twenty sentences with mistakes in them that will have then to be unlearnt.

13. VARIETY IN HOMEWORK

In setting homework to beginners it is best to give several different types of work, each one of which will take only five or ten minutes to do, rather than a long and formidable exercise. As far as possible the work should be what the pupils are likely to want to do in any case; for instance, drawing pictures, especially to illustrate jokes or unusual occurrences in the school. A class-wall newspaper regularly changed and demanding a constant supply of new material is a good incentive for this. Jokes and pictures may be cut out of magazines to fill up the newspaper; they need not be copied out; the work of finding them and choosing the most suitable ones for inclusion may be enough, though a class proud of its standard of handwriting may prefer to have everything copied out. As much work as possible should be set which encourages the coming together of the pupils in pairs or groups to help one another.

14. MANIPULATIVE EXERCISES

A natural development from the adaptation of model sentences, or substitution tables, is the exercise consisting of sentences that require manipulation; the changing of a set of sentences, or a continuous passage, from the singular into the plural or from positive to negative or interrogative, from the present into the past, etc. The teacher can make these exercises interesting by finding plausible reasons for them; for instance, if he wants negative sentences he can write on the blackboard a list of obviously untrue statements. Such exercises as these should always be prepared in class, either by doing similar but easier sentences, or by doing the actual sentences themselves orally, so that there are very few mistakes when they are written. Only when pupils have acquired a habit of writing the form correctly ought we to give them sentences in which there is a possibility of mistakes being made.

If they have been well prepared, it may not matter if the sentences are unrelated to one another, for then the pupil may be able to concentrate on getting practice in doing the trick; but the oral preparation in class should always be carried out in meaningful, mutually related sentences or conversation, so that the mind of the pupil can be fully concentrated on the meaning rather than on the form; thus everyone takes full, conscious part in the process and is not merely a passive on-looker. The final result of a set of exercises on a particular language form should be that each pupil writes a set of sentences which embody the form for his private textbook: either a copy of the corrected draft of the final exercise, or a series of new sentences. As time goes by the teacher may expect continuous narrative to be written by the brighter boys to enjoy and display their dexterity. In this way every pupil's work is adjusted to his capacity. Examples of this type of exercise will be given in the chapter on the teaching of grammar; it is enough to emphasize here that such exercises are not exercises—in the sense that exercises in piano-playing, singing and athletic sports are exercises—unless they are easy to do, once the trick has been grasped.

15. COMPOSITION EXERCISES

These manipulative exercises are, in themselves, simple

G

composition exercises, but they develop quite naturally into the type of more difficult exercise that is more usually meant when we speak of a composition exercise. Although the sentences need not tell a story, they are the better for being a related series.

An example might be a set of ten sentences to re-write twice, as in the four which follow:

1. I was tired and went home.
(a) I went home because I was tired.
(b) As I was tired, I went home.

2. I had a headache and therefore took an aspirin.
(a) I took an aspirin because I had a headache.
(b) As I had a headache, I took an aspirin.

3. I wanted to take an aspirin and therefore fetched a glass of water.
(a) I fetched a glass of water because I wanted to take an aspirin.
(b) As I wanted to take an aspirin, I fetched a glass of water.

4. The water from the tap was too cold; I therefore warmed it a little on the gas stove.
(a) I warmed the water a little on the gas stove, because the water from the tap was too cold.
(b) As the water from the tap was too cold, I warmed it a little on the gas stove.

The first sentence is given in each case and the pupil has to convert it into versions (a) and (b). When he has finished the ten sentences, he can be asked to devise original sentences of his own for conversion in the same way, to continue the same germinal story. When he has done this he has the basis of a continuous composition, which he can work out for himself without much possibility of making mistakes, yet he has to use all his skill and ingenuity in doing it; he can make it as easy or as difficult as he likes according to his ability. The exercise can be done again by substituting for " I ", " Mr. Smith " and " he ", etc., and yet again with " we " instead of " I ". After this each member of the class can be asked to devise ten new sentences on the same pattern as these, outlining a similar sketch of a story. Each sentence should be convertible into patterns (a) and (b); then a complete story can be written with the sentences using the original version of each sentence, or version (a) or (b), according to taste, linked together, of course, with sentences of other patterns which have been learnt.

16. ESSENTIAL QUALITIES OF AN EXERCISE

These exercises are used to exercise or practise language skill, and not as tests; they should be worked over or discussed in class before being given for homework. After that, they should regularly be given to be done again, either as they stand, by the members of the class who have found them difficult, or with other content and vocabulary and different situations by those who would find them too easy as they stand. Though allowed to choose which they prefer to do, some members of the class may be asked to repeat the exercise before attempting the more difficult adaptation. If any should protest at being asked to do what they already know, they may be told that a pianist or a clarinet player practises scales every day, and an acrobat or a football player does exercises to keep himself supple; these exercises are not at all difficult, but must be done by anyone who wants to develop skill and maintain it.

A good exercise should require close concentration, but no original thought; it should also give opportunity to practise in isolation a particular sphere, or element, of the total skill. The teacher should recommend particular exercises for particular weaknesses or mistakes made by particular pupils; in time most of the class should be able to prescribe their own exercises; a good exercise for a bright pupil would be to prepare a remedial exercise for a weaker one and supervise the carrying out of it.

17. REVISION OUT OF CLASS

The type of homework which seems not to be work at all is probably the best. Without any intention of the student, the most memorable moments and the language patterns connected with them pass through his mind, and he finds himself repeating them, perhaps with other people. Forced by the pressure of material forcefully taught and adequately repeated, some pupils work systematically in writing, others merely remember amusing incidents or jokes, or repeat to other members of the class, jocularly or facetiously, key sentences as a form of greeting.

The over-ambitious pupil who habitually reads ahead and meets, wholly unprepared and usually bewildered, difficulties that he is not ready for at the stage he has reached, often neglects the essential repetition of what he has done in class. He probably does this because he finds his work dull, so we must provide for him homework which is at the same time fascinating to do, not dishearteningly difficult, yet obviously valuable as a contribution to the development of skill. We should not neglect games and puzzles, drawing and chart-making, model-making, activity and observation, to give interest to the repetition work. Although language practice will ultimately save trouble, it may seem at the time too easy or irksome unless we cover it up. If what we set seems like anything but the homework we have usually known we shall probably be on the right lines.

18. THE IMPORTANCE OF MEMORIZATION

There is one type of homework which can be allowed to keep its accustomed importance; this is learning by heart. Memorization may not be quite deliberate, but after very intensive study of a passage in which the sentences are repeated very often, the class will almost know them by heart before the lesson is over. I have myself found that one of the simplest ways to learn an unfamiliar sentence pattern is to repeat a passage that incorporates it, many times over. I usually end by learning the passage by heart, although at school I was one of the worst memorizers. My French teacher gave us the same piece of dictation at least a dozen times within a few weeks, at one period, and I found myself thereafter forming sentences quite naturally on those patterns.

We can dictate poems and any other passages which we want to be remembered, and repeat each sentence over and over again during the correction process, so that very little is left to be done at home. Otherwise we may let the individual learn by heart anything that appeals to him, but we can see that he always has something on hand—a personal statement, a poem, a memorable joke or piece of wit, a fascinating sentence, a specimen letter, a famous historical remark, and so on. This memorization need not occupy more than ten minutes of any one preparation period.

19. OTHER SUBJECTS CAN BE DISCUSSED IN THE FOREIGN LANGUAGE

In India, and in other countries where a language other than the mother tongue has been used for higher education, it has been well and easily learnt by using it for learning about and discussing other subjects. It seems that the less we concentrate on language the better we learn it. A great economy of time, both in the teaching of the foreign language and in the teaching of the other subjects, can still be effected by spending language-learning time on the other subjects of the curriculum. There is no need to teach these subjects through the second language, but limited topics can be looked up in reference books or textbooks in it, and short talks can be delivered by the pupils in class; these talks can be based on notes made from the reference books. The teacher is part of the audience, and only speaks to correct usage and pronunciation.

In their last few years at school the pupils should be trained in reference skills, so that they can make proper use, as educated people, of public and university libraries, consult encyclopedias and dictionaries, use bibliographies intelligently and

understand charts. They should be able to draw useful conclusions from charts, which they must be able to put into
words and explain to others.

20. THE TEACHER'S WITHDRAWAL

When the teacher sets his first piece of work for private
study he is beginning the process of parturition which will
eventually result in a fully independent knowledge and use of
the language in his pupils. Just as the bud in spring contains
the germ of the stopper that will eventually seal off the leaf
from the parent stem and cause it to fall in autumn, so the
teacher must be aware, from the beginning, that the homework
he sets, whether in the form of group work or solitary study,
must form a nucleus round which his pupil's independence in
the language must grow. By the time he leaves school the
pupil must have acquired habits of serious study; he will have
taken over the responsibility for the work he does, so completely that the teacher will be superfluous. This process is
not likely to be complete unless the teacher works consciously
to produce independence and responsibility in his pupil.

It has been known for a long time that the only way to
develop a sense of responsibility in a boy or girl is to trust him
or her with some real responsibility, however limited. Only
certain of them ever attain to the responsibility of keeping
order in the passage; all of them can be given real responsibility for the conduct, and ultimately even the planning, of
their own homework. If this is done, the pupil must, as a
logical consequence, have the responsibility of deciding
whether he does the work or not. Every time the teacher
punishes or scolds the boy for not doing his homework, he is
depriving him of some of that responsibility which rightly and
necessarily belongs to the boy.

There is really no reason, except convenience and fairness in
marking, why all the members of a class should do precisely
the same work at the same time; in mathematics they frequently do different work. If a boy has chosen to do a par-

ticular piece of work, it is only himself that he has failed if he does it badly or carelessly or forgets to do it altogether. The teacher can help him to realize this, and to face the consequences honestly, without having to be censorious. But membership of a group which expects and values good work is the best spur to conscientious effort. Building up a sense of responsibility in a class or in individuals is not a quick process, especially if it has not been cultivated by previous teachers. I myself found at school that very few teachers gave me the feeling that what I was learning was important to me personally, or that it was relevant to the world at large outside school. It led to the passing of examinations; these were generally understood to be the turnstiles to the world's work, but not otherwise relevant to it.

21. DEVELOPMENT NEED NOT BE COMPETITIVE

If we want to help a boy build up a sense of personal responsibility for his own work, we first have to help him to a sense of achievement and craftsmanship similar to the feeling of mastery that makes him want to improve his skill in a game or craft; he must feel that he has a personal stake in the language that is worth enlarging; he must have a sense of growing or development in the language. It is bound to be largely irrelevant to him how he compares with the other boys in the class; after he leaves school he will probably never see more than one or two of them again. It is not socially desirable nor economical to encourage him to try and outshine them, nor to make his success a comparative success. He needs to see the value of his own contribution to the total success of the group. In education, measurement is far too often vertical, giving us the situation at a particular moment, giving a comparison between the degrees of development of a number of different personalities at that moment. Yet the educationist is really interested, rather, in the rate or curve of development of his pupils, looking towards the ultimate achievement of maturity in them. For this, a horizontal measurement, showing development over a period, comparing the pupil's achievement and degree of maturity at different stages of his development, is necessary. A boy can be as interested in this as he is in the making of a model aeroplane or the building of a hut, if he is shown how to watch for it.

Under constant pressure to make up his mind about a pupil the teacher tends to see him as a static rather than a developing personality, and also, almost inevitably, to simplify his view almost to the point of caricature. The real test of the pupil comes when he makes use of the language either to follow a university course or in the exercise of a profession. The real test of the teacher lies in his pupil's ability to continue learning after he has left school. A more convenient test, and portable evidence of it, is the school-leaving certificate or matriculation examination, but we must remember that this is only a dummy for the real test.

22. THE FAIR-COPY NOTEBOOK

An important basis for a horizontal estimate, and an important training in building up a useful and coherent body of material can be the fair-copy notebook. The rough notebook could also be kept as evidence of development, but a boy who has done some very bad or untidy work may feel humiliated by being reminded of it. It is then wiser to destroy it, even if he has passed that phase and is now producing satisfactory work which he can be proud of. He will try to produce his best work to stand as evidence for his achievement and development. If he uses a loose-leaf notebook, pages can be taken out and rewritten, if the pupil would rather not be judged by them; also pages from magazines, duplicated or printed sheets of notes or charts, and other material can be put in wherever they are required.

The pupil should be encouraged to illustrate his notebook with drawings and charts in colour. Some teachers think this is a waste of time, but the alternative to drawing pictures in his English notebook is, for the pupil, not more mathematics or more chemistry, but pictures somewhere else. Drawings in his notebook help him to visualize and realize better the situations written about in it, but, more than this, perhaps their chief value is that they help the pupil to hold the sentences and situations he is trying to illustrate firmly in his mind while he does so; this is a valuable aid to memorization, and is evidence of comprehension; it may even assist or further comprehension. In addition, care in illustrating a notebook is a sign and a channel of the concentrating of emotion and affection on the work in the language.

23. THE VALUE OF SOUND RECORDINGS

In the same way as the notebook, so recordings of the pupil's voice, made at regular intervals on the tape recorder, can help us to estimate his progress in fluency, pronunciation and intonation in speech. Where there is a tape-recorder or gramophone available—and suitable accommodation for making use of it out of classroom hours—very useful work can be done also by the pupil, alone or in groups, listening to ready-made recordings, or to recordings made by the teacher for the class. Where private or group listening is impossible, five or ten minutes of recording can usefully be played each day to the whole school, or to sections of the school, to accustom the ear to hearing the patterns of the language, and to fix them in the mind ready for use in speech. More information on this point has been given in the chapter on ear training, but it is a useful form of homework or private study through which the pupil can develop independence and self-reliance and accustom himself to habits of observation and study, without being obliged to venture out to his depth.

24. FURTHER STUDY OF PASSAGES DEALT WITH IN CLASS

Dictionaries will not be needed in the early stages, because the teacher will introduce every new word by using it in relation to the pupil's situation as described in earlier chapters.

He will use each word and repeat it often enough for its sound to be familiar before it is ever seen in print or in writing. As time goes by, however, more and more of the work of repeating what has been presented by the teacher will be left to the pupil. He will be shown how to set about getting experience of new words and expressions, in listening and reading; he will be given exercises to speak and write, and then he will be shown how to make opportunities for himself by working out his own exercises; he will be shown how to use the dictionary to find out subsidiary and related meanings and usages.

Most of this work will at first be the reading over of passages which have been read and discussed in class. To help them begin such work effectively, the teacher may ask the class, at the end of the lesson in which they have studied the piece, to tell him which words they think of looking up in the dictionary that evening. If some new words or expressions are missed, he can draw attention to them and repeat them clearly five or six times, without giving meanings or explanations. He will suggest a few questions they may ask themselves as they study the piece. He will suggest their thinking of questions to ask him the next day, and he may invite them to look out for words and expressions which they are not sure of and need further examples of, or sentences they would like him to paraphrase for them. He may ask them to suggest words which they already knew, which might have been used in place of those words in the piece which are new to them. He will ask them to note those words and phrases which they find difficulty in pronouncing.

In the following lesson he will himself answer as few of these questions as possible; he will refer them to the class for answering before he attempts to answer them. In time he should be able to hand over the chairmanship of such sessions as these to a member of the class and retire into a corner to be called on as an expert witness only in case of necessity. As time goes by much of this work will be done in groups, but the teacher may need first to help the pupils to develop habits of independent study, and himself to supervise the work of the groups in rotation, to see that all individuals take part.

25. THE USE OF DICTIONARIES

Dictionaries in use should be entirely in the language being learnt; only for subsidiary reference should translating dictionaries be used. The teacher should never be ashamed of using the dictionary himself; he should be to the class an example of someone still learning, who is much farther along the way but still makes no claims to complete knowledge. When once dictionaries have been taken into use the teacher should seldom explain a word; he should merely give examples of its use, or rather, use it as if the class already knew it, six or seven times. At the end of the lesson he may refer his pupils to the dictionary for equivalents or exact definition. It is really better if the teacher almost never explains a word, even in the early stages; but after a number of examples of the word in sentences which make its use clear, he can ask the class for equivalents or definitions. He should not ask them to use new words in sentences until he is sure that they have heard them used enough for mistakes to be unlikely.

An explanation of the meaning of a word in words which the pupil does not understand is obviously valueless, but an explanation in words which the pupil cannot attend to or grasp is just as valueless, and even an explanation in words which the pupil does know is less useful than is often supposed. All explanations of words have the disadvantage, which giving meaning in the home language has, of diverting the attention of the pupil away from the word itself on to other words which are presumed to be known already and therefore need no spotlighting. We really want to spotlight the new word itself, doing work in its proper place in the language, not abstracted and put in a show-case, not smothered by its label and definition, but used and used again, as dramatically as possible. To teach the word "poor", for example, the teacher may beg from pupil to pupil, saying, "I'm a very poor man," and get boys to do the same, or turn out his pockets, showing that his left pocket is poor, but his right pocket is rich, or not so poor as the left pocket, but his note-case is fairly rich. This focuses attention on the words "poor" and "rich" in contrast with one another in sentences that convey meaning usefully. The word must first be learnt, its application and pronunciation grasped intuitively; its meaning may be guessed at or left in abeyance. Later, in the study hour, the interest aroused by hearing the word repeated will take the pupil to the dictionary for confirmation and precision of his impressions.

A student at a training college, teaching a third-year English class, had prepared his lesson carefully; he came to the word "poor" in the text; he was ready: "Poor means unfortunate, miserable, in indigent circumstances."

26. THE NECESSITY FOR WIDE DISCURSIVE READING

From rowing at the university I learnt that to be tough and agile enough to win races one had to spend a lot of time rowing long distances; a high degree of skill and endurance over short distances at regattas in the summer depended on a great number of miles having been rowed conscientiously, steadily and unflinchingly during the winter. Just as correct writing of a language depends on large numbers of correct sentences having been written, so quick and accurate reading depends on a great many pages having been read. There is no need for the reading to tax the powers of the reader nor to offer any sort of challenge save the challenge of endurance and the challenge to make the subject-matter one's own; the same patterns of sentences must be read with attention and understanding very many times over, until the impression such sentences make on the mind is immediate, powerful and clear.

The average pupil might be able to get enough practice in reading by reading and rereading çach passage in his text-book twenty, thirty or forty times over; but excessive familiarity makes conscious attention more and more difficult. It is wiser to give the pupil a book which he finds relatively easy to read, and interesting. An intelligent student can be given a book with difficulties which he has not met, and be trained to disregard them, or infer what they mean from the context. In the course of reading it through he meets as many repetitions of the common structural patterns of the language as he would in thirty or forty repetitions of each lesson in his textbook; his interest is held and his reading is fully significant.

An Indian friend of mine tells me that when he was preparing for the matriculation examination as a boy, his teacher called him up and told him he must read a great deal if he wanted to pass. "Read *The Vicar of Wakefield*," he said. My friend proudly replied that he had already read it.

"How many times?" asked his teacher.

"Only once, sir," answered my friend.

"Read it again," said the teacher.

My friend came, a few days later, and reported the completion of the second reading, but his teacher sent him back to read it a third time, and so it went on until he had read the whole of *The Vicar of Wakefield* twelve times. My friend said that this had been enough training for him to pass his examination easily, and reading from then on had been a pleasure.

I have found, in learning a foreign language, that reading and rereading a paragraph, or the first few paragraphs, and then—when they have become perfectly familiar—the whole of the first chapter, is introduction enough for the rapid reading of the rest of the book. I only use the dictionary for the second reading, provided there is not too long an interval between the readings. I try to avoid using it for the first reading altogether.

27. THE DEVELOPMENT OF FLUENCY IN READING

Fortunately there are plenty of simple or simplified books available in English for learners to be able to read a great deal without their having to read the same book many times, and there are books graded to suit every stage of the learning process; but I should still recommend any language learner to read some of these books several times over to gain speed and ease in reading. If a teacher can find one book that a backward reader really likes he may get him to read it over and over again. A simplified story that has been written within a limited and graded vocabulary appropriate to the stage the pupil has reached should be read quickly and easily; if it is not, the teacher should prescribe books intended for a stage earlier, or get the pupil to read easy paragraphs from the textbook many times over until he has developed enough speed and ease in reading to be comfortable in books at his own stage.

The predominant need is for the pupil to read a great deal; wrestling with difficult vocabulary and structure may be left until he has achieved fluency in reading and has had a good deal of experience in reading the language at some level.

However slow and unambitious this process may seem, it is the quickest in the long run. It is not, after all, very different from the practice and repetition we are prepared for in the early stages of any other skill. The reading and rereading of texts which have been prepared and studied in class, and the reading of stories or informative material which has been prepared for easy reading and needs no preparation in class at the stage for which it has been written, is suitable for homework or unsupervised study.

When the pupil can read the newspaper, or material at an equivalent standard, fluently, without having to look up any essential words in the dictionary, he should be encouraged to read as much as he has time for every day. Set homework may then be quite unnecessary. He should note, in a notebook, only those words which hold up his reading, and either look them up in a dictionary or ask the teacher to use them significantly for him. Or he may simply leave them alone, written in a list, without their equivalents beside them. He looks at them daily —reminding himself of their behaviour and meaning by looking at the piece he found them in—until he has come to be familiar with them and can understand them.

He does this reading to gain fluency and speed, reading what he can understand as rapidly as he can; he should ignore what he does not understand, as long as he can make sense of the passage as a whole. The time for him to learn new words and new constructions is when he is studying a piece of good prose intensively under the guidance of his teacher. Any patch of the newspaper which is beyond him but interests him, he should hand to his teacher for dealing with in class. He will find, however, that much reading of the same words and similar expressions in the newspaper will make them familiar anyhow and their meaning clear, without his having to bother with them consciously; one day he will notice them bobbing up in his mind like corks. The pupil can absorb a good deal more unfamiliar or unprepared material in his discursive reading than we sometimes think, and the brighter pupils may be encouraged to be more ambitious in their discursive reading than I have here suggested. More information on this subject will be found in the chapter on reading.

28. CURRENT AFFAIRS PERIODS AND RESEARCH WORK

As soon as newspaper reading has come to be within the reach of the majority of pupils, current affairs periods supported by bulletin boards and files or scrapbooks of newspaper cuttings become possible. Free discussion of topical problems, as they come up, or five-minute talks from individuals, or concerted talks on different facets of a subject given by groups, followed by discussion, can be the basis of these periods. The teacher may act as chairman, confining his speaking to the keeping of discussion going; or he may sit to one side as an onlooker, only correcting and stimulating the verbal expression of the class. This type of work is more appropriately discussed in the next chapter, under the heading of group activities, but the research and reading involved in the preparation of these periods can be a natural development from the training in private study which the pupils should be given from the beginning of the course onwards. The teacher will find such classes easy to lead, and a great stimulus to expression, especially if he has borne in mind, throughout the earlier years of language learning, that he is preparing them to do this kind of work in their last one or two years of language study at school. Such current affairs discussion periods help a class of young students, entering a university where the medium of instruction is not their mother tongue, to achieve experience and fluency in the language, and at the same time increase their general knowledge and their awareness of contemporary problems. If such classes as these are taken seriously by the students and conscientiously prepared for, they can lead to the formation of those habits of wide and responsible reading which are essential for an informed and responsible democracy.

29. RULES FOR SETTING HOMEWORK

The rules for the setting of work for unsupervised private study can be analysed as follows:

1. No new work should be studied as long as the elements of the language have not been mastered.

2. Exercises should be done that give exercise, or practice, in skills that have already been partly learnt. They should require concentration but no original thought. Copying will be done at all stages.

3. Material which has been dealt with in class may be memorized or worked over.

4. Silent reading of prepared texts or simplified reading books may be asked for.

5. Research work may be carried out in reference books, either in libraries or at home; visual material may be prepared for use in class, or material collected for talks, discussions or projects.

CONCLUSION

In general, the teacher has an opportunity in his setting of homework to guide his pupils in their methods of working both in class and out. Through his restrained direction of the pupils' unsupervised work. by his assuming the character of a friend and collaborator rather than a hostile critic when he goes through their work, he can help his pupils to assume more and more responsibility for their own homework, for its being well-planned and suitable, for its being well done, for their own progress and development in the language in general; he should never allow them to slip into a habit of feeling a responsibility only to the teacher and to what he can detect. The teacher must come over to the pupil's side of the problem and face it with him together as an ally, not as an enemy or a policeman out to catch him.

H

6

Co-operation in Language Learning

1. LANGUAGE IS A SOCIAL BOND

Language is a social affair; it is the most important binding element in society. Language can hardly exist in solitude; human society depends for its existence, as we know it, on language. In so far as I speak a language I belong to the community of people who speak that language whether I want to or not; if I know the language well and have absorbed some of the common stock of knowledge that every schoolboy knows who speaks that language, if I know the proverbs and homely sayings and have delighted in the succinct wit of those who speak the language habitually, if I enjoy their jokes, I have sat down beside them and shared some of their consciousness. To learn a new language is to join a new community. The similarity of the words "community" and "communication" can sum this up for us.

2. THE SOCIAL NATURE OF MAN CANNOT BE IGNORED

Soon after leaving school I tried to learn Italian alone. I failed. Analysing the failure afterwards, I concluded that it had been due to absence of human response or comradeship in learning and speaking. In writing a beginners' course to be done alone, some years later, I saw the need for the natural interchange of personality, normally subsisting between teacher and pupil. So I wrote at the top of every lesson that no single person should attempt to do the course alone; whoever thought of starting the course should get a friend, or preferably two or three friends, to join him in the struggle;

dialogue would form a part of every lesson, to give each learner a turn in asking questions and answering them, making statements and responding to them; the dialogues should be repeated several times, with each learner taking each part in rotation, until all felt that they had had enough experience of all the sentences to be able to understand or speak them without reflection. Later I came across people who had followed the course, and all considered that they had been very much helped by the advice to work with others; it had made each lesson a happy social occasion; the work was lightened by being tackled as a team, or shared; those who were tempted to drop off after being away from home and their lessons for a week or so, felt obliged to catch up, so as not to leave the others without partners; anyone who had been obliged to work over a lesson alone had felt the need for a partner and was glad to help another member of the group to catch up, so as to have someone to work with again.

A language cannot live for us if it produces no response and has no effect on other people. We are not yet sufficiently spiritualized to be independent of our bodies or our human nature.

3. MEANING AND SOCIAL PURPOSE IN WORK

Shortly after the war I visited a motor factory where remarkable results had followed putting disabled men to work in a specially adapted workshop to make parts of motor-cars within a few weeks of an injury. Formerly many of these men would have been away from work for a year or more and would have returned permanently crippled. Exercises would have been done perfunctorily and with only half the attention; the man was isolated from society in being away from his normal place of work and tended to become apathetic. Here, with others in the same condition, he was taking his place as a valued member of the community once more; the community was recognizing his disability and showing care and forethought in helping him to overcome it, showing him in the clearest way possible that he and his contribution of work were needed. This was accentuated by the worker's feeling of participation in the war effort. He could make thousands of movements with the muscles which were not damaged and restore the injured limb as a whole to working order before it atrophied, whereas even a few exercises would have been a struggle.

This has helped me to see that to use language in a natural, useful way, in a significant social setting, is to overcome the main problem of language teaching, the unreality, dullness and remoteness of language drill.

An exercise that is only an exercise cannot hold the attention for long; it is soon done slackly or perfunctorily or too stiffly; it produces fatigue far more quickly than useful and interesting work does. But work done in association with others, as a function of belonging, can be done willingly and naturally. Because it is done for a purpose we are more conscious of the purpose than of the movements of our bodies. In this situation we learn quickly and easily.

If we learn a language, concentrating exclusively on the words and how we pronounce them, concentrating on the language itself instead of the impact it makes on the hearer—the technique and the tools, instead of the work to be done with them—our use of the language is bound to be stiff, we can hardly help straining ourselves, and learning becomes artificial. If we concentrate, on the other hand, on the effect of language, if we let it establish a place for us in a community and relate us to other people, if we do work with it which others need and recognize, we find that we lose our stiffness, avoid strain and gain skill rapidly, and our language learning becomes a joy.

4. THE PROBLEM OF LARGE CLASSES

It was years before this varied experience, and reflection on it, bore fruit in a marked change of emphasis in my own class teaching. One day I was teaching a class of about forty-five or fifty boys as a demonstration for some teachers to watch. By my utmost exertions I was able to keep contact with the class, but the attention of some of the boys was continually wandering and had to be brought into the orbit of the lesson by a quick question or some notice; the moment I passed from them to others their eyes would glaze over again. Suddenly it seemed absurd for me to be trying to keep the whole class interested in the same thing at the same moment, so I set a third of them to read a previous lesson silently, while I concentrated on the rest. If those who were reading stopped and listened to us for a moment, their eyes were not vacant; when their attention wandered they looked back at their books.

In the discussion with the teachers which followed, I showed that there was a challenge to our ingenuity in the unwieldy class and the slipping attention of the jaded pupil. Many teachers said that oral work was impossible, because they had neither the strength nor the stamina. Was the struggle, after all, with the enormous expenditure of energy, really necessary? I had already seen something of group work and had even practised it for certain purposes, splitting a class into pairs for practising question and answer simultaneously, for example, and for project work, but never to free me to concentrate on the work of a small group. What I had heard about and read about others doing had never before seemed to be for me more than an occasional expedient. Now, with the force of a conversion, I began to see that the organization of a class in groups is the only satisfactory solution of the problem of the large class. It has also certain valuable educational advantages which I had not foreseen or read about when I saw the challenge and took it up with a horde of boys disillusioned from waiting for the teacher's attention and so seldom getting it, yet being denied their own activity or thought.

5. MAKING USE OF THE SOCIAL NATURE OF MAN

Making boys and girls sit beside another and learn a means of communication, without allowing them to communicate with one another, forcing into their hands a social link but forbidding them to join themselves to their neighbours with it, giving them a vehicle for the interchange of opinion and information and even encouraging them to load it, but then not permitting it to leave for any destination, is equivalent to installing a telephone in a house and not connecting it with the exchange, giving a rope to a party of mountain-climbers but forbidding them to link themselves together with it, or starting a lorry service and loading the lorries but keeping them in the garage; frustration must follow.

The teacher, on the other hand, who is on the look-out for ways in which communication between pupil and pupil in the language can be encouraged and developed, for ways in which they can help one another, and for new vehicles for the carrying of loads of information to destinations where there is a shortage and a need, not to no destination at all or to destinations where there is already too much, soon finds that the apathetic look leaves his pupils' eyes, and they begin to plan and follow up their own work.

Instead of forbidding them to do whatever is natural and necessary for them to do at their stages of development—whatever it is their nature to do—we should consider whether these urges are necessarily the enemies of learning, or whether there is not, after all, some way in which they can be made use of and diverted to the benefit and cohesion of the community and not to its disruption.

A boy's instinct to communicate can be satisfied in group discussion and in the writing of reports for the community and messages to individuals; his desire to assert himself can be harmlessly exercised in debates, in the leadership of discussion groups and in the presentation of proposals for the conduct of the form's business; his wish to help others, and be helped, may be met in the co-operative working of exercises and various types of homework; his need for responsibility may be made use of and cultivated by giving him genuine responsibility for his own work whether done in isolation or in co-operative groups. His need for activity can be realized in project work.

6. CO-OPERATIVE WORK OUT OF CLASS

The pupil can soon find that co-operation and the solidarity of the group help to make the burden of work out of class lighter, and reduce the tedium of repetitive work. If the text-book gives no dialogues or conversations, the teacher writes them or—better still—he helps his pupils to write them and practise them together until they are known by heart. If the textbook does give some, he can make sure that pairs or groups of pupils work on them together; when he is satisfied that they do this habitually, he may show them how to make up their own—at first, stereotyped—conversations for recital, in pairs or groups, in front of the class.

A good beginning can be made at this work by showing them how to convert their personal statements into dialogues. This adaptation work can be almost mechanical; each will have learnt a personal statement such as this: "My name is Govindarajulu; I am eleven years old, my mother's name is Lakshmi and my father's name is Satyanarayanamurthy. We speak Telugu at home, but I speak Tamil too. We live in Madras, not far from the railway, at Perambur. I go to school at the C.C.C. High School and our Headmaster's name is Hanumantha Rao." Two such statements can be combined to form a dialogue, with the help of simple questions, as follows:

A. "Good afternoon, my name is Govindarajulu; what is yours?"
B. "My name is Gopalakrishna; how *old* are you?"
A. "I am eleven years old. How old are *you*?"
B. "I am eleven too. Have you a mother and a father?"
A. "Yes, I have; have you too?"
B. "Yes, I have a mother, but my father is dead. He died two years ago."
A. "I'm very sorry to hear that. My mother's name is

Lakshmi and my father's name is Satyanarayanamurthy.
What is your mother's name?"

B. "My mother's name is Sita. We speak Tamil at home;
what language do you speak at home?"

A. "We speak Telugu. Do you speak only Tamil or do you
speak Telugu too?"

B. "I speak a little Telugu. Do you speak any Tamil?"

A. "Yes, I do. Do you live in Madras?"

B. "Yes, we do."

A. "So do we, we live in Perambur. What part of Madras
do you live in?"

B. "We live in Perambur, too," etc.

Similar dialogues, at first rehearsed, but gradually less and less
rehearsed, can be spoken by every pupil with every other pupil
in the class, so that A makes up a dialogue with B only once,
but, shortly after, with C and then D, etc., right through the
class, each dialogue bringing new elements together.

As the personal statements become longer and more complex, the dialogues can be repeated more elaborately and at
greater length. This means an almost limitless number of
repetitions of essentially the same dialogue with different personal details, and a new social relationship, threaded on to
each repetition. Interest in it is kept alive by the interest of a
new relationship of personalities and a new contrast of personal detail and qualities.

The repetition is not purely mechanical, for it is fulfilling a
natural social function; the forms of words are subordinated
to the purpose they are used for. The ordinary exchange of
social civilities involved in establishing and maintaining contact with a succession of strangers at a reception or cocktail
party is not less repetitious than this. Time at the beginning
or end of each lesson can be set aside for the recital of these
dialogues to the class until the method of work has become
familiar. As soon as this dialogue work is beginning to become
a routine assignment and the pupils are experienced enough to

do it without close supervision, they can be left to do it as a group activity in or out of school; the rest of the group may observe and check the speakers.

This work may begin by being stiff and stereotyped, but if the teacher sees that departures from the pattern are encouraged as soon as they are possible, and helps them to compose other dialogues on the same general pattern, first in class and then in groups, he will find that the invention of the pupils soon brings in originality and greater freedom. In any case, even the most stereotyped dialogue is greater freedom than being absolutely tongue-tied.

7. THE OPPOSED PRINCIPLES OF INDIVIDUALITY AND COMMUNITY

One of the central problems of education is the reconciling of the importance of the individual with his obligation to society, of giving full play and development to his particularity, yet relating that particularity to its setting and significance in relation to other human beings. Present-day man, though more isolated and rootless than any of his ancestors, is yet joined by more far-reaching and complex ties to larger numbers of his fellow-men than ever before. When most people lived in village communities or in easily grasped communities within small towns, the relationships of human beings and their dependence on one another were visible and conscious; but now a bus or an electric train will take me from one end of a vast conurbation to the other in half an hour; I no longer know my neighbours; I am only half-conscious of them as a vaguely hostile fringe of beings taking in similar milk bottles.

Is this manifest contradiction between the individualistic way we live our lives on the conscious surface, and the actual dependence of our condition on a community we only half-recognize or admit to consciousness, the basis of our unease? Is it for this that we take to wearing similar clothes, drinking the same drinks, joining vast collections of people to watch football or cricket matches? We probably collect the same bits of information from the newspapers, listen to the same radio programmes, watch the same television programmes and share the same insipid jokes as part of the rite of belonging.

8. THE RECOGNITION OF THE INDIVIDUAL'S SOCIAL IDENTITY

Many teachers seem content to believe that the pupils in the schools are unrelated and atomized individuals, that the acquisition of knowledge and the development of skill are private and independent transactions equivalent to the filling of the tanks of cars at petrol stations. The condition of the child or adolescent in some schools may remind us of Rilke's "Panther":

> "Sein Blick ist vom Vorübergehn der Stäbe
> so müd geworden, dass er nichts mehr hält.
> Ihm ist, als ob es tausend Stäbe gäbe
> und hinter tausend Stäben keine Welt."

By the time he leaves school he has spent so many years pacing to and fro looking through the bars of his cage that at last he sees nothing but bars, and is consciously aware only of separateness. Fifty years ago this was excusable, the submerged portion of the iceberg was still invisible, and largely undreamt of; relativity had not yet opened our minds to the possibilities of the interaction of solid bodies on one another, and thereby showed the way to studies of the dynamic interactions of human personalities. There is no space for further discussion of these problems here, but those interested may refer to *Whitehead's Metaphysics* by Ivor Leclerc (Allen and Unwin).

If we are to take our responsibilities towards society seriously and take present-day thought and knowledge into the classroom we must see that personality has abundant opportunity to react on personality, so that—through the interaction—each person develops into his own realization of a

mature, related and well-balanced individual. We shall hope
to see an individual who is neither intimidated nor intoxicated
by society, who is neither without landmarks in solitude nor
overwhelmed in society, who has learnt to discuss important
matters without quarrelling. This person will have been
helped at school to acknowledge and prize his relatedness to
others, but to realize through this integration his own individuality, to balance reflective thought with discussion, and
solitude with society.

9. THE CREATIVE SOCIETY

I have been encouraged recently to find that my own experience in the classroom is confirmed by the writings of
Alfred Adler.[1] Adler regards the individual as essentially
creative, but only reaching full maturity in work directed
towards a goal in association with others. For him the neurotic or immature person is an individual who has for some
reason failed to give himself to an aim, beyond or greater than
his own personal profit, in association with others. He speaks
of the "narrow stable" of the neurotic and shows how he has
been able to help children out of unhappiness and frustration
by giving them the courage to shed their fears in trust of
others, co-operating with them in significant work, in concentrating on the aim and not on the process. Geniuses, he
thinks, are simply people with the greatest degree of social
relatedness, the greatest capacity for forgetting themselves in
socially directed and integrated, if outwardly solitary, work.
In language teaching we see the greatest efficiency where the
pupil has aims beyond his immediate grasp that he can strive
towards in association with others. The application of these
views to education has been shown by Dr. Fleming in several
books, most recently in *Teaching: a Psychological Analysis*.[2]

---

[1] As edited by Heinz L. Ansbacher and Rowena R. Ansbacher in
The Individual Psychology of Alfred Adler, Allen and Unwin, 1958.
[2] C. M. Fleming, M.A., Ed.B., Ph.D., Methuen, London, 1958.

10. THE CO-OPERATIVE SOCIETY

The Christian and the Marxist—for different reasons and from different premises—look forward to a perfected society in the future, in which there will be true and complete co-operation, in which rivalry and the instinct for piling up private hoards of advantage—whether concrete or spiritual—will wither away. With 2,000 years of aspiration behind them the Christians have less excuse than the Marxists for being still so far from their goal; those Christian schools, in particular, that have an imperialist organization of headmaster at the top and a hierarchy of lesser potentates all down the scale below him, with zealously cultivated fields of rivalry and prestige, with fountain-of-wisdom type of teaching and organized emulation and graded scorn do little to bring this ideal nearer.

Large-scale industry, commercial organization and political interrelatedness demand social skills of a high order and a well-diffused sense of responsibility as much as they demand skill and knowledge in specialized fields and a common language. It is logical to learn the one in relation to the other: when we are learning a language which will make supranational organization possible, to cultivate the skills of harmonious living and working together which will make it successful.

We can do our best to reduce the spirit of rivalry, and the instinct for accumulating private stores of knowledge and skill, by showing our pupils how they can each develop quicker and better and acquire more knowledge if they work together and give generously in time and effort to one another. The stronger soon find that they can enjoy helping the weak; the weaker ones learn to look to society for help, not for scorn. The teacher who has let himself get trapped in the competitive system—often against his own better instincts—can soon develop a new outlook. He shakes off the examining, prying, peeping, policeman, judge, jailer—and even hangman or public executioner—attitude of the authoritarian type of education as if he were shaking off fetters. He rejoices to see that he has a duty to build up, and not to drive wedges into every weakness; to build up the skill and confidence of every individual pupil, but also to build up a healthy and well-integrated society with a habit of mutual help and interdependence.

11. PRACTICAL CO-OPERATION

A workshop atmosphere can be built up in any classroom; in each pupil a sense of responsibility for work done can develop. Children and young people want to learn; long years of sitting waiting for the cue from the teacher that so seldom comes, the lack of reality in the classroom and the isolation and unrelatedness of the individual effort that is called for, the sense of struggling alone and unaided, and the expectation of scorn or pilloried failure, produce an apathy, which is often labelled "laziness".

It was a surprise to me once, on my rounds of visiting schools, after weeks of monotony, watching apathetic classes turning the wheels of the treadmill in resigned disgust, to find myself in a class where there was no apathy. The girls were permitted to ask me questions; the number of questions was overwhelming—one girl had prepared twenty-one that she wanted to ask—so three or four girls were set to choose the most interesting of them to put to me. I was introduced to the editor and two assistant editors of the wall newspaper and shown the last number, and the sheets so far collected of the number that was in preparation; I was introduced to the custodian of the models, and to the archivist with her store of pictures assembled for the illustration of lessons and listed according to subjects. Several pairs of girls were asked to recite their dialogues based on their personal statements; one pair could not finish and were advised to try again next time. One girl handed in homework that the teacher saw at a glance was badly done. She did not say anything to the girl who had handed it in, but turned to another girl sitting on the other side of the room: "Why did you let Fatma hand in work like this?" she asked.

"Oh, I'm sorry, Miss ——, we went to the cinema yesterday evening, so I had no time to help her last night, and this morning I only just had time to do my own homework before coming to school."

"Well, you must understand that being in group 'A' carries responsibility; if you are not able to carry out your responsibilities you must move into group 'B' and make way for a girl who can. I'm too busy to look at this work; I should keep the whole class waiting if I tried to. Take her to the back of the room and show her what she's done wrong."

The two girls spent the next five or ten minutes whispering together at the back of the room while a group of three girls reported to the teacher and the class the arrangements they had made with the father of one of them, who was a railway official, to visit the railway workshops the following Saturday morning. Then the offending exercise book was brought up for inspection, glanced at and put on the pile.

"Yes," said the teacher, "I'll look at that now. You seem to have corrected most of the mistakes." Then she explained to me that the class was divided into three groups, the bright girls on the right, the backward ones on the left, and the middling ones in the middle. They were all paired for doing their homework: each of the bright girls was paired off with, and expected to help, a backward one, and the middling ones were supposed to help one another. Girls who no longer needed help from a brighter girl were moved out of the "C" group into the "B" group, so that they would do their homework with a girl of about the same standard. Similarly, girls who were unable to help the weaker ones, or who failed to develop a satisfactory sense of responsibility, were moved out of "A" group into "B" group. The aim was to reduce the size of "C" group progressively during the year. For some purposes the groups worked together as groups; for example "A" would prepare and perform a relatively difficult dialogue or miniature drama, "B" a less difficult one, and "C" a quite simple one.

I asked if the "C" group did not suffer under a sense of inferiority and "A" group from swelled heads. "No," said the teacher, "I constantly remind the class that most of those in group 'C' are there because they have missed a lot of school through illness and other accidental causes, or because they have not had certain advantages; anyway, they are the members of the community who need help and we must see that they get it. Those in group 'A' are kept from getting spoilt by being given responsibility and by a great deal being expected of them. I try to show them that they have not earned their gifts, but that they must be grateful for them, and show their gratitude by sharing them, as much as they can, with others who have not been so fortunate."

12. THE MAKE-UP OF GROUPS IN A CLASS

This was one way of grouping a class; the system worked well in the hands of that teacher and with those girls. It might not be suitable for every class or teacher. On the other hand, it is a mistake to overlook other ways than one's own of organizing classes. I should be uneasy in working it myself and could hardly believe that the children could be kept from smugness. A more normal arrangement is to divide a class into four or five groups of roughly parallel attainment, with advanced and backward pupils in each group. The groups can choose their own leaders or the teacher can choose them, in the early stages of such work; but ultimately the aim should be to give a chance to every boy or girl to lead the group, in rotation, at least for certain purposes, so that they can all learn to experience the responsibilities and prestige of leadership. The pupils should choose which groups they join, as far as possible, by giving first, second and third choices on slips which are kept confidential by the teacher.

This is better than just arbitrarily allotting them to groups, as it gives them the feeling that the group they are in is the group of their choice, if only of the second or third choice. Groups of friends co-operate better and even seem to perceive and learn better than groups of people—whether children or adults—who are indifferent to one another.

13. THE ORGANIZATION OF THE WORK OF THE GROUPS

The groups can be kept fluid, their composition and leadership changed from day to day, or they can be left more or less permanent, led by the leading personalities or by those most capable of leading the groups in language work of various kinds. One can constitute the groups differently for different purposes; for instance, for practising dialogue a relatively small group of three, four or five pupils is handier than a large group, because it gives more opportunity for the individual to speak, but a larger group may be better for discussion or for dialogue as long as only two or three can use a new pattern correctly. If the class is divided into groups of ten or twelve for practising what has just been taught by the teacher, they can be subdivided into smaller groups of three or four as soon as the weaker pupils have had enough experience of the new language form to practise it correctly without close supervision. The size of group most suitable for the presenting of texts or for working up and presenting spontaneous drama may be five or six pupils. Here again it may sometimes be wise to begin the work in a group of ten, twelve or thirteen, and then subdivide it into groups of five, six or seven, as soon as enough pupils have begun to grasp what is needed for leadership.

When a class is divided up into pairs for practising the asking and answering of questions the clamour need not disturb other classes. Each may speak in a low, controlled voice, audible only to the other member of the pair. The mechanical division of the whole class into pairs can be rather stiff, and not dynamic enough for frequent use, except as an opportunity for further rapid practice of a series of pattern sentences, already learnt in larger groups. The sentences learnt in this way can be repeated again a few times by friends living near one another, at home, for homework.

If the teacher practises a group of ten or fifteen in a series of sentences for a few minutes he can break it up into smaller groups of four or five when he leaves it for the next group. These may break up finally into pairs, to practise the same series further. This arrangement keeps the interest going longer by changing the personality relationships, helps the pupil to feel his own progress and increasing mastery of the pattern, and makes it possible for the teacher or the group leader to observe if any members of the groups are evading the pressure of responsibility. If a pair fails to get through the series it can be split up and each single pupil attached to another pair to be given a chance, in turn, with the others. If one of the two is particularly slow he may be practised by the group leader in the series and after a few minutes' repetition, the pair can be reconstituted for further practice.

The teacher can present a new language pattern to the class as a whole for ten minutes during one period and repeat it at the beginning of the next. After five or ten minutes' work in question and answer, according to the need of the class, he can divide the class into four groups, one of which he continues to practise in the new form. The other groups do writing work, or one group may practise quietly in pairs in the corner a sentence pattern learnt the previous week. Or a group may practise songs in a corner, or on the verandah, if there is one. The writing work may be the copying out of sentences from the rough notebook into the fair-copy notebook, or it may be the doing of a written exercise. One group may do silent reading; a good way to stimulate reading at home is to let the pupils read a story for about ten minutes in class in this way, let them get past the introductory paragraph and thoroughly interested, and then break off and tell them to finish the story at home.

After five or ten minutes' practice with the first group the

I

teacher moves on to another and leaves the first group to practise the pattern alone; after a further five or ten minutes' practice he passes on to a third group. By this time the first group may have done enough practice of the new form—or as much as they have patience for—and can settle down to writing. The teacher should always leave the group to conduct its own question and answer practice, as soon as he thinks the group leader can take over or the group otherwise manage without him.

The teacher should try and find an opportunity to take a quick look at the copyists, while passing from one group to another. This is more to give them the feeling that they belong to the whole process than to criticize or check what they are writing, though he should notice anyone making mistakes and get the group leader to go through the work and correct it where necessary. He may join in with the singers or speakers of the songs or rhymes from time to time, and perhaps take up the whole class into singing the chorus of a song for a few moments. A skilled teacher may aim to achieve a constant flux from class to group and back to class again, gathering up threads or dispersing them, as the development of the lesson and the needs of teaching require, like the conductor of an orchestra.

As the pupil grows older and moves up the school, he will be able to work more and more effectively in groups; class teaching will grow correspondingly less and less usual and less and less important. The teaching of advanced texts may gradually be taken over from the teacher by groups, or he may teach a text to a group in detail, giving plenty of individual attention, while the other groups are engaged on other work; he may direct the group to library reading and let them prepare a co-operative presentation of the piece. More details of this sort of work will be given in Chapter 10. Group methods of teaching composition will also be described in detail in Chapter 9.

CLASSROOM DRAMA

14. THE PLACE OF DRAMA IN LANGUAGE TEACHING

Interest in drama as a means of education and healing has increased and found confirmatory justification in the last thirty years. It began, or seems to have begun, with Moreno's reports of being able to help children and adults, wrenched from their homes and community attachments by the first world war, to achieve new social relationships through co-operation in spontaneous drama, to put down new roots and regain their mental balance. Moreno showed that the relationship between mental balance and social balance was close, and that both could be set right in the dramatization of social and emotional needs.

Since then dramatization has been adopted as a means of social and moral regeneration in prisons and schools for juvenile delinquents. It has been used as the basis of group psychotherapy, replacing individual analyses as a way of economizing time and effort; several patients at a time can help one another to externalize and deal with their difficulties in attitude and behaviour under the direction of one psychologist. Some psychologists even say that group psychotherapy by discussion and dramatization is superior to individual analysis, as it is quicker and more permanent in its results.

In recent years role-playing has established itself as one of the most convenient and effective ways of studying conduct and achieving insight in human relations, as part of the training of managerial staff in business, industry and the civil service. We may be surprised at this recognition coming so late when we remember that in military manœuvres and in the imaginative play of children before they go to school, or in their sampling and rehearsing of various roles in life spontaneously in their out-of-school hours, dramatization has for generations been an important means of experiencing and learning.

Drama in school gives the opportunity to the individual to

try himself out, and see himself in various roles and types of conduct, to relate himself to others in doing so, to work in a team, to learn to rely on others and defer to their wishes and opinions, to integrate himself into a community quickly and satisfactorily. It helps him to speak clearly and expressively, and to use language fluently in connection with dramatic action. Spontaneous drama and what is written by the pupils themselves can help them to experiment with and confront, express and reveal, and ultimately adjust themselves to their inner and secret conflicts and longings, and thereby form a healthy, co-operative community. It can be, under skilled direction, a way to the finest aesthetic achievement and catharsis.

(1) *School-made Drama*

Very few teachers who have not seen skilfully directed and inspired drama work in school can guess at the possibilities of the medium, or at the beneficial effects on the minds and characters of the children who take part in it. In particular they would probably be surprised to see what can be achieved in spontaneously worked-out and acted drama and plays composed by the children themselves.

I myself stumbled on an indication of this more than twenty years ago soon after I began teaching. I had to help the boys of a school between the ages of eleven and fourteen to amuse themselves one wet half-holiday afternoon. After doing charades rather perfunctorily for a little while we started to act the scene the older boys had just been reading in Caesar's *Gallic War* of the landing of Julius Caesar in England; there was hardly a definite decision to do so, it began with pushing benches along as war-canoes towards the stage at one end of the room. The war-canoes somehow turned into Roman galleys. Before long we found ourselves composing absurd couplets for Caesar to declaim from the prow of his boat and for the brave officer to declaim as he sprang into the water and climbed up the beach. Choruses were composed for the

British chiefs to shout and sing, spears and cardboard shields were quickly improvised, manœuvring and spear play were practised.

At the end of the afternoon the boys broke up with regret, vowing to spend an hour every evening in rehearsal and composition; copyists were already at work copying out the parts. For several days the leading characters thought of little else: the carpentering shop went over to the exclusive manufacture of shields, spears, bows and arrows; there was a great deal of discussion as to how chariots and boats could be simulated; all available pictures of Roman armour and equipment were searched for in the library; the English periods were commandeered for the writing of more and more ludicrous couplets, the best produced being chosen for incorporation in the master script which was kept by the master scribe. I was myself slightly stunned by the energies let loose and by the degree of social cohesion that developed out of this co-operative project.

But, alas, after only a few days, word went round that the annual school play was to be prepared for, and no rival theatrical activities could be tolerated. We had to give up our mad lark for the hard and serious work, involving weeks of rehearsals, absorbing practically all their spare time, to be started. The official play was a trivial comedy, the sort of thing that parents are amused to see their children performing in, but quite outside the interests of boys of that age. All the enthusiasm and co-operation that I had been surprised at in the spontaneous play, and that had caught up classroom periods into the scope of play, vanished, and in their place there was a dreary round of mechanical rehearsals that extended school-time intolerably into the play time; rivalries and bitternesses developed; frustration and boredom took over, and the final performance on parents' day was a dispiriting experience. At that time I had no knowledge of the work which was being done in developing spontaneous drama and co-operatively written drama in schools, but I could see that what I had unwittingly helped into existence, if only so fleetingly, was educationally fruitful and fructifying, while the mere learning by heart and performing of a worthless play had been educationally stultifying and to the last degree wearisome.

(2) *Ready-made Drama*

Another experience which I had in the same school has helped me in all my teaching since. The headmaster asked me to spend one period a week with the top form on play-reading. I thought to myself: "If play-reading, then Shakespeare," and remembered the enthusiasm I had developed for Hamlet at the age of fourteen. Other teachers in the school said: "Certainly not Shakespeare. Shakespeare is too difficult for school at all, it ought to be kept for honours degree courses at the university."

I thought of the queues I had seen the previous week waiting outside two theatres in London to see plays by Shakespeare and asked myself what these people, who were certainly not all university graduates, expected to get from a play of Shakespeare, and what it was that made the experience worth while to them, so that they felt good when they came out; I supposed that very few could have answered an examination, and if they had, in fact, had such a possibility in mind while they were watching the play they would probably have objectified the experience to such a degree that they could not have enjoyed it. I doubt if I could have put my thoughts into quite these words at that time but this is what I sensed, if not coherently thought.

Moreover, I thought over the effect of seeing a street accident; one is conscious of the central drama to a much greater degree of intensity than one is normally aware of what one sees; subsidiary events can only be noticed or remembered in so far as they lead into and contribute meaning to the central event. If one is questioned about them afterwards in the police court one sees again the crucial action that seemed to lead into the accident, but whether the man driving the delivery-van had a moustache or not one cannot remember, nor anything else that did not at that moment seem to contribute to the final result, yet one's opinion on the accident was valid. If, however, a film of the accident were played over half a dozen times one would gradually become aware of scores of minor incidents that excitement and concentration on the main lines of the drama had cut out as one saw it the first time.

It seemed to me that in reading Shakespeare with younger boys we must concentrate on the main lines of the drama and leave everything else deliberately slightly out of focus as a photographer does when he photographs racehorses in a race; the grandstand behind is blurred and only a few waving arms foggily contribute to the impression of excitement as the minutely focused and brilliantly lighted winner and the slightly less sharply focused second and third runners go thundering by.

I told the boys that we were going to read Shakespeare and that they were to ask no questions about the meanings of words unless they really missed the point of the story. We acted enough of the action to help comprehension—Falstaff appeared with a pillow stuffed into the front of his coat and was waylaid by his friends armed with rulers—but we spent no time on stage management or costumes. The keynote was speed, and we read eight plays in a year. I believed, at the end of the year, that those boys would never again be deterred from liking Shakespeare by any conscientious schoolmaster noticing and treasuring separately and equally every word and its meaning.

They had absorbed and experienced what was within their reach. What was beyond their reach had been mercifully left there. Teachers can hardly expect to communicate to immature pupils an experience of a play that they themselves have achieved after half a lifetime of reading, studying and seeing performances of the play. A play is essentially an impressionistic medium by virtue of its quick passing, like a horse-race; many of the problems of Shakespeare only occur to the reflective mind in the study; preoccupation with every detail of the setting or scene distracts us from the central theme and a general understanding of that.

(3) *Spontaneous Drama*

The most readily applicable kind of drama in language teaching is spontaneous drama, which many teachers might not dignify with the word drama at all. Yet it is an essentially dramatic way of working and leads quite naturally into more formal drama. There are various ways of stimulating the imagination to carry the body with it into the enactment of an imagined scene. The teacher may tell the class a story and tell each of the groups into which the class is divided to enact it; this will not only show comprehension, but will help the separate groups to reach comprehension, in discussing how to act the story, or in simply acting it under the direction of the group leader who has understood it better. In watching the other groups give their interpretation of the story, all will come to realize it more fully. Besides this, it is an exercise in group composition.

The teacher may, however, simply ask the groups to enact in turn a story well known to them from their own literature. Or he may give them a story to read and then enact. A difficult passage in a text which the form is studying may be easy to grasp if a group is asked to take up the roles of the characters in the story and perform the actions described in it for the eyes of the rest of the class to follow while the passage is being read.

But dramatically rendered situations may arise from almost any attempt to carry the class out of the classroom through the imagination. The development of a three-dimensional picture, in action, from a two-dimensional picture—from the onlooker's point of view—will be discussed in the next chapter. But a boy who has difficulty in visualizing a situation which he has seen in a picture, or has merely read about in a prose text or in a poem, can be helped most quickly to comprehension by being pushed and pulled into enacting a part in the situation that has puzzled him. Here we may distinguish between two types of spontaneous drama: in one kind the teacher gets one boy to be Tarquin, another Horatius, two others his companions on the bridge, another Lars Porsena, and two groups to represent the citizens of Rome and the armies of Clusium; this is for initial comprehension and may be static. The other is to show that the piece has been comprehended and to render it memorable, when the form gives a dynamic performance, possibly to display it to another form.

Another time we may ask: "How does a tiger kill an antelope?" and get one boy to be the tiger and another the antelope, or "What do you do if you have a bad headache?" and so on. We may be looking at a picture of a railway station and see two people looking at the time-table; we ask, "What are they saying to one another?" and perhaps, to start them off, say: "Mrs. Brown is saying to her husband, 'I told you our clock was twenty minutes slow, and now we've missed the train.' And he is answering, 'It's all right, my dear, there are plenty more trains.'" From this point we can ask the class what Mr. and Mrs. Brown will do till their train starts and we may agree that they will probably go to the waiting-room or to the restaurant to drink a cup of coffee. Then the scene in the restaurant can be enacted, with Mr. Brown wanting to read the newspaper and his wife wanting to go on grumbling and the waiter bringing them coffee. Afterwards, it may be repeated with variations by each group.

Another possibility is for the teacher to give each group a scene to enact and allow them a few days to prepare it, with or without his help. When they are ready he will let them perform their versions in turn; they may either do them in succession in one lesson, or separately spread over several, as something to look forward to at the end of the lesson. The teacher might say, "Someone comes and knocks at your door late at night. What is it? Are the police looking for a murderer who, they think, has taken refuge in your house? Or is

the second language in the library and in home reading; they can give research assignments or projects that include references in the foreign language to groups when they are preparing topics for presentation to the class. If the subject teachers are shy of using a foreign language to discuss their subjects they may periodically indicate to the foreign-language teachers the scope of recent work done and suggest lines on which research reading and discussion in the second language would be valuable. If this is done regularly and systematically the language teacher will seldom be short of reading or discussion material or of subjects for written composition.

7

Visual Aids to Language Teaching

INTRODUCTION—THE NEED FOR CULTIVATING THE IMAGINATION

In trying to teach a language in a classroom we are forced to do without a good many of the stimuli to natural use of the language that the everyday environment and the situations of normal civilized life force on the person who learns a language naturally, living among native speakers of it. He joins them in their daily work and in their amusements, he establishes friendships with them and hears them express themselves in all the circumstances of their daily lives; gradually he joins in the verbal accompaniment to their activities, and hardly notices how he is helped in doing this by his contact with concrete objects and situations.

The imagination is hardly needed in the early stages, and, when it is needed, the imaginative leaps called for are securely based on innumerable experiences in which language and situation help one another in relating language, and what it stands for, intimately together. When he begins to read the signs on shop windows, he is helped to do so by his need to buy food, cigarettes, newspapers, etc.; when he begins to read the newspaper, his reading is supported by conversation on the same topics amongst the people round him, even if he hardly takes part in it himself.

The teacher in the classroom has to try and make up for this lack of natural stimuli, and usually calls on the pupil's imagination to help him. Unless the teacher realizes the extent to which he is making demands—and sometimes excessive demands—on his pupils to do this, and consciously takes steps to make these imaginative leaps natural and easy, he is likely to leave them behind, discouraged and perhaps apathetic, only faintly stirred, and not caught up, in the mazes of words he parades before them.

Most unsuccessful language learning is due to failure of the imagination: failure of the teacher's imagination to realize that words alone may not suffice to carry the pupil over into the imaginary situations he is trying to bring him into, and failure of the pupil's imagination to create or picture the situation in his mind that the words are intended to build for him. Most teachers see the need for making use of visual aids in one form or another to help the pupil to imaginative experience beyond the reach of the classroom; not enough teachers realize the need of using visual aids imaginatively. That is, they use the objects and situations shown in a picture, film, or other visual representation of reality as if they were the actual objects and situations themselves; whereas even the best and clearest representation remains a representation and requires to be related to—or based on—experienced reality by some effort of the imagination, however slight. The teacher can help the pupil to make the effort by reminding him of parallels in his own first-hand experience and showing him examples, until he is satisfied that the leap has been made. How this can be done by simple spontaneous dramatization in the classroom has been shown in the chapter on co-operation in language learning, Chapter 6, but gesture, mime, facial expression, or just doing what is shown being done in the picture may be enough to bring a picture or other kind of representation to life.

A. TWO-DIMENSIONAL AIDS

1. *The Blackboard*

The simplest classroom aid of all is the blackboard. It has great possibilities for pictorial representation, yet most teachers seldom use it except for writing lists of words or paradigms on it. If they are shown the value of quick sketches for giving meaning or situation, helping the pupil to picture what he is hearing about, they usually excuse themselves on the grounds that they are no artists; they are afraid of making themselves ridiculous in front of their pupils. They prefer to describe what the pupil is expected to see in his mind's eye in the home language; yet, although meaning may have been conveyed, the essential work of picturing a scene, of perceiving visually, has been left to the pupil.

Picturing a scene that is being described even in one's own language requires an effort; this effort is not infallibly made by all the hearers even if there is no apparent difficulty in doing so. It is not easy to listen attentively to a description, even if the language of the description is quite simple, largely because language is not an appropriate medium for relating objects to one another in space and conveying shape and texture; yet language may help us to a very accurate perception, once the general disposal of masses and shapes has been perceived spatially. So a drawing on the blackboard, if it is to act as a lay-figure or skeleton on which to spread a verbal description, need not be more than schematic or skeletal, something for the imagination to crystallize out on, to help keep the elements of the scene separate but related.

I once saw a training-college student trying to tell the story of Grace Darling. He struggled to keep the rocks the lighthouse was built on and the rocks the ship was wrecked on separate, he tried to explain how the boat went out of sight of the people in the wrecked ship when it sank into the trough of the wave and how it came into sight again when it rose on to the crest of a wave. The expressions "trough of the wave" and "crest of the wave" were new to the class and not easy for inland boys to visualize, yet no other words would replace them adequately; "the ship which had been wrecked" was a difficult phrase to grasp at first, yet easy enough to attach to the perceived situation of the stranded ship, once it had been perceived. There was blank incomprehension on the faces of the class, so the principal of the college suggested that the trainee should draw a picture of the scene. He drew a pitiably small lighthouse on very schematic rocks and monstrous regular waves like the waves of sound in a physics diagram; the rocks the ship was wrecked on dwarfed the ship and the people dwarfed the ship and the rocks, but suddenly the scene slid into focus as a boat bigger than the lighthouse and the ship, and its rocks, began to move out over the schematic water; it was perched on the top of a wave, then it was rubbed out and reappeared in the trough between two waves. We seemed to have seen it slide down from the crest into the trough; the line of sight of the people in the wrecked ship was drawn to show that they could no longer see it.

The problem had been to establish relationships in space rather than to visualize accurately; the visualization could, perhaps, be left—it was, in fact, largely left—to the imagination. The trainee might have said, "Let this chair represent the lighthouse and that one the wrecked ship; my shoe is the boat, and this piece of chalk is Grace Darling; these three benches are the waves; the duster represents the people on the wrecked ship." This would have given the spatial relationships quite satisfactorily and would have had the added advantage of three dimensions instead of two; it would have been difficult to remember which chair was the lighthouse and which the ship, but this is a perfectly valid type of visual aid, using symbols rather in the way they are used in charts. The symbolism would be improved by taking a different type of object to represent each different object that had to be represented; for instance, the teacher's desk to represent the lighthouse and his chair the ship. A drawing is better than a representation of this kind because in a drawing we can represent each object by a visual symbol made to resemble the object, so that no effort of memory is needed to remember which is which; exact representation is seldom necessary.

In this particular lesson about Grace Darling what astonished me was the degree to which I myself was helped by the drawing to concentrate on what the trainee was saying and doing; the attitude of the class changed from bored indifference to eager participation, although the drawing was as incompetent and unrepresentational as a drawing could well be. Of course, good drawing does the work of the lesson better than bad; but bad drawing is better than no drawing at all where the pupil needs help in visualizing.

(a) *Techniques of Blackboard Drawing.* The best type of blackboard drawing is a rapid sketch, expressive like a caricature or the drawing in a good humorous magazine, but not necessarily accurate. The essentials are indicated only, and no unessential details are shown. The great advantage of a blackboard drawing is that it takes shape under the eye of the pupil; teachers lose this advantage by preparing the drawing in advance. A drawing done in advance is best done on a piece of card and pinned up, but it still has a different purpose from the purpose of the blackboard drawing.

The blackboard drawing built up, like a living organism, in front of the class, has a special life of its own; drawn with a running commentary from the teacher, it is in itself a means of relating language to experience; the words and their meaning penetrate into the mind with unusual clarity; concentration, if the drawing is rapid and lively, is extreme; the participation—even of a large class—may be complete. However complex the drawing may ultimately become, the dullest member of the class is not puzzled or dismayed at its complexities, because he has seen its development, line by line, from easily grasped beginnings.

A figure may be rubbed out and rapidly redrawn in a new position to give the illusion of movement. Camels may come over the horizon. The sun may rise behind mountains. A man standing in front of a house may put out a foot and begin to walk towards it; he can be rubbed out and redrawn half-way to the house with legs and arms swinging, and then rubbed out again and drawn standing in front of the door, with one arm raised to the door; we knock on the blackboard and the class can almost swear they have seen him knock on the door. It is as well if any actions thus shown on the blackboard are mimed by the teacher and then by one or more members of the class, so that there is no room for doubt as to what is intended. No time is lost by doing this, as comprehension is tested and ensured at the same time. "Knock on the desk!" we may say to everybody.

(b) *Application of Blackboard Drawing*. I have always found drawing in this way on the blackboard a sure way of rallying the scattering attention of a class unaccustomed to concentrate; it is a way of giving point and focus to the spoken word. As I draw very badly, it at once puts me on a level with the class, and brings out their sympathy and friendliness. I was once able in this way to make a very unruly class of sixty-five little girls attentive and quiet. Their teacher's voice and physical presence were insufficient to silence or overawe them. But I was able to get their attention by drawing pictures of cats and inviting members of the class to outdo my cats, and then telling a jury to number the cats in order of excellence. The fact that I was having an off-day in my skill at representing cats with a few conventional curves did not seem to affect their value as a focus for attention.

After a time I went over to dogs, but my first dog was universally shouted down as more like a sheep; eventually we achieved a fine quantity of good quality dogs, some with spots, some with short tails and some with long; there was scornful rejection of the notion of a dog with stripes, and cats with short tails were also not tolerated.

By the end of the lesson we were able to agree, with some surprise, that we had got used to hearing and using, if we had not yet quite learnt, the ordinal numbers *first, second, third, fourth* and *fifth*, and expressions such as *better than, worse than, the best picture of a cat, that dog's more like a sheep than a dog, dogs with short tails, dogs with spots, stripes*, etc., and a great deal that had been half-learnt before had been well practised and made quite clear and conscious.

K

The teacher must never draw away silently on the blackboard, wrapped in concentration over his little masterpiece; he must constantly comment and invite comment on what he is doing: "I've drawn that arm too long." "Does an arm look like that?" "Can anyone draw it better?" "Have I given him any eyes?" "Now I've drawn one eye, the other eye's on the other side; we can't see it," or we can make it come Picasso-like round the corner, to have it at once sent back again by a literal-minded class. Ears and hands can be put on in the wrong place, to the scandalized delight of the class. All this gives opportunity for natural and compelling speech; or it gives an opportunity to bring in humour and humanity into the otherwise rather sterile classroom.

2. *Ready-made Pictures*

Ready-made pictures, either made by the teacher or members of the class out of school, or bought for classroom teaching, or simply cut out of old magazines, can be divided into two categories. There are those intended and designed primarily for teaching, and there are those used primarily for decorating the classroom and giving a background that conveys a visual impression of the country where the language is spoken. Both are important, but they have different uses and should be handled differently. Pictures printed in the textbook play a subordinate role.

(a) *Pictures intended for Teaching—their Design.* Pictures which have been designed for teaching language should show representative objects, especially such objects as are not likely to be familiar to the pupil, which he can hardly confront and sample through any other medium. The teacher should never allow himself to forget that direct experience of objects and situations at first hand is bound to be more effective for entering into a situation through language than second-hand experience arrived at with the help of pictures. There is therefore no need to show in pictures what the pupil ought to be learning to scrutinize and experience with his own eyes and hands.

But, besides objects, the pictures specially prepared for classroom use should show as much diversity of situation and action as possible, so that we can say "What is that man doing, and why is he standing there?" and "What is he going to do in a moment?" "What has that woman just done?" and "Where has that boy come from?" And this last question reminds us that we have not finished when we tell over the contents of the picture; a good teaching picture should give us the opportunity to make use of what is not visible in the picture at all, but can easily be inferred from it: "When the bus comes to that bus stop, where those people are standing, what will they do, and how will they pay their fares?"

The pictures should not be put up on the walls and left there from lesson to lesson; the success of expression in the presence of pictures depends on their being fresh and interesting when they are put up; we should have the impression that we have caught these people and held them for a moment, busily engaged in their various pursuits, this sunny or showery morning. The pictures should on no account be allowed to become stale by being seen when they are not being used.

(i) *The Use of Pictures.* It is seldom necessary to say: "This is a bus," or "That is a picture of a railway station." The words should rather be used as naturally as possible with reference to the objects they stand for, as if they were quite familiar already, even if they are not. This is perfectly satisfactory, especially as pictures are not to be made use of until the classroom background and direct experience through it have been exhausted. We should say perhaps: "Have you seen a railway station?" "Well, did it look like that?" "They are looking at something. What are they looking at?" "They are looking at a piece of paper"—"a notice" we may interpolate—"What sort of a notice is it?" We may ask "Is it the kind of notice you have on the school notice-board?" "It's rather like the notice we have there to see the times of the lessons, isn't it?" "We call a notice that shows us times of lessons or trains a time-table. Why are that man and woman looking at a time-table?" "When do you look at the school time-table?" "Do you look at it when you know the times of your lessons?" "No, we don't. We look at it when we don't know the times, or have forgotten which lesson comes next, or which classroom it's in." "Yes, that's right, these people want to know two things. They want to know when the next train goes to the place they want to go to, and they want to know which platform it goes from." Of course, if we are using the picture for the first time fairly early in the course we shall use simpler sentences than this. Then we put it away for a few months, use other pictures in the meantime to practise the same structures in other situations and contexts, and when we come round to the same picture again, we use more complex sentences, developed forms of the same structures, and new structures.

There is hardly any other way to take children in their imagination into an English street or railway station, or to a dock-side or into an English house, with its furniture, table-ware and fires, if they have never seen England.

(ii) *The Use of Pictures for Practising the Tenses.* One way to get plenty of practice of the tenses is to ask about what the people we can see in a picture are doing, have done, will do and will have done in two hours' time. A more mechanical way that ensures the conversion of all present tenses into past tenses is to roll up the picture, after we have spent half an hour or so in talking about what is going on in it, and ask what the people were doing, whether they caught their train or missed it, whether the man standing by the bookstall bought a book or a newspaper, etc. Or one may keep the picture in front of the class and say, "Of course, this picture was made some time ago; what were these people doing?" "This picture shows the kind of thing people do every day. They will do the same things tomorrow," and the whole lesson can then be in the future tenses. Or we can say: "This is a scene that has been imagined by the artist. What would the people do if they did what the artist has put into the picture?" and do the lesson in Conditional Tenses.

I prefer, however, to make my use of the conditional more natural, saying: "That man is just going to get into the train, what would he have done if he had missed the bus and got here too late for the train?" Or we can say: "What would you do if you were there?" For teachers who feel unsure of themselves in this kind of discussion the more mechanical way may be safer until they have trained themselves in this way of working and got enough confidence to feel able to do the other.

(b) *Pictures intended for Decoration.* These pictures are not such a direct teaching aid as those designed for teaching; they can be used as a point of departure for discussion, but not for detailed discussion; they have a very important part to play in establishing atmosphere and background and in establishing what the psychologists call mental set. They may show views of the country where the language being learnt is spoken; they may be photographs, or paintings or drawings reproduced. They should also show, besides views of places and things, various kinds of people at their daily work, amusing themselves, travelling and going to their work. They can be cut out of magazines, but rather larger pictures than these are desirable if they can be obtained.

No picture should be kept on the walls too long. Stale pictures come, in time, to be almost invisible unless they are works of art. If there are twelve pictures available, not more than three or four should be hung at any one time and they should be changed once a fortnight.

When they are first put up they should be discussed briefly with the class, so as to ensure that they are fully realized. If they are photographs we may draw attention to a tower or a house or the fact that there is no traffic in the streets by asking what time of day it is, or what time of year. If shadows are short and leaves are on the trees it is near midday in summer. A correct diagnosis hardly matters, but, to give one, the pupil must observe the picture accurately. Less topographically informative pictures may be discussed for what they suggest, or whether the members of the class like them. Discussion should not be prolonged too long nor insisted on at all costs if there is nothing to say, as this would make the putting up of new pictures an ordeal instead of a delight. One possibility is to let each member of the class choose a picture, in turn, from the class collection, and introduce it to the class, either by talking about it for a few minutes or asking questions designed to draw attention to any interesting features in it. A valuable source of pictures for the classroom walls—perhaps the most valuable of all—is the work of the class, either in the art class, or as a part of project work or other language-learning activity.

The Display of Pictures

Pictures should be kept carefully and displayed neatly where they can be seen well. The pictures are easy to handle and store if they are mounted on large sheets of brown paper. If they are labelled on one corner of the brown-paper mount, they can be identified or found by simply turning up the corners. There is no need to turn over the whole pile.

Wherever careful provision has been made in a classroom for the display of pictures and there has been planned and regular use of pictures as background and for teaching, I have seen concentrated attention and signs of well-being in the class. In one school, two boys presented themselves to the teacher in the staff-room ten minutes before the lesson began and asked what would be needed for the lesson. "Pictures of meadows with cows in them and a farmyard," said the teacher to one boy, "And that cut-out model we have of a farmyard," she said to the other. So, when we went into the classroom a few minutes later, there they were displayed, the pictures hung from hooks in a batten of wood along the wall, the model farmyard set out on the teacher's desk. She told me that the boys all had periods of duty in charge of the pictures and the models which belonged to the class. They had to keep them in order, clearly marked and catalogued, and get ready the right ones when they were needed. There was an extraordinary sense of purpose and efficiency in that classroom; it was not the teacher's lesson, the lesson belonged to the class, and the teacher was there as their expert helper and guide. Where morale is high, as here, from well-organized team-work, learning is effective.

(c) *Pictures printed in a Textbook.* Pictures printed in a textbook, especially if they are well-drawn and brightly coloured, can contribute enormously to the attraction of a textbook and can set each lesson in its appropriate visual setting; they can remind the pupil, when he is revising, of incident and scene that he associates with the lesson, but in my experience pictures in a textbook are seldom appropriate for teaching. If the teacher holds up his copy and points to details, most of the members of the class are unable to see, and his finger and hand are likely to obscure most of the picture. Besides that, the publishers, in a praiseworthy attempt to make each picture go a long way, often crowd a great deal of detail into a small space, and I have found that for some children this is confusing. A simple drawing on the blackboard of the essentials of the picture—details being added only as they are needed—is much better for teaching, and the picture in the book can be used for reference, after the lesson has been introduced, and for revision. I have assumed that the picture in the textbook is well and clearly drawn; often they are blurred or clumsily drawn. These are bad because they show lack of concern; they are of no value for any purpose whatever; such a textbook should be discarded.

3. *Projected Pictures and Projectors*

(a) *The Cinema.* The great disadvantage of the moving film for ordinary teaching is that it gives no time for reflection; the audience has to submit to the influence of the film and accept what it gives until the film is over and the total impression can be judged. The moving film can hardly be used for an informal commentary by the teacher and a discussion as it goes along, unless the sound is cut out. Even then the movement is too rapid for effective discussion to be possible. Once the teacher has made up his mind to this disability, however, he can decide to make use—for language learning—of precisely those qualities that are a disadvantage for normal teaching.

In the natural process of learning a language we hear natural speech forms emerge from action; the less reflection there is on language the better. Reflection allows comparison with the mother tongue, and this produces only difficulty. Some people say that they have learnt a language simply by going to the cinema a great deal and seeing films with dialogue in the language they want to learn. Where there is identification with the actors and a corresponding entering into and sharing in the action, the audience are bound to work the speech patterns through their minds as they watch the action and take part in the action in their minds. Language passing through the mind, with or without our speaking, in association with a clearly realized situation, makes the kind of marks or impressions on the mind that result in the learning of language. I understand that Dr. I. A. Richards has prepared lengths of film in which certain actions are shown in association with relevant language; the ends are fastened together so that the film forms a loop and can be repeated continuously. So far, I believe, only cartoon film has been used for the purpose. Normal photographic film might be even better: there is a greater degree of authenticity and richer possibilities for situation and action to hold the attention while language falls into its natural place in the background.

Adapting Ordinary Films to Classroom Use

We can overcome the defects of a normal film for classroom teaching purposes by playing the film silent—with the sound switched off—and giving a simplified commentary within the vocabulary range of the pupils. After playing it through once, or perhaps twice, we can play it through with the sound switched on. Although a good deal of the language may still be beyond the class, they will understand the situations and what is going on; this will bring a good deal more of the language within their range than they would normally grasp, or even notice. The film can be played through several times like this, and finally it can be played through with the sound switched off again, for members of the class in relays to give the commentary and reproduce conversation as far as their knowledge allows. Variations of this would be for the teacher to record a simplified commentary on a tape-recorder, or for a group of five or six members of the class to study the film and prepare a simplified introduction and commentary for the film and record it on a tape-recorder. This sort of work will hardly become a regular feature of language-teaching pro-grammes until suitable films of the right length and graded difficulty have been prepared.

(b) *The Film-strip Projector*. The modern film-strip pro-jector is small, compact, portable, and even for the least mechanically gifted person, easy to handle. Thirty-five-milli-metre slides can also be shown in most models and loaded into a magazine containing thirty-six slides, in advance, so that they can be shown one after the other without any hitches or trouble or waste of time during the lesson. Any teacher who does colour photography can show his photographs very easily to a class in this way. If he has visited the country or countries where the language he teaches is spoken, he can add greatly to the interest of his classes, and to the ease and fluency of the discussions of those aspects of the country, and the way of life there, that he can illustrate. But the film-strip is the handiest medium for projection; the little rolls of cinema film will go into the pocket and can provide thirty or forty clear pictures on a whitewashed wall or screen, big enough for a class of fifty, or more if necessary. The images are sharp and clear enough, with a good projector, to be seen clearly by a small group even in an undarkened classroom. In a room with no suitable white wall I have projected pictures on to a sloping portion of the ceiling. Another possibility is to paste two sheets of white foolscap paper side by side on the inside of a cupboard door and open the door of the cupboard when one wants to project. This gives an image large enough and clear enough in daylight for a group of twenty, provided one avoids projecting the pictures near direct sunlight.

I have been able to use comprehensibly, in accompaniment to a film-strip, language which is far beyond the normal range of comprehension of the class, and get an effective response. One can use the Continuous Present Tense for what one is showing, the General Present Tense for generalizations from that, the future tenses for what may be expected to be seen in the next frame, and the past tenses for what has been seen in previous frames, and one can turn back to see whether we have remembered correctly.

The great advantage of the film-strip projector is this possibility to stop at a picture as long as one likes—to search it for clues, reflect, comment on it, discuss it, ask what it is leading on to and recall what came before it—and then turn on to see if one's expectations are to be realized, or back to an earlier picture to see if one had remembered accurately. Thus one has, in addition to the two dimensions of a normal picture, the added dimension of time under one's control. The film-strip is at once past, present and future. Vegetables are on the table; the class says "cauliflower"; we turn back and see Mrs. Brown buying a cauliflower in the greengrocer's shop; it is cauliflower. "Do you like cauliflower?" "What colour is it?" "What does it feel like when you bite it, hard or soft?" "Where does your mother buy cauliflowers?" "Do you know how much she pays for one?" And so we thread the picture through the daily lives and experience of the class until Mr. and Mrs. Brown and their daughter Mary, by periodical repetition of the film-strip and constant embellishments of the story, come to be as much a part of the lives of the members of that class as if they had come into the classroom in the flesh.

Simple and obvious as this may seem, I, for one, only came to see the possibilities of film-strips for direct language teaching very slowly, and few, if any, have yet been specially prepared for the teaching of foreign languages. Some cartoon film-strips for showing simple actions and teaching the verbs, prepared for children learning to express themselves in their own language, seem to me to be almost valueless because the actions are all actions that can be more easily demonstrated by the teacher than shown in a picture; the great advantage of the film-strip projector, to show a developing situation, is lost.

Factual film-strips to show how things developed or how they were made—the medieval castle and village, for example; the internal combustion engine, latitude and longitude—have a different but equally valuable use in the classroom. They can be discussed and explained; they can be concentrated on, as language is used to bring their subjects within the consciousness of the pupil.

In this way language is performing its rightful and useful function in digesting and absorbing knowledge and experience, and it is at the same time making its imprint in a significant way, so that the mind flies to the right words instinctively, as the fingers of an experienced typist fly instinctively to the correct keys on the typewriter.

(c) *The Epidiascope.*   If one has a page from a book to show to a class so that all can see it at once; if one has pictures, either in a book or too small to show to the whole class, which one wants to comment on or discuss, the epidiascope can make them large enough. One can even show very small objects conveniently on the screen.

As the light does not pass through a transparent slide or film, however, but is reflected off the picture or object through a mirror or system of mirrors, a good deal of light is lost and the epidiascope—unlike the film-strip projector—cannot be worked successfully in an undarkened classroom. It needs complete darkness and a good screen. Some get hot rather quickly, so that a page of a book or picture cannot be left in too long or it begins to burn. This restricts its use but, in any case, it is a comparatively bulky piece of apparatus and cannot easily be moved about from room to room. It can never be the handy classroom stand-by that a film-strip projector can. It can be switched over to showing glass slides, but these are heavy and easily broken, and are no longer made in great variety. It can be used in a similar way to the film-strip projector except that slides or pictures from a book are less manageable than a film-strip and neither can be left on the screen so long; one has to keep discussion of each picture short. Pictures shown in this way, like the pictures used for decoration and background, and unlike those used for teaching, may be starting-out points for discussion and convey information briefly, but can hardly be discussed in detail or analysed.

In spite of its limitations, however, it is still the best apparatus for showing still pictures on slides to a large audience, and it gives the possibility of throwing beautiful coloured pictures from encyclopedias and other reference books on to a screen so that a large audience can see them; and also, if the pictures have been very much reduced for printing, we can see them enlarged to their natural size. In teaching Yeats' poem "Byzantium" to a university class once, I projected some coloured reproductions of Byzantine mosaics from the encyclopedia with an epidiascope while I was reading the poem. Yeats' impression of Byzantium had been gained from similar—perhaps the same—mosaics, and some of the difficulty of the poem shrank away, with these life-size and portentous figures, on a gold background, in front of the class.

4. *Maps, Plans and Charts*

Practice in the interpretation of schematic representations of reality, such as maps, plans and charts, graphs, isotypes and other representational figures, columns or objects, and statistics, is a valuable exercise. It is an important part of the process of learning to wrap the tentacles of the mind round the concrete phenomena of which they are the abstractions, salivating them mentally, and flowing round them, as the amoeba flows round its food. This is perhaps the chief business of Geography or Social Studies, but the mental saliva is language and the process of absorption involves a linguistic exercise. This can be as important an exercise in a second language as in a first. Reference material to take the pupil beyond the limits of his own language, and further out into the world of knowledge than his own language allows, may only be readily available in the second language.

As soon as we can say: "Govind is in the middle of the room," or "Ahmet is in the corner of the room," I like to be able to point to the map and say: "Nagpur is in the middle of India," or "Ankara is in the middle of Turkey," and "Birmingham is in the middle of England." "What town is in the middle of France, Austria, Africa, etc.?" and we search the map for candidates. Or we say, "Marmaris is in this corner of Turkey," pointing to it, "and Erzurum is in the opposite corner of Turkey, up here. Erzurum is in the north-east corner of Turkey, and Marmaris is in the south-west corner." "What other towns are in the south-west corner of Turkey?" "Denizli, Bodrum, etc., are."

This sort of work, simple enough in the early stages, can develop imperceptibly into a co-ordination of all the pupil's knowledge and experience, and the working of his mind, in the second language, parallel to the co-ordination he is achieving in the first. Merely from the narrowly linguistic point of view the constant use of maps extends enormously the scope of the classroom as a language laboratory; mountains, rivers, seas, currents and oceans, countries, provinces, towns and their population, siting, relation to the country adjacent to them, dependence on foreign trade, susceptibility to foreign influence, conquest, threats and dangers, are brought within the reach of the language teacher. This gives him endless subjects on which to practise and extend the linguistic apparatus he is bringing into use in the classroom situation, especially if he works in close collaboration with the teacher of Social Studies or Geography, who can suggest topics on which the class is already well-informed.

A plan of the town in which the school is helps us to talk about how the different members of the class come to school every day, the shortest way to the post office, the railway station, the police station, the town hall, etc. As soon as possible a pupil should be asked to direct another boy by verbal directions from the school to these and other destinations on the map. The boy supposedly walks or waits for a bus at the bus-stop, and travels in it. He represents his progress on the journey with the point of a stick or a finger on the map, turning left, if the guide says "Left", even if he knows he meant to say "Right". This can often provide an amusing five minutes, but need never take up much time in any one lesson.

The interpretation of graphs, charts and statistics, first of all in speech, in the class, and afterwards in writing, is a form of composition. In just the same way the description of the findings from an experimental testing of a new hormone weed-killer in association with fertilizers, and expressed in the form of figures or a graph, would be, although it is at the same time an exercise in agricultural science. Population statistics, trade figures, market prices, agricultural production and railway traffic figures can be collected by committees of those interested in the particular fields; they can be rendered graphically in graphs, isotypes, bar graphs or other symbolic representations, and then interpreted to the class as a combined operation by the committee.

Both the search and the interpretation of the facts are linguistic exercises of the greatest value. What may not be so easily realized, however, is that the preparing of the graphic representation of the facts tends to impress on the subconscious mind the language patterns that have been used in the collecting process; and at the same time the language patterns that will be used to explain the facts are helped to begin to germinate in the mind as the pupil works at the drawing of the shapes that represent what he will have to say. The very movement of the hand seems to straighten out the grain of the thought, so that it lies the right way for expression when the time comes.

B. THREE-DIMENSIONAL REPRESENTATION

There must always be a loss of some kind in a two-dimensional representation of a three-dimensional original. Sometimes this loss is compensated for by gains of a different kind, but in the language classroom three-dimensional representations seem to have a decided advantage in stimulating the imagination and helping the pupil to enter into reconstructed situations imaginatively.

1. *Dramatization, Mime, Gesture, Facial Expression, etc.*

Actual representation of an action, dramatically, represents the action better than any picture can, because, with it, we have movement and the third dimension, for lack of which a picture is sometimes unsatisfactory. But besides this we also have the fourth dimension of time. Without repeating the remarks on dramatization, in Chapter 6, the chapter on Cooperation in Language Learning, it is still possible to deal with drama in its presentation aspect—the presentation of situation dramatically—and refer to the importance of gesture in the teacher, and his ability to show a scene and communicate an experience of it rapidly to his class by acting it, with suitable gestures, movements and facial expression.

The teacher and, after him, the pupil can act a blind beggar or an enraged cook, or a lame man getting on to a bus, or a woman running for a bus holding a baby on one arm and dragging a child by the other, holding her handbag in her teeth and trying to attract the attention of the conductor with cries of rage, entreaty, sorrow, exhortation and cajolery, punctuated with sharp agonized interjections to the children to be quiet, to run faster, or to stop sucking their thumbs. No human predicament need be regarded as beyond the teacher's reach; a boy told to groan in agony as if from a severe stomach-ache learns this pattern of speech, that summarizes his assumed condition, more quickly than by any amount of explanation. One boy after another can do the same action, and either say what he is doing, or say something appropriate to the part he is acting; at another time different boys can do different actions and give their actions the right verbal accompaniment. Especially in the later years of the course, scenes in prose passages that are to be studied can be brought alive for the class by being presented, first of all, in dramatic form by a group that has been studying them in detail for this. More will be written about this in Chapter 10, on Reading and the Study of Prose Literature.

2. *Puppetry*

A convenient extension of classroom drama is puppetry. Children who are too nervous to speak fluently in front of a class can often speak quite fluently if they are behind a screen and speaking for a puppet they are manipulating with their hands, or if they are reading a poem while others manipulate puppets in dumb show. The making of puppets is a simple and fascinating activity that can be directed and carried out through the language being learnt, the activity helping to fix the language pattern of the instructions and incidental explanations in the mind. The delight children have in bringing their own creations to life can be exploited by getting them to make and give personality to their own puppets in dialogue and miniature drama. Puppets, once started in the beginners' classes, can be continued right up through the school with growing degrees of elaboration in the making and display of the puppets, and growing degrees of sophistication in décor and production and in the nature of the plays produced. If here is insufficient time in school, a spare-time puppet club can be formed which can fulfil the needs of the school for puppets, on order, and even carry out puppet shows.

3. *The Sand-table*

(a) *Use of a Sand-table.* It is curious that a sand-table should be commonly used for teaching small children and for teaching officers and men in the army, but comparatively seldom used for the intervening higher forms in schools. I have mentioned elsewhere a lesson in which I taught a prose passage to a linguistically very backward and tongue-tied fifth-year class of fourteen- and fifteen-year-olds by means of a heap of sand I had had made on the teacher's platform in front of the class. I was able to teach all the new vocabulary required by the piece, during the process of making the landscape, and cutting the camels and Arabs out of cardboard, and setting them out among the sand-hills.

The muscular and tactile experience of moving the sand into shapes and blowing it about to simulate a wind seemed to help and quicken comprehension; energy and concentration that would have been needed to set out a basic picture of the scene in the mind were reserved for discussion and enjoyment of the finer points; we had time to discuss the metaphorical use of language and the effects which desert travel might be expected to have on a man. At the same time, through frequent repetition during the lesson, made possible by the saving of time from explanation, the sentence patterns of an unusually beautiful piece of prose came to be impressed firmly on the mind. I have taught the same piece with the help of simple sketches on the blackboard, but there is a decided advantage in having actual solid material to work with, and three dimensions, instead of only two.

As soon as the lesson was over, we poured the sand back into the sack, gathered up the camels and Arabs and threw them, with the newspaper we had poured the sand on, into the waste-paper basket. The scene could now live on in the minds of the boys. One of the advantages of the sand-table is

L

that it is transitory. It is an approximation, a hint, sufficient to set the imagination working; thereafter the imagination may be expected to take over the duty of keeping the scene in the mind's eye and the sand landscape can be dispersed, as superfluous. A sand-table does not take the place of the imagination, or sidetrack it: it stimulates it.

(b) *The Dimensions and Making-up of a Sand-table.* Although, as I have described, a simple heap of sand on the floor, on the teacher's platform, or in the corner of the room can be quite an effective aid, it is more convenient to have one's sand in a regular receptacle known as a sand-table. This may be an ordinary table given a rim of cardboard which may be fastened with drawing-pins, or simply kept in place by the weight of the sand, or it may be a specially constructed tray, with or without legs. Houses and smaller buildings, bridges, quays and jetties may be made of wood, or of clay or papier mâché, allowed to set hard, and possibly gathered up after each using and kept from one landscape to another. Rough brown cardboard is just as suitable, and quicker to make into bridges, warehouses, etc. A small piece of green tissue paper a few inches in circumference, according to the size required, can be used for bushes and trees; one screws the edges together to form a point, leaving the centre of the piece roughly spherical, and sticks the point in the sand; some hundreds of trees and bushes can be made in a few minutes by half a dozen boys, once they have had a little practice. Sawdust can be dyed and scattered lightly over the surface for colouring the slopes of hills or fields. Blue sawdust can be used in this way to represent water. A few stones can be embedded in the hills to give them a craggy appearance, moss and tree bark may be used to give the impression of a rugged landscape. The sand should be slightly dampened before it is moulded into shapes; it will then hold these shapes for several days. Each single operation of moulding the slightly dampened sand into the shapes of hills and valleys involves recognition and comprehension of the sentences of the instructions, or a sharing in the realization of them.

"Let's make a line of hills here, not too steep"—if steep hills are wanted, they may be moulded out of clay and let into the sand, or the sand may be built up on bricks—"You two, Arul and Balu, help me with these hills; you, Chicku, make the hills on the other side of the valley, with Dillip. You others can make the sea at that end of the sand-table, by clearing away the sand to the bottom of the sand-table and covering it with blue tissue paper"—holding up the blue tissue paper— "You can make a river run down this valley into it. Use either blue tissue paper torn into strips for the river or that blue tape that you'll find on the table over there. If you think this river isn't really blue, you can use grey tape. Does our river look blue?" "It looks blue in the distance, but it looks grey or brown when you stand on the bank," may be the answer. "All right, we're looking at this landscape from a distance; we're not standing on the river-bank; we're looking at it from above, as if we were in an aeroplane, aren't we?" "Now, Arul, hold this piece of grey tape, we'll make a road with it. I think it will have to cross the river by a bridge; so will two of you make a bridge out of cardboard? You'll find some cardboard over there, on the table."

All these sentences, or modifications of them, are bound to be repeated again and again as new landscapes are planned and made. The work may be partly done out of school, to save time in class, but the initial work should be carried out in the language that is being learnt, and, as far as possible, the language should be used for co-ordinating the work in its later stages. This can be helped by the pupils having their instructions, or what they themselves have decided to do, dictated to them and written on work-cards that they keep in front of them as they work at making up the village with its church, inn and parish hall, or at the harbour with its jetty, warehouses and customs sheds, or the railway station with its sidings and goods-yard. If the teacher likes, he can give a series of likely pattern sentences, or he may record on the blackboard, and have copied by the class, the sentences that were actually used as they began work on the landscape.

When the landscape is finished it may have done most of the work it was designed to do, but it still can be the basis for useful discussion. If it was designed to illustrate a story there can be many collateral stories drawn out of it and a good deal of incidental discussion of social questions, problems of behaviour, etc. One landscape should not be kept in being too long, however, until everyone is tired of it.

The Classroom Window—Link with the Real World

Although what we see from the classroom window is not representational and is not within the control of the teacher, nor is it directly experienced contact with reality, yet we can consider it as a visual aid; the window frames a sample of the life of the world outside the school; it is often the only accessible link we have with everyday life. Teachers try hard to explain something about a bicycle, or about someone going along or across the street without noticing specimens of what is being spoken about, through the window. From some classrooms streets, houses, shops, traffic, a railway, factories, trees and gardens can be seen, and actions are actually going on.

Instead of fearing the classroom window as a possible source of distraction, the language teacher may welcome the opportunities it gives for natural and effective use of language related to easily perceived samples of living. The teacher may sometimes spend ten or twenty minutes at the window, talking about what can be seen, and afterwards make a rough representation of the principal features on the blackboard for further discussion.

C. MISCELLANEOUS VISUAL AIDS

Every language classroom should have a calendar to make talking about the date easy. There should also be an old clock with hands that can easily be moved, or simply a clock-face, for learning to tell the time. We can make our own clock-face out of cardboard, or let members of the class make one, or failing that, we can just draw clock-faces on the blackboard, but a clock-face with hands we can move easily is better. A little work with this often over a long period is better than a short period of intensive work and then neglect. A clock-face makes it easy to teach and practise the use of the past and future tenses. A mirror is a valuable aid in teaching pronunciation; if each member of the class has a small pocket mirror he can observe the shape of his mouth, as he pronounces sounds that give him difficulty. Once the pupil has got used to what the correct shape feels like, and has learnt to bring his lips automatically to that shape when he thinks of or speaks the sound, he has overcome the greatest difficulty in pronouncing it correctly.

8

The Teaching of Functional Grammar

To judge by the way some people speak, there is no place for grammar in the language course nowadays; yet it is, in reality, as important as it ever was. "It seems to have gone underground, as it were, like a communist cell in a country where the party is banned," an onlooker at some oral lessons might say. Other onlookers may notice nothing, and ask at the conclusion of a lesson on the General Present Tense or the Present Perfect, or even on Conditions, whether the lesson had any aim at all; it seemed to be nothing but idle and inconsequential chit-chat on whatever caught the teacher's eye. The experienced demonstrator who has set up the beginnings of an instinct[1] for a speech pattern in a class is sometimes hurt that his art has passed unnoticed; yet this almost imperceptible passing of a new mode of expression into the experience of his pupils is, in fact, a measure of his skill.

The pupil must be firmly grounded in the exercise of correct grammar, if he is to attain any skill or effective use of the language, but he need not know consciously formulated rules to account to him for what he does unconsciously correctly.

[1] I am using the word "instinct" for shortness in the sense of acquired habit or unconscious feeling for correct usage throughout this chapter.

The teacher must have a clear idea of the grammar of the language, its structure and usage; everything he teaches must be based on it; he should always be conscious of introducing or practising some point of grammar; he must carry the stages of development of the language in his head so that it becomes a well-integrated growth in the mind of the pupil; but he should only pass this on to the pupil, in the form of an explicit scheme, in retrospect, as a form of revision, as a means of organizing knowledge he already has, as a way to establish pattern and order among diverse and perhaps confusing impressions.

1. GRAMMAR AS THE RECOGNITION OF PATTERN

One of the satisfactions of language learning lies in the slow clearing of the fog, the slow falling into place of the scattered and, at first, seemingly unrelated clusters of sounds, the gradual emergence of pattern where formerly there seemed to be none. If the teacher tries to by-pass this process and serve up to his pupil a systematization not worked for and not developed out of the learner's experience and its organization, he deprives him of this satisfaction; worse than that, the opportunity to get practice in digesting and ordering what he has learnt, in arranging his knowledge and his mastery in manageable segments will have been missed.

Learning a language is not only learning a particular language; it is learning to be sensitive to language in general; learning to be alert to language signals; learning not to be dismayed by strange forests of words, but to search for ways into the forests, clearings, tracks and footpaths. We can drive rapidly through a forest in an hour or so on a broad motor road, and know something of it afterwards, but to know the forest itself intimately we must walk or ride through it in every direction—preferably, at first, with someone who knows the forest and its trees well—and hack our own paths through the densest thickets; we must live in it. Categorizing will be a recognition of the unity underlying many particular experiences. Grammar is a recognition of the pattern and unity underlying verbal experience.

Grammar is a description in words of verbal behaviour, just as a drill book is a description in words of parade behaviour. A new recruit is not asked to sit down at a desk and con over the drill book, and then get up and do what it says. He is drilled by an experienced drill sergeant; but the experienced drill sergeant keeps the drill book in his pocket and constantly refers to it off parade, to be sure that he is not departing from the rules laid down there. Description in words of something concrete like a scene or behaviour is the rendering in one medium of what has existed in another. There is bound to be some loss; this loss can be filled in by the imagination of someone who has been that way, or seen that kind of thing before, but it is a struggle to see clearly in the mind's eye something we have not yet seen in reality. A description of a way through a town we have never visited is almost impossible to follow and realize, and very difficult to remember; but a description of a way through a town we have visited, of which we can picture the chief landmarks as we are listening, is comparatively easy to follow.

Particularly disappointing, as one begins to learn a language, is the description of it in a language one knows. All seemed so plain as one read it, but it is so hard to apply. Switching one's mind perpetually from the language one is learning to the one that holds the description slows up the rate of perception and delays the forming of habits. A description in one language of the phenomena of another needlessly magnifies and distorts the differences between the two languages and the strangeness of the new one. If each is kept separate, and comparison is postponed until the knowledge of the new language is wide and instinctive, they are seen to be separate territories to be known and understood for themselves in their own terms. In much the same way Holland is to be learnt for itself and Belgium and France for themselves; perpetual comparison with one's own country as one travels round them keeps them foreign and us insular; they should be appreciatively and hungrily absorbed as new territory for the spirit to inhabit and rejoice in, but not as foreign or inimical.

We learn a language most easily, most naturally and most healthily when we learn it as if it were our own, from the inside, as a native does. If, on the other hand, we begin with the schematization of grammar, we cultivate that onlooker attitude which makes subsequent participation difficult. Women seem to learn languages quicker than men. Women seem to accept and not question too much what they absorb, if they are not academically trained; they are impatient of theory; men are always trying to analyse, to reason out what they are learning. Men look for landmarks and like to be constantly reassured that the way home is open; women seem content to make their home anywhere.

2. ACQUIRING AN INSTINCT THROUGH NATURAL ABSORPTION AND USE

When learning Turkish I was particularly helpless before the *kalksam*, *gelsem* form. In my grammar there was a warning that the pupil should be very careful to distinguish *kalksam* from *kalkìrsam*, *gelsem* from *gelirsem*, as they were quite different, but no attempt was made to explain wherein the difference lay. I often asked for explanations, but Turks could not explain it, any more than an Englishman can explain to a foreigner the use of the Present Perfect Tense, unless he has been trained as a language teacher. People who had learnt Turkish as a foreign language usually compared it with some usage in their own language; but this confused the issue for me.

It was not until one evening, when I was sitting in a restaurant with some Turkish friends, prevented by a heavy fall of rain from going home, that I determined to turn the enforced inactivity to good purpose, and get the better of this baffling tense. I began using sentences with the form in them. *Kalksak, eve gitsek* (suppose we were to get up and go home), etc. The sentences which failed to give meaning in relation to our circumstances that wet night were rejected by my friends; those which did work, I tried to copy with sentences that seemed to hold the attitude to circumstances which the form implied. Dropping those that failed to pass muster, I went on trying more and more possibilities. At the end of the session I was still not able to put my experience into English words, but I had begun to form a sort of blind instinct for the form which I continued to exploit in my talking over the next few weeks. Whenever I began to tell myself that *gitsek* meant *let's go* or *how would it be if we were to go?* I found that a sort of cloud came down on my knowledge of the form, obliterating some of my experience of it. I had to go on rather blindly for some time longer, risking mistakes and asking to be corrected if I saw a blank face.

3. THE TEACHER'S PART IN PLANNING NATURAL ABSORPTION

This technique I later found to be the basis of modern techniques of linguistic analysis with informants. The essentials of the process were: first, the isolation of a speech pattern; secondly, the application of it to felt situation, errors in application being corrected by experts; thirdly, not forming a concept of the new language experience in terms of another language; fourthly, the gradual development of an instinct for the correct forms. All of the processes need not have been initiated by the learner; time and effort would have been saved if, when I came to need a speech pattern, it had been presented to me in carefully planned sentences applied to my circumstances by a skilled and observant teacher. When the teacher noticed that I was beginning to acquire a correct instinct for the form and was no longer inhibited by the speech habits of my own language, he could have discussed with me the use of the form in such a way as to help me to order my experience in words, that is, bring it to consciousness. If he felt it necessary he could then have helped me to state a rule, or have given me that of the grammar books, preferably the Turkish ones.

4. DIFFICULTY OF APPLYING DESICCATED DIRECTIONS TO LIVING SPEECH

I have cited my experience in learning Turkish because I myself learnt a great deal more about language learning from learning Turkish and beginning to learn Estonian and Arabic than I learnt from learning Greek, Latin, French or German, which, however different they may seem from English, belong nevertheless to the same family of languages. Besides that, there were no reliable textbooks available to me in learning Turkish, and no experienced teachers of the language; so I had to devise my own course, using at first an educated man with a good knowledge of English as an informant.

5. LANGUAGE AS SIGNIFICANT PATTERN

Another feature of Turkish which gave me a good deal of trouble, as long as I relied on my grammatical, schematic approach to the language, was the interrogative and negative particles. The interrogative particle was nominally *-mi*, or its equivalent according to the vowel system of the verb; the negative was *-me* or its equivalent, but in practice in many positions both interrogative and negative were shown by *-mi* or *-mı* (a back ə). The interrogative was final, or followed all but the personal ending; the negative particle was slipped between the stem and the main body of the tense ending; so that *gelecek mi* meant *will he come?* and *gelmiyecek* meant *he will not come*; *gelecekmisiniz* meant *will you come?*, *gelmiyeceksiniz* meant *you will not come*. Reckoning to myself whether the *-mi* had immediately followed the stem or whether it had followed the tense ending, and trying to remember which was which, brought speech to a standstill and made reading laborious. As soon as I got used, however, to the questioning tone and uncertain situation of *geldi mi?*, *gelecek mi? gelirmisiniz?* and the emphatic final negative of *gelmedi, gelmiyecek, gelmezsiniz*, confusion vanished. Not only that, but I found myself moving the interrogative particle up and down the sentence according to changes in emphasis without consciously learning to do so: *Eve mi çabuk gitti? Eve çabuk mu gitti? Eve çabuk gitti mi?* or even *Dün akşam mı eve çabuk gitti?*

A further complication was that the negative of the imperative and the verb noun were identical: *gelme, don't come,* or *gelme, a coming;* further, *gelmem* could mean *I don't* (or *won't*) *come* or merely the verb noun personalized, *my coming. To my coming* would be *gelmeme* and so would *a not coming. My not coming* would be *gelmemem* and *to my not coming* would be *gelmememe.* This laid out on a page would be enough to make the mind reel, but in a sentence referring to a situation that was perfectly clear no difficulty was noticed; I found, as time went by, that I need not count the *me*'s in the phrase *gelmememe rağmen, in spite of my not coming,* nor was there any difficulty in separating the meaning of this from *gelemememe rağmen, in spite of my not being able to come,* instantaneously and without reflection, even though the form was seldom used. When the pattern was repeated I found I took up the mental attitude quite automatically, in the same way as I had earlier taught myself to fire five shots with the machine-gun, by learning to recognize the pattern, and not by counting the shots.

It is this sort of sensitivity to significant pattern that makes it easy for anyone who has learnt English from the inside to understand a pattern such as: "This man should have been being treated for arthritis, not rheumatism," even if he has never heard that actual pattern used before, provided the situation referred to is clear—that the man is not getting better and needs a change of treatment. Someone who has acquired his knowledge of the language from outside, through the grammar book, will attempt to analyse the pattern; if he is successful he will tell you that such and such a grammar book asserts that the form does not exist, and the sentence should therefore not have been said.

6. LINGUISTIC ANALYSIS

There has in recent years been an increasing interest and faith in linguistic analysis as a guide to language teaching.

This seems to have arisen from speculations over the success of the intensive language-teaching programmes undertaken in various armies during the war; it was assumed that they were based on scientific linguistic analyses. As Mr. J. B. Carroll, of Harvard University, in his book written after a careful study of the teaching of languages in the United States,[1] has pointed out: "It is only a half-truth to say that the new programs are based on the teachings of linguistic science. Though linguistic analysis has played an important role in these new language-teaching programs, *linguistic analysis is not a method of instruction*;[2] linguistic analysis merely has something to say about *what is being taught*. The linguist can indicate to the learner a number of rules which will help him to acquire the language more rapidly than if he had to work out these rules for himself. The linguist can also point out the relation between the sounds of a language and its orthography and many other details about the structure of the language system which is to be learned. In case the language is one about which little is known, the linguist provides a technique for ascertaining the details of the language system." Mr. Carroll points out, further, that it is not surprising that linguists have advocated a "mimicry-memorization" method to fix new linguistic habits firmly in the behaviour of the learner. "But," he adds, "it is gratuitous on the part of the linguist to affirm that endless drill and repetition constitute the *only* way in which new linguistic habits may be strengthened. . . . The psychologist can cite many cases in which learning occurs after only one trial. . . . We are fundamentally in ignorance of the best ways of strengthening new habits, and must therefore appeal to the psychologist to give us new evidence on this score."

These valuable words remind us that discussions of what we are to put into a container are trivial as long as there is no consideration of the capacity or qualities of the container. The language teacher, while grateful to the linguist for his arrange-

---

[1] *The Study of Language*, Harvard University Press, 1955, p. 190.
[2] Mr. Carroll's italics.

ment of the structure of the language into an orderly and logical system, must hold himself free, under the advice of the psychologist, to determine how and in what order he teaches it.

7. SOME UNJUSTIFIED ASSUMPTIONS

A few examples may warn us against the dangers of taking over the results of the work of the linguists uncritically. The linguist analyses a language into structural items of language and arranges them in what he regards as a logical order; this may be an order of ascending complexity. The language teacher takes the list and concludes that the structural points of the language—the tenses and the sentence patterns—should be taught in this order and one after the other. Yet it does not necessarily follow. It is sometimes easier to learn two diverse forms in opposition and together, and sometimes a relatively complex pattern is easier to use naturally in a classroom than a simpler pattern that gives little opportunity for immediate application and interesting repetition. On the whole, its recognizability and memorability as a pattern is what makes the learning of a new language form easy.

Seeing the structural patterns of the language arrayed one after the other, and remembering how in bad textbooks they were often introduced without care or planning, and even sometimes allowed to creep in without being introduced at all, we may be tempted to conclude that no new pattern should be introduced until the previous one has been completely taught. But it is not necessarily so. It is true that structural material should be graded and each item properly and separately introduced; different patterns should not be piled on top of one another; a recently introduced pattern should not be covered up by the impression of the next, before it has had time to set in the mind. New material should be carefully spaced out so that the load on the pupil is not too great in one section of the book, and so that there are no sudden and arbitrary increases of difficulty or complexity. No competent writer of a textbook should allow any form to creep in before he—or the pupil—is ready for it, and before it has been properly led up to. But to go a step further and say that no new pattern may be introduced until its predecessor has been completely learnt leads to rote learning and intolerable monotony.

8. LANGUAGE PATTERNS NOT TO BE JUDGED IN ISOLATION

One danger of concentrating too exclusively on the linguistic view of a language may be that we see the difficulty of learning a particular structural pattern exclusively in the pattern itself, whereas the difficulty may lie very much more in the pupil or his situation; for instance, in the remoteness of the ideas that are commonly associated with it, or the awkwardness of introducing it into the classroom situation at the moment when the book demands it. Sometimes a form may not have been learnt because it was difficult to practise within the conventions of teaching which were accepted at the time when the pupil tried to learn it. It has been noticed, for example, that some users of English as a second language fail to master the question form and never or seldom construct an interrogative sentence correctly, even after years of fluent use of the language. The conclusion sometimes drawn is that the pattern is a particularly difficult one, because the subject is taken from its normal position before the verb and placed after it. The reason might just as well be that the learner, during his school career, had too seldom been in a position to ask questions, though he may have answered them often enough; or his learning may have been too exclusively through reading stories and connected pieces of prose in which there was very little conversation.

I have referred to the initial difficulty which I had in learning to associate the particle *-mi* in Turkish with questioning, and in separating the particle which showed the interrogative from the often identical particle which showed the negative. This was at least as strange a signalling habit for me as the reversal of subject and verb is for someone who is not used to it, yet the difficulty in perceiving and using it disappeared as soon as I had had enough opportunity to experience it passively and actively in natural question and answer, and to initiate it myself in a wide variety of situations. One answer which has been proposed to this problem is to avoid teaching foreigners questions at the beginning of the course, so that they should not fall into error.

Yet mistakes in asking questions are quite likely to be made by someone who feels the need to ask a question but does not quite know how, and improvises on the basis of what he seems to remember, and afterwards learns his improvisations. It is wiser not to postpone the teaching of questions until the pupil begins to improvise his own questions by making statements with a quizzical look on his face or a rising intonation or some sort of dumb show; we do better to see that he hears us asking questions in the normal way as soon as a situation arises that calls for a question, and we must ensure that he is given plenty of opportunity to ask questions when he feels the need to, and is corrected when he makes mistakes.

9. DIFFICULTY IN DEFINITION DOES NOT NECESSARILY IMPLY DIFFICULTY IN TEACHING

A usage may seem to be difficult because it is hard to define or account for. Linguistic analysis is an explaining and defining skill; some of those who interest themselves in it feel uncomfortable if they are not explaining or defining everything they teach, and in no time they have rank on rank of words and arrangements of words like Kennedy's Latin Grammar in front of them. Although the linguist himself may know that language patterns are not best learnt from explanations, his enthusiastic followers may forget it, though difficulty, if we are teaching a language through situation and speech, does not lie in the patterns and words alone. The successful language courses of the present day—those that conform to the findings of educational psychology—are those that are modelled as closely as possible on natural speech in a compelling, unconstrained setting. To postpone useful everyday speech forms that are needed for the carrying on of the normal purposes of language in society is to introduce constraint and artificiality. It is true that constraint and artificiality cannot be entirely banished from the early stages of language learning, but they should not be gratuitously brought in.

To summarize the situation, the difficulties which the linguistic scientist sees may trouble the pupil only if he is given the opportunity of reflecting, as the linguistic scientist reflects, over language; yet the skilled teacher prevents this. He attaches language which gives experience of a pattern almost unnoticeably to his and the pupil's activity. He should sweep the pupil on through so many examples, so many experiences of the form, that there is no time to stop and reflect on anything but the situation. He only pauses when the form has been at least tentatively established in the pupil's mind. Once the pupil is used to the form he is not likely to question it much, until he is brought by the teacher to do so. When this is done, it will be to achieve a synthesis and an over-all view of his knowledge after he has learnt the chief structural material of the language.

10. PREOCCUPATION WITH USAGE IMPEDES FLUENCY

A conscious knowledge in the pupil's mind of the ways in which the linguistic scientist or the grammarian accounts to himself for the existence and behaviour of particular language patterns or of the main structure and working of the language may set up a barrier of self-consciousness between the language and its uses in the learner's mind. This is analogous to the inhibitions set up in the body by calling to mind, during the performance of some physical activity, the way in which the limbs and muscles move. The pupil must be helped to fluency at all costs and as quickly as possible. It is much better that he should say "beginned" for a time, and get confidence and a feeling of having a stake in the language, than

M

that he should be silent through fear of making mistakes. If he is afraid to commit himself or speak freely he always feels that he is outside the language and unfit to use it. Trying to speak to grammatical rules is an intolerable strain on the mind; it can only be done by a few scholars, and makes conversation slow, laboured and tedious for speaker and hearers alike.

11. EXAMPLE OF GRAMMATICAL BASIS TO INITIAL TEACHING

Time should not therefore be wasted by the teacher, while teaching any new language patterns, on explanations of how the form is used or in what circumstances; all this information is needed by the teacher, however, and should be applied by him to the planning of his presentation of the form and of the exercises that follow and consolidate the impressions. We can take as an example of such information an analysis of the General Present Tense which could be taken by the teacher, or the textbook writer, as a programme for the work he proposes to do on the tense. He would plan to begin with sentences dealing with what is permanent in the situation of the pupil, in contrast to the fleeting and incidental happenings that he has been dealing with in the Continuous Present Tense. He would talk about the permanent features of his daily programme, and contrast them with his immediate activity—revising the Continuous Tense—discussing the languages he speaks, the activities and interests he cultivates, and the work and activities of his parents, relations and friends. Then he would move on to sentences dealing with the permanent nature of things; that sharp knives cut well and blunt ones do not; that cars go along the road on wheels but men, dogs and horses go on their legs, unless they get into a car or lorry; that rain falls, and does not go up again in the form of water, but water vapour or steam goes up; that water flows downhill but not uphill; that grasses and all plants grow upwards but not downwards; that apples taste sweet or sour, but never salty and rarely bitter; that English people usually sit on chairs, but Indians more often sit on the floor on mats, or on low divans or benches; that the sun rises in the east and goes down in the west.

At length, when he thinks he has brought the usage within reach of the class, he may give an exercise designed to make the association between the form and the attitude of mind it records permanent; it will be the kind of exercise which requires concentration and manipulation of the parts of the sentence, but gives very little opportunity for mistakes. It calls for very little independent thinking, nor does it require new patterns of words that are not outlined in the sentences themselves. The form and usage should be allowed to rest in the pupil's mind for a time after this, while other work is undertaken; or the teacher may repeat situation and language material previously learnt, which will show the contrast to the new language pattern and the new type of characteristic situation that has been brought within the pupil's reach by the form.

12. REVISION AND SYSTEMATIZATION OF MATERIAL ALREADY LEARNT

The teacher may never forget a pattern which he has taught, or allow it to go out of use by not being repeated, on the grounds that it has been taught and therefore finished with. It will never be forgotten if it is never allowed to go out of use. He will see that examples of the pattern come into every lesson, and he will occasionally give exercises designed to practise the pupil in the form in contrast to other forms. He may from time to time test him in his ability to recognize where the form is needed by asking him to fill in blanks left in sentences. There is no space here for an exhaustive set of examples; a method of revising the tenses and keeping them constantly under review will have to suffice to show what can be done. At about the third or fourth year of work on the language, for instance, assuming the normal school programme of five or six periods a week, the teacher may decide that he has taught enough of the tenses to justify their being arranged in a system, and he will begin a systematic revision of the verb patterns so far learnt.

Children of fourteen or fifteen and over can be very interested in analysing, as a process of perceiving and recognizing, the language they have already learnt, although they may not have been able to do it as they learnt it. A systematic overhaul of their knowledge will help them to see that they have, after all, learnt a great deal; they can be helped to see habitual errors as untidinesses to be cleared up, and they can go ahead with more confidence to exploit their stake in the language. Bearing this in mind the teacher sets to work to construct an analysis of the tense system in English. Going through the tenses systematically will help the teacher to detect and eradicate any misconceptions that may otherwise remain unnoticed.

13. ANALYSIS OF TENSE SYSTEM

It must be made clear to the pupil, either initially or in the course of—and as a result of—the whole process of revising the tenses, that the use of one tense or another is determined by the attitude to the action in the mind of the speaker, rather than by the application of a mechanical grammatical rule to the time of the happening. As the present is most real and nearest to the speaker, the present tenses are most used and are therefore usually taught and revised first. If considerations of time are not uppermost in the mind of the speaker, the General Present Tense is normally used. If there is no special reason for using one of the highly differentiated tenses, a more general tense is always used. As has been shown above, only complete sentences and, as far as possible, sentences which have real meaning for the learners, should be given to illustrate any principles of grammar. We should never teach paradigms or naked verb forms without meaning; even sample sentences should have relevance to the life of the pupils or the situation of the classroom, or the imagined situation of a story. No piece of language material which cannot be absorbed should be given to the pupils.

The teacher begins by repeating the conversational patterns he used for teaching the General and Continuous Present Tenses, showing the contrast in their uses, and how the one can support the other. Then he rules a line down the middle of the blackboard and writes the word SIMPLE on the left-hand side of the line and CONTINUOUS (or TEMPORARY) on the right-hand side; when he is sure that the class have once more grasped the essentials of the difference between the two tenses he gets from them a pattern sentence to write on each side of the line, as follows. He writes up what is true for himself:

	SIMPLE	CONTINUOUS	ACTUAL
GENERAL	I speak English	I am speaking	(or
PRESENT	and German	English now	TEMPORARY)
	(in general)	(at this moment)	PRESENT

He goes on developing this scheme over several lessons, perhaps over several weeks, setting exercises on each pair for homework after each session on them, and perhaps an exercise to include also what has gone before. Finally he will have a scheme something like that on p. 170: he can draw attention to the essential pattern of each tense, and the ways in which it differs from the others, by underlining the verb element in each sentence.

As soon as he has worked out a complete scheme for one verb, he can set each of the groups in his class to work out a similar scheme for another verb; after that, individuals can be asked to work out schemes for yet other verbs, using, as far as possible, sentences which are true for each individual who works out a scheme.

In this way thirty or forty verbs can be dealt with, corrected and discussed in the groups, handed in for final correction by the teacher, rewritten where necessary by the pupil, and circulated through the class for the awkward verbs to be copied into notebooks. From now on a fairly frequent and typical assignment for homework may be: "Work out a scheme of tenses for the verb *to begin*." The essential qualities of the

	SIMPLE OR GENERAL TENSES	TEMPORARY OR CONTINUOUS TENSES	
GENERAL PRESENT (in general)	I speak German I do not speak Chinese Do I speak German to you? No, you don't.	I am speaking English now I am not speaking German now Am I speaking German? No, you aren't.	ACTUAL PRESENT (at this moment)
SIMPLE PAST	I spoke to Mr. B. yesterday I did not speak to Mr. B. last week Did I speak to him last Wednesday? (action and time finished) No, you didn't	I was speaking to him at 6 o'clock I was not speaking to him at 7 o'clock Was I speaking to him for long? (action and time finished) No, you weren't	INTERRUPTED OR BACKGROUND CONTINUOUS PAST (at that moment)
PRESENT PERFECT	I have spoken to Mr. B. this week I have not spoken to Mr. A. this week Have I spoken to your mother this week? (action finished, time unfinished) No, you haven't	I have been speaking to you for 10 minutes now I have not been speaking German Have I been speaking Spanish? (action and time unfinished) No, you haven't	BACKGROUND PRESENT PERFECT (until this moment)
PAST PERFECT	I had spoken to Mr. B. before I came here I had not spoken English before I came to school, etc. (action finished, time unfinished then)	I had been speaking for half an hour when his wife came in, etc. (action and time unfinished then)	INTRODUCTORY OR BACKGROUND PAST PERFECT (until that moment)
SIMPLE FUTURE	I shall speak to Mr. A. tomorrow I shall not speak to Mr. B. tomorrow, etc.	I shall be speaking to him tomorrow at 6 when you come to the meeting	BACKGROUND OR INTRODUCTORY FUTURE (at that moment)
FUTURE PERFECT	I shall have spoken to Mr. A. before I see you again (action finished, time unfinished then, in the future)	I shall have been speaking to you for an hour when I stop, etc. (action and time unfinished then, in the future)	BACKGROUND OR INTRODUCTORY FUTURE PERFECT (until that moment in the future)
FUTURE PERFECT in the PAST	I told him I should have spoken to you before I saw him (action finished, time unfinished then)	I told him that I should have been speaking for an hour when I stopped (action and time unfinished then)	BACKGROUND FUTURE PERFECT in the PAST (until that moment)

various verb patterns are brought out in constant concentration on their significance. They are always presented in association with the tense names, in such a way that the names become familiar and help those who can be helped by such labels, but they do not stand in the way of those for whom they might be a stumbling-block.

As soon as the teacher considers that the class has had enough practice of this kind to make the various verb patterns and their significance familiar and their relations clear he may get samples of verb schemes written up on four or five blackboards, if he has them, or he may arrange for each member of the class to copy out four or five samples on paper so that discussion of the qualities of each tense may take place in the class with enough examples in front of the pupil to make discussion significant. Then rules can be worked out, discussed and agreed upon; possibly—if time is short and the class large—each group can take one pair of tenses and present the agreed rule to the whole class when it has been worked out. These rules can then be copied out by each member of the class, the findings of the groups being circulated for the purpose. Even if the teacher corrects and amends them drastically they will have been worked for.

14. LEARNING TO ANALOGIZE NATURALLY THROUGH DEVELOPING PATTERN SENTENCES

As soon as the teacher has got the verb system well started in this way, and without necessarily waiting for his plan of work on it to be finished, he can start similar exploration in other directions. If he is clever at managing his groups and getting the best work out of them, he will set research tasks for each group to undertake for the benefit of the whole class, in working out the ways in which different types of words are used; the names of parts of speech will only come to be attached to the various categories as they show themselves to be more portable and generally useful than descriptions such as: "the kind of word that goes with a noun—usually before—

and describes it or makes it more definite, or shows which one of several it is"—or "the kind of word that goes with a verb and gives it a new sort of meaning". Lists of sentences can be worked out summarizing the work done.

The use of gerunds and their dual nature as verbs and nouns, for example, can be shown in a series of sentences as follows:

My father likes fish (with a sketch of a fish on the black-board).

My father likes fishing (with a sketch of a man fishing on a river-bank or from a boat).

My father likes my fishing (with a sketch of a boy fishing).

My father likes books (with a sketch of a book).

My father likes reading books (with a sketch of a man reading).

My father likes his reading in the evenings (sketch of a man reading by a lamp).

Through series of sentences of this kind, with sketches to concentrate the attention on what the word represents, a verb-noun is shown to stand for something picturable—countable, perhaps—and nameable, an action or situation rather than a concrete object, but still something that needs naming, which can be the subject or object of a sentence, while at the same time standing for an action or situation and able to have an object like other verbs. Participles can be dealt with similarly.

15. DEVELOPING AWARENESS OF GRAMMATICAL CATEGORIES BY DIRECT EXPERIENCE

Once the habit of identifying words by the work they do in the sentence has been established, it is a short step to see that groups of words can do what a single word had hitherto been seen to do, and stand for one person or object. Names such as *adverbial* or *adjectival clauses* or *phrases* need not be expected from the students, but exercises can be given in changing sentences by taking single-word adjectives out and substituting groups of words for the single word that will describe the person or object more accurately. This can begin with a personal name to stand for a particular person in the sentence; the various possible substitutes for this can be shown, so as to make clear the underlying identity of word, phrase and clause. For example:

1. Tom is eating an apple.
2. That boy is eating an apple.
3. That tall boy is eating an apple.
4. The boy with the blue shirt is eating an apple.
5. The boy who is wearing a blue shirt is eating an apple.

This manipulative work can be done on a large number of sentences without the names *adjective*, *adjectival phrase*, and *adjectival clause* being insisted on, but as time goes by these names will come to be welcome as handy labels for what have now been clearly seen to exist as nameable and identifiable categories. Later, another category can be added to those above, and seen to be related to them: a participle and participial phrase.

6. The boy wearing a blue shirt is eating an apple.

Chains of such sentences can be set going by the teacher pointing to a particular boy or an object, or someone seen through the window and asking for an adjective and a noun as the subject of the sentence from one boy, a noun and participle from another, a noun and adjectival phrase from another, etc. It is important for the pupil to see that the person, however many words we use to describe him, remains one person. The first examples will, of course, have to be worked out in detail on the blackboard, but as time goes by, this sort of work can be turned into a competitive game for group work. It may be much easier merely to recognize the category name as an order to proceed to the next item on a familiar programme than it is to search about in the mind for unrealized and elusive examples, and very much easier than producing definitions of grammatical categories which are hard to describe. Yet after a certain amount of work of this kind, examples come from the class naturally and spontaneously, and definitions spring to the mind if they were used often at a preliminary stage—perhaps in a very simplified form—as summaries to take the place of the grammatical names that have not yet been learnt. In time they come to be a natural adjunct to consciousness of the grammatical category.

This is not to assert that all the pupils in the class will be able to name and identify an adjectival or adverbial clause infallibly at the end of the process. But the manipulative work which they will have done, and their experience in sentence construction, will have given them a handiness and confidence in managing the English sentence which has its own value; above all, the sentences will most of them have been constructed out of their own direct observation and experience and will therefore have made the maximum mark on their minds. It is of much greater value and significance that what has been learnt about the ways of words together should have been struggled for than that it should be exhaustive.

The pupil learns to look at the grammar book and its explanations critically, as parallel to his own work and thought on the subject. They may summarize what he has done but never replace it as a short-cut to ready-made opinions. Ready-made opinions learnt blindly are seldom permanent and require a great deal of effort to retain for even a short time. But in any case, simply knowing a collection of facts about the grammar of a language is not in itself a fructifying influence in the mind; to be of any value each known fact must represent the solution of problems, the achievement of light, the unravelling of knots, the winning through to a distant and elusive goal in spite of difficulties, the comparing, sorting and ordering of categories, and the sifting and balancing of evidence.

16. THE TEACHER WORKS OUT HIS OWN EXERCISES

There are good books of exercises for this stage of work; but as they stand, they are likely to scatter the attention and discourage the pupil. The teacher must make up his own exercises, to introduce them, on the same lines as each exercise in the book. The sentences he uses should, as far as possible, be meaningful and take into account the student's age and his cultural and linguistic background.

When the type of exercise has become familiar, and the student has manipulated sentences which really convey meaning and hold his attention, he can do the exercises in the book alone. He can then enjoy doing them as an intellectual exercise, an exercise in the manipulation of words, even if the sentences have no coherence the one with the other or relevance to his experience. In time, after some years of using a good book of grammar and composition exercises, the teacher will come to have a set of useful exercises related to his pupils' abilities and background that will only need slight alteration for each individual or class.

It is in this sphere that the research work of the linguist is invaluable. The linguistic expert can help us to find out where we are linguistically. In particular the exercises which we set our pupils to do should be based on what we know of the language habits formed by their mother tongue, and our phonetic work must also be planned with full knowledge of its phonetics. Very little purpose is served by the explicit comparing of languages in the classroom, but we can work to overcome habits carried over from another language. In spite of all this, however, one cannot overlook the fact that the success of the courses for new Australians after the war was partly due to no account whatever being taken of the various linguistic backgrounds of the students: they were just given an intensive and planned exposure to English.

After a course of functional grammar such as I have just described, however, and provided the pupil has enough intellectual maturity to be interested in abstractions, some comparison can usefully be attempted. This will be to draw attention to experience he has already had of the working of the language, not to take the edge off his powers of observation or undermine his adventurousness. The teacher may begin by making up and giving passages that show the different coverage, for example, of such pairs of words as *right* in English and *recht* in German; or *warm* in English and *warm* in German; *sympathique* in French and *sympathetic* in English; *grass* in English and *ot* in Turkish; he may ask his pupils to go into the reasons in Tamil which cause Tamil speakers to say *keep* when they should say *put* in English or to use the future for the General Present. Comparisons between the Perfect in German and the Present Perfect in English are useful at this stage. It would be impossible for this work to be comprehensive, and the teacher need not do more than show the very different scope of words and structure that seem to be equivalents in the two languages.

Common sense will warn us against trying to do this too early. I was bored by a well-meaning man who tried to explain to me the different provinces of *aber* and *sondern* in the territory covered by the English *but*, before I was ripe for the information; yet, later, I was fascinated, while noticing for myself that *aber* was used in other parts of the sentence than initially, to realize that *however* was the equivalent of *but* in English, for use in the middle of a sentence: something I had never noticed before. This kind of work is interesting but it should not be allowed to take a more important place in the language-teaching programme than the occasional visit to the natural history museum in the biology programme.

17. AN EXAMPLE OF NON-CONGRUENCE OF PARALLEL STRUCTURAL PATTERNS

A simple example may also make clear the unsuitability of comparison between equivalent but dissimilar structural patterns in two different languages. The equivalent of:

To do one's hair, is, in German:
Sich die Haare kämmen.

I am going to brush my hair in a few minutes, is:
In ein Paar Minuten kämme ich mir die Haare.

I want to do my hair in front of the mirror, is:
Ich möchte mir vor dem Spiegel die Haare kämmen.

Do your hair quickly, is:
Kämme dir schnell deine Haare.

If I had only known how late it was I should have done
my hair much earlier, is:
Wenn ich nur gewusst hätte, wie spät es sei, hätte ich mir
viel eher die Haare gekämmt.

Each time we switch from English to German there has to
be a complete reorientation of our thinking; each time, the
German form of the sentence seems to be a monstrous dis-
tortion. Yet if the German sentences are developed from the
basic German language pattern, and related to one another
without reference to English, each development seems natural
and inevitable, and the pattern soon seems not to be foreign
at all. In this way the analogizing process comes to be a
natural and unconscious one instead of having to be thought
out afresh for each new variation, in terms of a rule that exists,
somehow, in another dimension of thought. An attempt to
find German equivalents to the word *put* makes a difficulty
where none otherwise exists.

18. THE NEED FOR CULTIVATING A NEW AWARENESS
    OF SPEECH

It is important to remember that a grammar, or a linguistic
analysis, is based on personal observation; it is a systematization or codification of what accurate and attentive observers
have noted to be normal usage. Yet it is not at all easy to
observe speech; indeed, accurate and systematic study of the
spoken language has really only become feasible with the
invention of sound-recording apparatus. Even now, specimens
of it are not handy or easy to take into the study. This is
probably why the emphasis in linguistic analysis and grammatical studies has until quite recently been primarily on the
written word. What was not written was not only not taken

seriously, it was ignored. Many grammarians still live in this stage of development in linguistic science, and look with suspicion on whatever has not been given the dignity of print. Even if speech is recorded for study, it is often prepared speech or self-conscious speech, and the modes of thinking developed during centuries of study of the written word cannot be adapted overnight to the study of the spoken word. This is partly why it is difficult to get teachers and textbook writers, brought up on a study of the written language, to produce courses which are really based on the spoken language and on the kind of impressions which speech makes on the mind; they still insist on analysing what they see on the page, instead of judging the impact the sound makes on the ear as a complete pattern or signal. Perhaps it is this type of print-bound thinking that makes some people suppose questions to be too difficult for the first lesson, or imperatives too difficult for the first year, and *give me a book* more difficult than *give a book to me*.

Grammars are still largely written by people sitting in a study imagining themselves into sentences which do not correspond to any actuality; grammarians have not always seen that their first duty is to call a situation to mind, out of which the needed sentence could spring. In going observantly about our daily lives we can notice more than we are able to remember or imagine in the study. A group of teachers on a refresher course once, for example, noticed that there was a blank in the grammar we were using, against the Passive of the Perfect Continuous Tenses; after some discussion we accepted the verdict, as we could not think, on the spur of the moment, of any possibility of or need for saying: "I have been being taken." The next morning, while driving in the office car to the course, I said that the car was making a rather peculiar noise. "Yes," answered the friend who was driving, "the car should have been being repaired all this week, but it was needed for this course." The situation called for the pattern, and it emerged without reflection, rehearsal or hesitation;

without any situation to compel it to birth we might never have thought of examples.

If we hear examples that fit the need and the circumstances so exactly that no other expression would have suited, we commonly do not notice the expression. A considerable degree of complication in structure can be tolerated in speech, through the help of intonation and stress, which would be incomprehensible in writing. This needs stating because it is generally assumed that the structure of the spoken sentence is necessarily simpler than the structure of the written sentence. As one who has frequently had to convert lectures—sometimes recorded on tape—into written articles, I can vouch for the intractability on paper of some sentences that could easily be followed when they were spoken, and had not struck anyone as complex or obscure.

We can make this clear to our pupils, and show them how to compare and evaluate the verdicts of various grammars; we can show them how to avoid slavish adherence to the verdicts of particular grammar books and yet achieve a clear, vigorous and graceful style, free from errors of taste or pedantic complexities. If we have helped them to use the grammar book intelligently as a guide, but not regard it as a prison, we shall have given them the right start in the language, and their work in grammar will have been a valuable introduction to analytical and diagnostic thinking; they will have begun to learn something of the nature of language and the work it does for us in the world.

CONCLUSIONS

So that the utmost economy in time and effort is assured to the pupil, there must be the most rigorous organization of the language course on a skeleton of grammar of which the teacher must be fully conscious throughout, but which the pupil need not be aware of until he has reached a stage of maturity—say at the age of fourteen or fifteen—at which problems of language and expression, abstractions and schematizations, appeal to him. If the earlier work in the language has been soundly based on grammatical principles and organization, everything seems to fall into its preordained place when the process of analysing and categorizing begins. What has been learnt is thus opened up and demonstrated.

The teacher's work, based on the presentation of language patterns in an orderly succession, must be to bring out of the learner's situation and his daily experience of the real world the appropriate reactions in language for his state of linguistic development; yet the teacher must never lose sight of the need to repeat the simpler patterns of the earlier stages. He must use them as a basis for, and relate them to, the more complex patterns of the later stages.

For this he would need to have, or acquire during his training, a comprehensive knowledge of the language, its phonetics, intonation and grammatical structure. He would have to be given systematic training in the presentation of language material at all stages, and in developing linguistic opportunities out of all kinds of situations. He would have to be fluent and resourceful, at ease in the language and able to control his vocabulary. Such teachers are rare, and perhaps always will be.

Where the number of skilled teachers available is small, no general improvement in language teaching can be expected unless steps are taken to support and improve the teacher. This can be done by radio or gramophone lessons, in which the teacher is, at first, an instructor and stage-manager rather than a teacher. If teacher and pupil all learn together and the teacher is given plenty of supporting material, both written and recorded, and further instruction in refresher courses as well as in the evenings or at week-ends, he can gradually develop enough skill to teach quite effectively alone; for the best way to learn is to teach what we are trying to learn ourselves.

9

The Teaching of Composition

INTRODUCTION

There is no impermeable line to be drawn round the subject of composition. An introduction has already been made in the chapter on homework (Chapter 5), and preparation for composition has been implicit in all oral work so far discussed. The teaching of grammar through exercises, oral and written, is exercise in composition, and only a conventional line, if any, can be drawn between grammar exercises and composition exercises. When discussing homework we saw that a pupil should not sit in front of his paper with his mind a blank, unable to write anything. He should never be in a position in which he is forced to work out sentences in his own language and translate them in his mind into vocabulary and sentence patterns which he has not really assimilated in the second language. This is to set a task which is beyond him at his stage of development and is more productive of error than of useful language skill. It has also been pointed out that he should always be within reach of skilled help whenever he is doing composition work which is on the limit of his powers.

The teaching of composition is inextricably bound up with the teaching of texts of both prose and poetry, so that the succeeding chapters will complete the treatment of oral and written composition, and show that composition of some kind can develop out of every type of work on the language. If time and effort are to be conserved and economically expended, we must plan the course as an integrated whole, and not allow any element of it to become dissociated from the others. This can easily happen when one teacher takes composition, one grammar, and another the study of prose texts, and perhaps still another the study of poetry. If it is, for any reason, necessary to have special periods under a separate teacher for written composition, the other teachers must lose no opportunities for requiring composition at every point where it is useful and appropriate. Every foray into the language, every operation for the possession of word and language pattern, all perceptive submission to the effect of language, should lead naturally and inevitably into active application of what has been absorbed, in independent speech or writing.

A. THE BASES OF SUCCESSFUL COMPOSITION WRITING

1. *The Promotion of Fluency of Expression*

The most pressing duty of the teacher of composition is to help his pupils to develop an effective and easily functioning instrument, an instrument not only of expression of what they know they know, but also an instrument for fishing in their minds and bringing out what otherwise may remain hidden and unproductive or dormant there, known but unrecognized and unidentified. There are teachers who test and estimate, commend and condemn, choose and reject, on the assumption that the human mind is a static, precisely measurable quantity of matter or a potential force like the horsepower of a car. They do not see it as a dynamic, growing organism, capable of sudden and unexpected efflorescence in the right temperature and humidity or of curling up and encysting in an unfavourable physical or mental climate. The successful teacher is one who finds, or helps the individual pupil to find in himself, not only what had hitherto passed unnoticed or unrecognized, but probably, too, what was not even there previously, except potentially, until the situation and the need called for it.

2. *The Necessity for Copying*

To promote a free flow of language and ideas the teacher must do nothing to destroy the confidence of the pupil. He must give him every opportunity to learn and practise the language units that he will need for free and unhampered expression. Not only that, he must see that he uses words accurately, in full consciousness of their meaning, and conscientiously. He must never allow a parade of words to be used only because they have triumphed elsewhere, particularly if they have not been genuinely digested and absorbed into the pupil's own natural mode of expression, once he has established one. Yet copying, in one form or another, as shown in Chapter 5, will be a necessary phase of the early stages of learning to write fluently; it will even continue in some form or other to the end of the process.

Original composition can develop from modifying a set of sentences copied from the blackboard, so that they apply to the pupil's situation. For instance, an Indian boy may have copied from the blackboard:

> John always drinks a glass of water when he wakes in the morning.
> He usually wakes at about half-past six.
> He often goes for a short walk before he has his breakfast.
> He sometimes eats porridge for breakfast and sometimes cornflakes.
> He occasionally eats only a little fruit in the morning.
> He seldom drinks coffee.
> He never goes out without having any breakfast at all.

He will adapt this as follows:

> I always drink a glass of water when I wake in the morning.
> I usually wake at six o'clock.
> I ofteh eat iddlies for breakfast.

I sometimes drink coffee for breakfast and sometimes tea.
I occasionally eat dosais for breakfast.
I seldom go for a walk before I have my breakfast.
I never go out without having any breakfast at all.

If he has the time and the inclination he can make up similar sets of sentences to apply to his friends, and copy them into his notebook too. This work can be developed further by doing grammar or composition exercises of the manipulative type, which involve copying two-thirds of the original sentence at first, and progressively less. For instance, the following sentences have to be modified to suit the changing of the adverb of present time to an adverb of past time.

1. I have written two letters and a postcard to my elder sister this week (last week).

2. I have seen her twice since Christmas (last winter).

3. You have shown me two letters from her this week (last Monday morning).

4. She has sent me some pocket money more than once this month (last month).

These sentences will be rewritten as:

1. I wrote two letters and a postcard to my elder sister last week.

2. I saw her twice last winter.
Etc.

The pupil copies most of the words in the sentence exactly, changing only the verbs; he copies into the sentence words given him for the purpose, and has to recognize and take out those no longer applicable.

A little later a more developed form of the same exercise can be done:

1. I have written two letters and a postcard to my elder sister since I heard that she was ill (as soon as I heard that she was ill).

   2. I have seen her twice since she left home (before she got ill).
   Etc.

This entails the rewriting of the verb in the same way as has already been done—the pupil can turn back to the page if he wants to—and the straight copying of the new, complicated part of the sentence, which needs to be learnt; this part can easily be understood by comparing it with the previous set.

The next exercise could be to write a new beginning to the sentence, which could be as follows:

   1. (a) I have sent my elder sister some flowers since I heard that she was ill.
      (b) I sent my elder sister some flowers as soon as I heard that she was ill.

   2. (a) I have forgotten to write to her since she left home.
      (b) I forgot to write to her until last week.

The new beginning can be as easy or as difficult as the individual pupil can make it; the brighter ones may be encouraged to enjoy trying their skill on something original; the less able ones may be restrained from flights of fantasy, and even helped to a correct and sober sentence. This may have to be done in class the first few times.

The same type of copying/composition is involved when a connected narrative is given with some words missing, perhaps the verbs or their tenses, and the whole piece has to be written out in full with the correct, or other equally suitable, words written in. A similar, but slightly different kind of copying is required when dictations, that have been corrected on the blackboard and in the exercise books as the dictation proceeded, are copied out afresh from the blackboard to facilitate fluent reading of the piece. A dictation can finally be copied into the fair-copy notebook to add to the store of memorable pieces of writing being collected there.

3. *Preparation for Composition Writing—General*

The teacher can help his pupils more than he might at first realize by seeing that composition writing is, from the beginning, a social and co-operative affair. The making of pieces of writing is a craft or skill that is appropriately carried out in a workshop atmosphere, with a workshop type of self-discipline. The pupil is helped to write clearly and reasonably by having constantly in front of him other minds as targets for his writing. We can hardly expect a learner at shooting to hit the target often if he is seldom or never allowed to see exactly what he is aiming at, or have his hits reported to him. A piece of written work is usually the better for being wanted by someone specific for a particular reason, to satisfy a particular interest, and because the last piece read was appreciated. The help and criticism of others, and reflection in their presence, or in the light of their reactions, are valuable grindstones for the developing powers of expression. Ideas which are half-formed must be brought out and developed to their conclusions under the pressure of discussion; ideas which seemed good in private speculation frequently seem crude and unsound under the scrutiny of others, or put beside alternative propositions.

This is not to suggest that the pupil should be trained to yield to group pressure; when the group is working on a problem as a group, a group decision—possibly a compromise —should be reached, but when an individual is trying to reach coherence and clarity in a line of thought through discussion with others, he should be allowed, and indeed encouraged, to develop his own line unless and until he is himself convinced that he is on a false trail.

There is no need for co-operative work to lead to the suppression of individuality; where each pupil is himself active this is unlikely. The teacher can guard against the possibility by seeing that a group at work on a piece of co-operative research or planning allows to each individual freedom to develop his own particular sector of the work in his own way, within the general agreed plan. The responsibility of each member of the group can be worked out and clearly defined before the work is begun, even though some of the investigation and preliminary discussion, and even the final presentation, is done in pairs or groups. Besides this, part of the presentation may always take the form of individual contributions to a common pool, either in speech to the class or on paper in the records of the work.

4. The Preparation of Particular Topics

If the teacher wishes the whole class to write a composition on a particular subject he must prepare them in two ways: (1) he must satisfy himself that all members of the class have enough ideas on the subject to form the basis of a successful piece of writing, and (2) he must also be sure that they have the linguistic equipment to deal with the material. If he finds that the majority have neither the ideas nor the equipment to express them, he must either postpone that particular subject until later on in the course or he must set about preparing them for effective expression. This preparation can take two forms:

(1) factual
(2) linguistic.

In a preliminary discussion of the subject all members of the class should

(1) be helped to think about the subject; and
(2) given vocabulary and sentence patterns in which they can crystallize out their thoughts.

1. If the subject seems to be beyond the mental grasp of the class, the teacher can either modify it or postpone it until they have developed enough maturity to be interested in it. If, on the other hand, he thinks that they would be interested in talking or writing about the subject if only they knew a little more about it, he may set them various assignments which will open up their awareness to it. Possibly a group of five or six

members of the class could be asked to prepare the subject and initiate a discussion on it with a few short talks and some illustrative material. The group should lead the discussion in such a way that the subject is opened up factually to the whole of the class; references may be given to be followed up by those whose interest has been aroused, as part of their personal preparation for writing. Such references can even be divided amongst the class so that each individual or each group is able to deal with a slightly different aspect of the subject.

If the subject has been well worked over in discussion there is not likely to be any hold-up in writing for lack of ideas. The slower members of the class can be helped with a few introductory sentences suggested by the class or perhaps worked out separately with each of them by the group leaders. If they still have difficulty in expressing themselves, either they have not yet learnt enough of the language to be ready for free composition, or else the subject requires the use of vocabulary and sentence patterns which lie too far outside their linguistic experience at that point.

I once saw a young teacher reading a difficult book on psychology with a fifth-year class and requiring them to write compositions on the various topics dealt with. I asked him why he did it. He said that he had been told that a teacher usually taught well what interested him; this interested him very much, and he thought that if the class could read and understand, and write about, this book, they could do anything. I had to admit that this was all true, but there was one consideration that might outweigh it all; supposing the subject-matter were outside their experience and range of interests, and at their level of maturity the words carried no significance; into their minds they would perhaps have a precocious vocabulary and set of stereotypes of ideas and academic expressions, but if their minds had not developed in proportion to contain them, his pupils would forget them as soon as they stopped reading the book and answering questions on it. The class seemed to be flattered at being deemed

worthy of so dignified a book; as the Werewolf of Morgen-
stern was flattered at being declined:

> Dem Werwolf schmeichelten die Fälle
> Er rollte seine Augenbälle—

but it was clear they were out of their depth.

2. If the subject is linguistically beyond the class the
teacher may postpone the setting of it until he has built up
their knowledge of the language further. On the other hand,
he may decide that they are mentally and emotionally mature
enough to grasp and think about the subject, and fluent
enough in the language in general to justify dealing with it, but
that they require a wider vocabulary in that field and greater
fluency and confidence in using certain language patterns. In
this case he will set exercises in those patterns and discuss the
subject in such a way as to give them confidence in handling
them, and any unfamiliar words, significantly. This linguistic
process can, of course, be combined with the factual preparation; it is only desirable that the teacher should keep the two
processes apart in his mind in such a way that he can satisfy
himself that the preparation of his students is adequate in each
sphere.

He should still, even after he has spent some time on factual
and linguistic preparation, be ready to admit that the attempt
has been premature and beyond the capability of the majority
of the class, and give them a period of work on easier material.
There is no useful purpose to be served in letting them write a
composition which is too full of mistakes to give them practice
in writing correct sentences fluently and confidently, or too
stiff and unfamiliar for them to get experience by welding into
an ordered whole elements which they have thoroughly
mastered. Teachers are often unwilling to recognize that a
class which, according to the syllabus or the programme they
have themselves worked out in advance, should be doing
original written composition is not in fact ready for it; the
best interests of the class, however, are served by recognizing

and responding to the facts. Any work which they can do well, and which calls out their capabilities to the full, will do them good; it will help them to develop quickly and healthily. Work which they can only do badly and which is so far beyond their capabilities that none of their actual ability is called into use, discourages and cramps them. All learning of expression should be done on material, both linguistic and thematic, which is well within their reach.

5. *The Destination of Written Composition*

One of the falsifications forced on the learner by the traditional or customary modes of teaching composition is that writing is directed only to the teacher, instead of to the relatively wide public to which all forms of writing which we undertake in later life, except letters and perhaps reports, are normally directed; yet how or what we write is very much conditioned by the public we have in mind when we are writing. Particularly quenching to the fires of inspiration is the transcendental status of some teachers as omniscient or superior beings; the composition is, all too often, a carrying of inferior coals to Newcastle.

Children often have the greatest difficulty in writing letters to their parents or compositions for their teachers, because there is no common ground of understanding or interest to base communication on. I found it difficult to write letters home to my parents when I first went to boarding-school at the age of eight. Perhaps the first few letters, while everything was new, went well, but I soon began to notice that my family found some of what I wrote quaint and naïve; for instance, I described the first debate I attended in all the detail I could muster, as it had made a tremendous impression on me. I explained, painstakingly, that one side was called the motion and the other the opposition. My parents smiled and found me very simple; they explained that this was so in all debates, and I need not write that kind of thing.

From then on I never quite knew what would be too

obvious to them to be worth telling about. I knew they disapproved of a good deal that most people thought harmless; even in matters which were their chief interest, I knew that the wrong shade of opinion was likely to provoke indignation. Better play safe, I told myself, and did my best with my letters to give cause for neither amusement nor indignation: week after week, at the hour's letter-writing period on Sunday mornings, I wrote the address and the date at the top followed by "My dear Mummy and Daddy"; after that, prolonged scraping of the bottom of the mind brought little to light until at last there bobbed up, and I scratched earnestly down, "I am quite well." Another pause, sometimes enormously prolonged, with a good deal of gnawing at the wooden half of my pen, and then—flash of inspiration, consideration for others having been explicitly enjoined and all too easily forgotten—a safe candidate for approval: "I hope you are quite well too." There the matter usually rested; at the end of the hour I left the letter unfinished, hoping, in an agony of frustration, for some miraculous flash of inspiration before the letters had to be handed in at four o'clock in the afternoon. For years my parents' chief complaint was that I never finished my letters home; I never even scribbled my name at the bottom, hoping to the last for some aspect of my activities of the previous week to appear in a favourable light, suitable for transmitting home. None ever did.

I can still feel the frustration, amounting at times to despair and frenzy, as I pressed my knuckles into my temples to squeeze something out. If only one of the teachers who sat and read a book or wrote his own letters on his distant pedestal had noticed how little I wrote and had sat down beside me and talked to me kindly and interestedly and got me to tell him what I had done, or what any of my friends had done, during the past week! But if anyone had sat beside me—and I believe, on second thoughts, once or twice one of them did—he would not have listened to me, but would have felt obliged to help me by telling me all the official school events: who had won the cricket match the day before, and who had scored the most runs; the names of some old boys who had visited the school or distinguished themselves recently; matters on which my parents and I were, after all, at one in total and utter indifference. He could hardly have been expected to see, however kind and sympathetic he was, that the problem was not to push in something, but to fish for something to pull out; to help me to find words to thread my half-concealed and trampled-on dreams, projects and speculations on, and to find formulae to represent my own special view of the world about me.

6. *Keeping in Mind the Public Addressed*

In planning an exercise in composition, we should ask who is to be primarily addressed in it; not only should we show our pupils how to look for and identify, and see always in the background as they write, their probable readers; they may see them in the mass, or represented by certain known characteristic figures that they can keep more easily in mind. It will be all the easier to do this if the process of composing begins with an actual conversation on the topic with these live specimens. The best way to classify the writing work to be done is to group it according to purpose and destination rather than according to its intrinsic nature.

B. TYPES OF WRITING TO BE ATTEMPTED

There is a great deal of writing work waiting to be done in every direction, in school, if we can once give up the idea that every member of the class must necessarily write an essay of approximately the same length on the same subject at any one time. There is plenty of information that is waiting to be collected and digested and given out in easily readable form for those who will never have time to search out and read for themselves all that they need to know in outline.

1. *Reports*

For instance, we can justify reports of all kinds. These may be directed from individuals to the group, that is, to the class, to the teacher, and to both the teacher and class together. Or they may be directed from the group, either as a group or as a planned and co-ordinated symposium, to the rest of the class and the teacher.

If there is a discipline committee in the class, its chief work may be the taking of evidence on matters brought to its notice, and the preparing of reports for the class as a whole with the teacher in the chair. If there is a disturbance and a chair or a window is broken, the discipline committee sits as a court of enquiry and presents the evidence it has collected orally in the first place; the gist of it is noted down and published, after correction by the teacher, either on the classroom notice-board or in the form of a folder specially got out—like a government white paper—for the purpose and the occasion.

Other committees may exist for other purposes and report on their work and their findings. The visits committee may plan, perhaps with the help of a parent or parents, visits by the class to the railway station or a factory or the municipal offices, and report at each stage the progress of the arrangements. The drama committee may plan dramatic performances and write reports on its work and its plans. The entertainments committee and the games committee, the library committee and the music committee, and any other committees that can show a valid reason for existing, can keep records and make reports. Every piece of work can be made useful and significant and its value increased and placed on record in the form of short but clear reports. These may be stereotyped at first, based on models prepared with the help of the teacher, but gradually becoming freer. Some of this work, of course, is only appropriate where the language being studied is also the medium of instruction.

The most important and frequently used type of report writing will be the material prepared and presented to the class by a group as preparation for the study of texts or in the course of working out the findings of a project. This will be treated in greater detail in the next chapter, "Reading and the Study of Prose Literature". All this work has the merit of being directed towards the community, the class and the teacher; the teacher is associated with it as an expert adviser on language and usage, but he is not the destination, nor is he the judge of it. If his help is tactfully offered and kept to a minimum it is valued and eagerly accepted; the pupil will not feel himself to be being judged, but helped.

2. *Reviews*

Most teachers find it difficult to persuade all but the most intelligent boys to read outside the textbook and in excess of their immediate obligations. A scheme for reviewing the books available to the class in the range of difficulty they can face may help to open up the books through the experience and the words of fellow-members of the class. The books can be distributed to volunteers and part of a period set aside for listening to the reviews. A tradition of good-humoured heckling may help to ward off dullness. Afterwards the reviews can be written down by the speakers and slipped between the fly-leaf and the cover of each book for ready reference by those looking for a book to read. The review may be quite stereotyped at first; it may begin with reasons for liking the book; it may go on with a short summary of the story, or an account of the ideas handled or suggested by the book; it may then give some account of the chief characters and the general effect of them— whether agreeable or disagreeable—on the reader; and finally it may tell whatever is chiefly memorable in the story.

Practice in writing to such a scheme will give a coherence and shape to other types of writing afterwards. It will help concentration on the points of a good review if the class, either all together or group by group, criticizes the review and awards points according to a scheme of qualities. This type of writing is directed exclusively towards the class, with the teacher as adviser and prompter, helping each student in turn to do himself credit in front of the class.

3. *Advertisements and Publicity*

Articles for sale, school or class entertainments, voluntary excursions and school or form societies and clubs could all benefit by being brought to the notice of those who might be interested, if they were properly advertised. In particular, many a struggling school society could be strengthened by attracting larger membership and developing greater interest and enthusiasm among the existing members by effective promotion propaganda, explaining the scope, possibilities and significance of the work done in the society. Everyone interested may try his hand at preparing material, and a publicity committee can undertake the choosing of the best of it for actual use. This can at first imitate the persuasive writing of good travel literature or the folders got out by education authorities to publicize evening classes or by government departments to explain their policy.

Perceptive textual study such as this, with a view to doing similar work, is a very important part of learning to write. Where the language is the medium of instruction the teacher may usefully initiate and lead discussions on the particular qualities that make one type of persuasion more effective than another; this may lead to discussion of the value or otherwise of sincerity in this type of writing, and of the part played by the exploitation of desirable or undesirable qualities in the public aimed at. These topics will lead to discussion of the part played by organized official and unofficial persuasion in modern civilization. This may be a valuable opportunity to draw the attention of the class to some of the undesirable and even dangerous uses of the mass media of the press, the film, the radio and television to influence the masses contrary to their own true interests, though the positive side of their use to promote healthy influences need not be forgotten. Advertising and intensive propaganda are an important feature of our civilization. A comprehensive education cannot ignore them.

4. *Descriptive Articles on Matters of General Interest*

Hardly to be distinguished at first from reports, except that they cater for wider and more general interests, are descriptive articles, prepared for the class or school magazine. They may aim at interesting more than merely the rest of the class, perhaps the whole school and parents and the wider community round the school too. They lead into the type of free composition which, in school, usually goes under the name of essay, but they should be simple and interesting; they may present current affairs, local developments, descriptions of innovations in the neighbourhood such as a rebuilt railway station or a new sports pavilion, the harvest or the development of a new local industry.

They may arise out of the research of a local study or a project, but they will not necessarily be part of it. A student who has prepared a particularly interesting report on some activity or innovation in the neighbourhood for a local studies project may be invited to rewrite it as a magazine article—or several pupils to collaborate in rewriting it—but it will be seen to be a different type of writing, with a different aim and a different public in view, demanding a rather different type of construction and working out. This sort of exercise may show best the difference between the spare, desiccated presenting of the bare facts, almost in note form, demanded in a report, and the more expanded, reflective, but still economical writing which has to aim at conjuring up a scene to view by stimulating the imagination.

Once the class has had its eyes opened to the possibilities of the neighbourhood and their own experience as a source of material for factual and descriptive writing designed to interest and please, there will be no difficulty in finding them topics to write about; they will be more likely to find them for themselves. The composition period will then be a period when every member of the class is busy with something that interests him. There will be problems of construction that he is interested in solving; he will blow his mind to white heat to forge his propositions, and then take them to the work-bench to hammer them out. He will get help and advice from his neighbours when necessary, but wrestle with his own reluctant or willing consciousness to produce his own fluency and his own revelation.

The teacher will cease to expect every member of the class to be engaged in writing on the same subject; he will be content that they are all engaged in the same task of pondering or producing through words a new relationship to the world about them, and at the same time preparing for those sitting around them channels to new experience, access to facts, figures, activities and sensations that would otherwise remain local and ephemeral. To ensure plenty of time for reflection he should see that proposals for subjects are usually made well in advance.

5. *Letters*

Letters are different from all the types of writing so far discussed in that they are not public utterances. They are personal projections on to a single person, or a limited number of people—such as an organization or firm—usually personified in the mind of the writer to an image of a single person. A letter is one side of a duologue, a private conversation of which half is missing or postponed; it should never become a monologue, but it all too often does. Success in letter-writing depends on successful imagining of the presence of the person to whom the letter is being written. It is therefore wise to start off the child on his learning of letter-writing with targets within easy reach, on whom it is fairly easy for him to see the result of the writing. Some teachers of small children have a red cardboard or wooden post-box in the classroom in which letters to other members of the class, or members of parallel classes, can be posted; the postman clears the box at stated intervals and delivers them. This might not work with older children, but letters to pen-friends and the writing of requests to the teacher in letter form can give practice in the conventions of letter-writing. Letters ought not to be read by the teacher unless he is invited to do so; as an outsider, he may spoil their personal character; but if the teacher has a really good and close personal relationship with his pupils he may share many of the personal interests and aspirations of the majority of them. If so, he may be asked to share their letters. Even then, it is wiser not to spoil the unselfconscious projection of personality on to an intimate friend, or the communication of personal ideas, by correcting beyond what is strictly necessary for comprehension. A tactful suggestion of a way in which a sentence might have been more clearly expressed should be as far as the teacher should go in correction unless the letter is a more or less public utterance or has no particularly personal or private character.

If the teacher has accustomed his pupils to the conventions of letter-writing, modes of address, opening and closing remarks, politeness and consideration for the feelings of the person written to, during the first few years of work on the language, he can leave the letters in the later years unchecked, relying on the recipients to draw attention to any mistakes or solecisms.

Letters from the pupil to the teacher will not, of course, be unlikely if relations between them are good, and in a large class it may be the only practical way for the pupil to rely on expressing himself at length to the teacher and getting a considered reply. The teacher may make it a rule that any boy who wishes to tell him anything personal should save his time between two consecutive periods by putting the gist of what he wants to say in a letter. The teacher may give a written reply, or an appointment to speak to him. The teacher's tact and common sense may restrain him from correcting the mistakes that trouble him but may not trouble the writer; he should remember that to concentrate on this aspect of the letter may seem to the pupil heartless, if he has been trying to express to the teacher ideas—or possibly troubles—that seem to him important.

I have always thought that setting a class to write an imaginary letter applying for an advertised vacancy in an insurance company, or asking a rich industrialist for the hand of his daughter, to be a tiresome, artificial kind of nonsense that is unlikely to produce anything but pomposity on the one hand or facetiousness on the other, but experienced teachers whose intelligence I respect tell me they can bring that kind of thing off successfully, so I have nothing but my prejudices to fall back on, and an invincible reluctance to try it myself. For economy and exactness in language, practice in writing telegrams can be tried.

6. *Creative Work involving the Full Personality of the Pupil*

In all the types of work discussed so far there has been no compulsion on the student to expose or display himself; he can be as objective in his reports, advertising and descriptive writing as he likes; his letters can be matter-of-fact and businesslike. But there is also a place for a type of imaginative writing that lays him open to the gaze of the reader, and commits him to a confession of what he is and what he aspires to be.

It is possible for a person to defend the sacred citadel of his personality and refuse to expose himself to judgment, but no man can be fully mature until he learns to face what is in him and is prepared to hear and recognize the worst. Many a brilliant—or apparently brilliant—scholar or conversationist has written little or nothing, excusing himself on the score of humility or laziness, because he was afraid that what he would write might not be first class; having lived among the great geniuses of literature or history in his imagination, he is unable to face the possibility that he might himself be second-rate. He has preferred to criticize the writings of others, safe in his tower from which he has made no sorties. If we are to help our pupils to healthy all-round development, however, we must encourage them to put out hostages and risk losing them.

It is this free self-expression which helps the pupil to work out personal problems and relieve psychic pressures. It has therefore a very important part to play in the development of the individual. It should be started as early as possible but not before the pupil has enough command of the language to write freely without many mistakes. At first, this free writing should always be done in class, but as single pupils begin to write confidently and wish to spend more time on imaginative writing, we may encourage them to finish at home composition begun in class, and, finally, to write whatever they have a mind to, whenever the mood takes them.

Recognizing as we must that they are giving something of themselves, confiding themselves into our care, we must take our pupils' trust seriously and see that they have no cause, as far as we are concerned, to regret their confidence. The teacher should look through the work sympathetically and carefully, but avoid, as far as possible, correcting it unless it is to be put on the wall newspaper, in the form or school magazine, or in any other way put on show. Then it has to be dressed up so as to do its author credit; spelling and punctuation must conform to normal social etiquette, sentences must be clearly written and expressed so that the meaning and tone are easy to grasp.

A good deal of this work can be done by the writer himself if the teacher starts him off by indicating certain sentences which are not quite clear, and certain passages where a re-arrangement of the punctuation would avoid ambiguity. If the teacher thinks that the general idea is good but that it has been marred by an unsuitable tone, he may suggest the rewriting of the whole piece or a part of it, avoiding the underlying attitude marked by the—in his opinion—unsuitable tone, but not necessarily discarding the first draft until he can compare the two. Then both drafts can be submitted to a panel of critics to be discussed. Even if the writer still prefers, and adopts as his final draft, the one the teacher has disapproved of, he will have had his attention drawn to considerations that he might not otherwise have been aware of, and he is not likely to write in quite the same way again. The teacher will have made his point clear but have left the final responsibility to the boy; this is important because the boy must learn to carry such responsibility himself, and may even have to learn good taste by experiencing and ultimately reacting from bad taste.

The teacher must make it very clear that he is not condemning the boy in drawing his attention to lapses in taste. Most of the work on the pupil's language and style should take place in exercises, and in the types of composition given under the first four heads; then criticism is a natural and welcome part of the process of developing a good and useful skill in writing; it is not personal and is not normally painful to the learner. It develops in scope and complexity to include more and more facets of writing.

But when he has been working with the teacher for some time and is quite assured of his sympathy and interest he will probably be glad if the teacher says even of his most precious offering: "Look here, this is good stuff, and I like the way you've developed the ideas, but the real point of what you want to say hasn't quite come over. Can we make this last paragraph clearer?" Or: "I think this is the best work you've done so far, but there are still a lot of spelling mistakes that I suppose you don't want to live with for the rest of your life." Or: "I don't think this is quite up to your usual level, but nobody can write his best all the time. Would you like to start again from the beginning or would you rather just leave it alone and forget about it? I find, myself, that a bad start like this is best scrapped, and I'm never sorry I've started again once I've taken the plunge; but we can save something from the wreck, some of these ideas are good. Let's pick them out, and they can be the notes for a new try." In this way a boy can be shown how to struggle with difficulty and build success on what can be salvaged from previous failures.

Sometimes the pupil writes something particularly personal that reveals rather more of himself than he would like everyone in his form to see. If the teacher finds it good and thinks others would like to see it, he must first get the permission of the writer to pass it round; he should not try to persuade him if he sees that he is really unwilling to give it. It is above everything else important that the teacher should have the full confidence of his class if he is to get good writing of this personal type out of them, and especially out of the shyer members of the class. It may be precisely these who are sensitive and may have the greatest potential gifts of absorption and expression.

SUMMARY OF TYPES OF COMPOSITION

Nature of composition	*Public in mind*
1. Reports	the teacher or the class.
2. Reviews	the class.
3. Advertisements and publicity	the class and other classes.
4. Descriptive articles on matters of general interest	the class and the teacher, and ultimately a wider public outside the class.
5. Letters	either the teacher or a single individual.
6. Creative work involving the full personality of the pupil	the teacher or the class, sometimes both, and the wider public of form and school periodicals.

There is a place for each of these six types of composition, and none of them need be fakes. It is in many ways more important for the teacher to think out a compelling social purpose for a piece of composition than for him to think of a subject; for a social purpose brings subjects in clusters with it and provides the incentive and releases the energy needed for a successful and vigorous piece of writing. If a subject demands our full enlistment and devotion, if even the attention to the subject has arisen from a genuinely felt social and personal need, we can expect the energies to be directed all one way and not clash with one another in frustration.

If anyone is to write well he must write a great deal and must mean what he writes; he must learn to push himself energetically, even violently, into his subject. The rather facetious, whimsical style of Lamb has had a very unfortunate effect on English essay and light, belles-lettres types of writing, at least on the work of amateurs; even some more weighty kinds of writing are the worse for the influence, as if it were impossible to be serious and witty at the same time. Vacuity and inanity cultivated in writing during the school days are difficult to live down and grow out of. For this, a grim and despotic schoolmaster with a bitter tongue may be the quickest cure, and we should be thankful for at least this service from these purgative pedagogues.

C. THE SETTING FOR SUCCESSFUL WRITING

All original composition of the sixth category should be done in class, at least until the fifth year of English; work begun in class may, however, sometimes be finished at home by a keen and able pupil if he can be relied upon to work easily and quickly beyond the reach of the teacher's help. Work in the first three categories can be done at home earlier, that is to say, as soon as the teacher considers that the majority of the class can do the work without his help. Work in the fourth category may be thought out at home but finished off and written out in class, with plenty of discussion and criticism in groups, until each separate pupil has shown that he can write independently without too many mistakes. The licence to do this work at home may be a sort of promotion or mark of maturity, a sign of the confidence that the teacher has in the individual pupil's powers.

1. *Dealing with Difficulties in Expression*

Where the teacher finds that a pupil has difficulty in expression he may suggest words and sentence patterns, and recommend particular exercises to fix the patterns in the memory. He should often ask the pupil to tell him which forms of expression he finds difficult. By enlisting the pupil's watchfulness and sense of responsibility on his side, the teacher very much reduces his own burden of responsibility and the reliance he must place on his own diagnostic penetration. If he asks the pupil to suggest how many times he needs to write out a word so as to learn the spelling, or how many times he needs to write an expression to fix it in his mind, the pupil has an incentive to complete the process within the limits he has himself set; his concentration is therefore more complete and effective than if he has been set the task as a sort of punishment, coming to him unbidden from outside.

If a subject is proving difficult for the majority in the class, the teacher may stop all writing and get the class to co-operate in a joint composition that may be written out on the blackboard and then copied into individual exercise books to serve as a basis for individual effort. Or he may get one paragraph written in this way, and then divide the class up into groups for each group to write an agreed second paragraph. After this, the third paragraph may be written by individuals. If corrected compositions and agreed, corrected group compositions are always copied into the fair-copy notebook, there will be perpetual clearing up of mistakes and the driving of correct forms of expression into the mind.

It seems to me wrong to give simply key-words, phrases and sentences to be the basis of a composition improvised on a suggested theme, for even if the majority of the class could not work out such a list for themselves, the searching for the consecutive ideas, under guidance, and the compiling of a fruitful and coherent series may be within the powers of the class as a whole, one mind reacting on another. But even if the process resembles the teacher's thinking aloud more than a co-operative effort, the class will learn more from the transaction than from a blank list presented without comment and without any effort or reaching out of the mind of the learner.

2. *Group Composition Writing*

A great deal of the early work in composition—the actual learning of correct expression—can be done in groups. The group takes into the corner its list of sentences to be modified and rewritten; or it goes out on to the verandah or into the garden. It discusses quietly what has to be done. When agreement has been reached on each sentence, the agreed version is written down by each member of the class and compared with his neighbour's versions to make sure that there are no spelling mistakes or other slips. When all the sentences are finished the leader of the group either hands in his book or copies the sentences once more on to a piece of paper to be handed in to the teacher. It may be better, as time goes by, for him to ask whichever member of the group is least sure of the correct forms to do the copying, so as to give him a further opportunity of learning them; it will be regarded as a privilege rather than as a punishment if the group leader has always done it hitherto.

As the pupils develop experience they can gradually begin, first to modify, and then to compose for themselves, connected pieces of prose in groups; they may continue working in groups until their standard of performance as individuals is high enough to ensure correct and fluent independent writing.

3. *The Planning of a Piece of Writing*

The architecture or planning of a piece of writing is often as important as the actual writing itself. If the various points follow one another in a logical order in such a way that each point grows out of and strengthens or supports the one before it, the cumulative power of the whole piece may be very much greater than that of any single element in it.

(a) *Can Planning be Taught?* The question is whether planning or composing can be learnt as a separate skill from writing. A good many courses in composition are based on the supposition that it can; common sense must warn us, however, that the teacher does not help his pupils to learn anything by saving them the trouble of trying to do it for themselves. A naked skeleton presented to us to be clothed may give us experience in making clothes, but it will not give us experience in making skeletons. Nor is there much to be gained by practising just the making of synopses for a piece of writing that will never be written, as an exercise for itself. I have seldom found much come, either, of efforts to make a class sketch out their ideas in advance before they start writing. Most of the class find that they have no ideas until they start writing—the very act of writing seems to produce them—so they sit confused and despondent until the teacher says: "All right, start trying to write something," and the idea of a plan drawn up in advance is quietly dropped.

(b) *Training in Planning.* In my experience it is much sounder to get each member of a class to jot down notes for a talk, and then let him give the talk at the first available opportunity. After hearing and criticizing someone else's talk, he may be invited to go over his own notes and see if he wants to revise them. In this way critical awareness of the process of composition and construction is fostered, and most of the students come to their speeches having gone over their notes and thought about them several times; perhaps they have even discussed them and recast them.

It can be a regular exercise for every speech to be written down in full, after it has been delivered, for record purposes, and for the rest of the class—and perhaps members of other classes too—to have the opportunity to study it at their leisure. If the notes used for the speech are the basis of this writing, rearranged if necessary in the light of the experience of speaking on the subject, the student comes to practise the habit of making use of his notes for writing, and this gives an added purpose to the working out of the notes in the first place.

(c) *Further Exercises in Planning.* There are other ways of drawing attention to the problems of careful planning and construction. The elements of a good piece of prose can be identified and a new piece written on the same plan, if possible an episode within the pupils' own experience; something which has been studied in the textbook can be used, preferably something with a clearly defined skeletal form, with a clear beginning or introduction, statement, development and conclusion. Poems can be used after they have been learnt, partly as an excuse for renewed attention to the poems, and to direct close attention to their structure, and partly as a quarry for ready-made plans for independent writing. If we take the traditional poem *Gipsie Laddie*, beginning:

> It was late in the night when the squire came home,
> Enquiring for his lady.
> The servant made a sure reply:
> She's gone with the Gipsum Davie,[1]

we can use the first line to begin the composition: "It was late in the night when the —— came home, enquiring for —— " and then follow the outlines of the story with a chase on horseback or by some other conveyance, a request to come home, and a refusal, followed by an account of the eventual fate of the runaway. A prose version of the *Demon Lover* would be a contemporary story with the main facts reproduced but the supernatural elements reinterpreted as mental or psychological states or occurrences. I have used Wordsworth's *Daffodils* very successfully for this purpose, after it had been taught and become very familiar. I found it stimulate the imagination of the class to a remarkable degree and lead to a renewed understanding and affection for the poem. Compositions began: "I was walking along the road near the park one day when all at once I saw a Gul Mohur covered with scarlet blossom . . ." Or, "I was travelling along in a bus from Secunderabad to Hyderabad one day, when all at once I saw a mass of blue water hyacinths, stretching right across the marsh on the left of the road . . .," etc. Some left flowers alone and described street accidents, two women fighting, the fire brigade fighting a fire, or two horses playing in a field. I

[1] W. H. Auden and John Garrett, *The Poet's Tongue*.

refused to accept unpleasant sights as parallels to the poet's joyful experience, but all had the same plan: (1) beginning with an observer walking or riding into view of the scene or occurrence, (2) describing the setting, and (3) the way in which whatever or whoever it was that caught the attention of the observer moved, and (4) then, finally, describing the effect of what was seen on the mind and the memory afterwards.

(d) *Paragraph Writing*. The writing of paragraphs as recognizable units of composition can be practised separately, concurrently, and as a preparation for continuous composition writing. The teacher asks a member of his class to give his opinion on some subject more or less within his reach and first-hand knowledge. He replies with a sentence which the teacher asks him to write down. Then the teacher gets him, or other members of his class or group, to add four or five sentences that enlarge on or explain this statement, and one sentence to round off the argument. This can be a model paragraph which can be repeated with new statements proposed by the pupils individually or collectively in answer to the teacher's probings in class. They may be written down to be developed later, in or out of class, as occasion and their state of development allows. Some of this work, as suggested previously, may be done in groups.

CONCLUSION

The foundations of good written composition are laid in:

1. Oral composition exercises and continuous narration.

2. The writing of composition exercises.

3. The completing of passages, whether copied or written down from dictation, or composed co-operatively on the blackboard and then copied.

4. The narration, discussion and writing down from memory of stories told in class and reports, descriptions, etc., as recounted under headings 1, 2 and 4 of section B above.

5. The by-products of the preparation of advanced texts,

in collating and narration of material gathered from direct experience, interviewing, research work in libraries and discussion.

6. Group compositions.

If all these types of exercise and the continuous prose composition that develops out of them—both co-operatively, in groups, or singly, as individuals—are progressively practised and developed, the pupil and the group being encouraged always to be on the look-out for subject-matter for themselves, there need never be monotony or falsity; there need never be windy and pretentious writing on subjects too far in advance of the pupil's stage of development to have been genuinely felt and experienced. There need be no perfunctory, half-engaged writing, such as leads to slackness and imprecision of expression. There need be no sense of frustration due to the pupil's true interests and feelings never having been tapped.

If the teacher lets the need for expression arise from the natural interests of the pupil in the world around him, in supplying reading matter for others, and from his daily work in other subjects—physics, chemistry, history, geography and biology—he will never be short of subjects for discussion in speech or for composition writing. Moreover, he will have the satisfaction of knowing that he has directed the thinking of the pupil into every corner of his life, and given him a skill that will help him to perceive the world and its life, and reveal himself to the world.

10

Reading and the Study of Prose Literature

INTRODUCTION

Whatever the process we submit the mind to as we help it to develop through learning a foreign language, to adapt itself to strange impressions, to equip itself for taking in knowledge and thinking in the new language, we must see that the pupil takes with him the ability to manage without us when he leaves school and our part of the process is over. Back in his home environment he may not hear the language often, but if he is able to read fluently and perceptively, with some pleasure, he can keep the language alive in his mind; provided he has learnt the sounds and intonation well, they will sound correctly in his inward ear as he reads. If he reads constantly and widely he will increase his mastery of the language far beyond what he was able to reach at school; he will join native users of the language in reading their newspapers and books, submitting himself at the same time to the currents of thought which move through the culture of the language and are accessible in the printed word.

No one is likely to remember a language for long if he is unable to read it easily or if the normal writing intended for native readers of the language is beyond his reach. If we have taught him a limited sample of the language, a reduced, selected vocabulary with carefully graded structural material, and have not given him, with this basic knowledge, some experience in facing normal unrestricted language, he is likely to find even the newspaper difficult and books inaccessible. All work in reading is more effective and economical if the mind is systematically trained in absorbing ideas quickly and accurately from the printed page.

So we must help our pupils not to be afraid of difficulty. If they have come to expect the meaning of a difficult passage to yield to concentrated reading and rereading, they are willing to go on until the words and the sentence patterns begin to come into focus in their minds and take on significance, however inaccessible they may seem at first. They will be accustomed to the experience of reading, say, the daily news rapidly and finding that certain unknown words, seen often in similar contexts, come gradually further and further through the crust of incomprehension or inattention to a permanent place and significance in the mind.

It is more urgent therefore for the pupil to cultivate a habit of attentive and perceptive reading, once the main patterns have been made familiar in speech, than for him to have been drilled painstakingly in a complete or representative sample of the patterns of the language, though this also should be attempted. However little we have time to teach he will learn more if we train him to grapple with difficulty and to read adventurously, not being daunted or held back by unknown words or expressions, than if we allow him practice in reading only what is well within his grasp. On the other hand, as long as we are teaching him to read, we must use easy material, language which has been well learnt orally, and is quite familiar in sound and meaning, so that he can concentrate on acquiring the skill of reading, matching what he sees to the sounds he knows, without being distracted at the same time by meeting new vocabulary.

The teacher may well find these two aims, fluent, fully conscious reading, and adventurous, searching, half-conscious reading, hard to reconcile. In the first kind, every word is familiar; its meaning and function are clear; in the second, many words are taken on trust, the exact functions of many words in their sentences are left undefined; as he feels for the general drift of a passage, the reader comes to understand the meanings of words by their relation to this general drift; patterns many times repeated, hugged, as it were, trustingly but uncomprehendingly to the bosom as the reader races on, are found to have yielded up their significance by the end of the article or chapter or book.

To cultivate both these types of skill the teacher may plan his reading instruction with both in mind. He can begin with the first, and even when he begins to introduce the second—sooner with a quick class than with a slow one—the first may preponderate for some time, until gradually the preponderance of the second is increased towards the end of the course, as part of the teacher's policy of encouraging independence and responsibility as soon as the pupil is ready to be responsible for his own learning.

PART ONE

EFFECTIVE READING INSTRUCTION

The teacher may be helped to remember that there is more than one type of skill included under the heading of "Effective Reading", if he looks once more at Bacon's advice about reading in his essay "Of Studies". "Some books are to be tasted, others to be swallowed, and some few to be chewed and digested, that is, some books are to be read only in parts, others to be read but not curiously, and some few to be read wholly, and with diligence and attention. Some books also may be read by deputy, and extracts made of them by others, but that would be only in the less important arguments and the meaner sort of books, else distilled books are, like common distilled waters, flashy things!"

This can be summarized as follows:

1. Leisurely light reading.

2. (a) Rapid scanning, as when searching a newspaper for the latest news.

(b) Rapid scanning to glean salient points of a chapter or book.

3. Serious analytic (reflective) reading.

4. Deputy reading—abstracts, reports, etc.

As a preparation for thoroughly effective reading of all kinds, the teacher must see that the beginnings of reading in the textbook are always kept well behind the point his pupils have reached; they should learn to recognize all new words on paper and begin to write them only when they are thoroughly familiar as sound. In the first few years reading must be the quick recognition of what is well known, not the slow deciphering of a code or puzzle. Only as he finds his pupils reading ahead in the textbook and becoming more adventurous in their reading of supplementary readers should the teacher begin to put in front of them more difficult material containing unknown words and expressions. He may begin with only a few of the brighter ones in the class and gradually extend the privilege. As he does so he will increase their interest and involvement by the variety of skills which he sets them to learn. Bacon's categories may guide him here.

1. *Leisurely light reading* is cultivated in the reading of simplified texts; what have sometimes come to be called "non-detailed texts" because examiners do not require a detailed knowledge of them. The teacher should try and provide plenty of easy reading at a vocabulary level well within the grasp of the pupil, keeping mainly within the structural patterns learnt up to that stage. This reading is not intended to teach the pupil new language, but to exercise him in what he has learnt in such a way that his reading is fluent and fully conscious.

2. *Rapid scanning* is a useful skill worth cultivating for its own sake; if it has been cultivated systematically from the earliest point in the course at which it can be attempted, cooperative work on the study of texts—to be described later—can be greatly expedited and made easy. If newspapers are

P

taken into class at least once a week from the fourth year onwards, and special exercises in rapid scanning are given, skill will develop to a useful degree by the end of the course. Nearly all the background reading required for the presenting of a topic to the class by a group calls for proficiency in this type of reading.

3. *Serious, analytic and reflective reading*, such as the best sorts of literature call for, and the more profound books on politics, philosophy, religion, economics, technology and science, is best catered for by training such as that which is to be outlined later, in which discussion follows perceptive reading of a piece of concentrated and demanding prose.

4. *Deputy reading* is a type of reading too little cultivated consciously, though a good deal of school work is based on its results. The ordinary school textbook in most subjects is a summary of someone's reading of a large number of more detailed works. It is desirable that not all of this work should be done in advance by the teacher and his ally the writer of the textbook. An enterprising teacher will contrive to confront groups of his class with a selection of material similar to what the textbook writer condenses into his familiar, sad-hued pemmican. If he does so everyone in the class has a chance of contact with original sources—if in a limited sphere—and the rest of the class can benefit by the fruits of each of these contacts. This is much more *zweckmässig* (or shall we say purposeful) than the artificial production of an epitome for the teacher in relation to nothing in particular.

Reading Circles. At an advanced stage, where the student is faced with a formidable list of books which he is recommended to read, he may reduce the problem to manageable dimensions by uniting himself with others, faced with the same daunting cliff of reading, to divide the field. Each one takes a book, reads it, makes notes on it and speaks about it at a meeting of the group; later he may connect up his notes to form a summary and an estimate of the book.

If the book is being read with a particular study in mind,

the relevance of the book to the study should be shown and those chapters or pages enumerated which have the closest bearing on the subject of the study.

In this way a comparatively large number of books can be passed in review before the members of the group; each member of the group has had an introduction to all of them and has had their relevance to his interests or to the study he is at work on investigated for him; at the same time he has read one book attentively and diagnostically, with not only his own interests and studies in mind, but those of the other members of the group, so that his reading has had a social significance and has been given thereby intensity and direction. Later, if he has time, he may read those portions of the other books marked out for him by the other members of the group; he may even read the whole of some books which he finds are, after all, within the range of his ability and interests.

Practical Steps to Improve Speed and Accuracy in Reading. The teacher, even at a fairly early stage, may take steps to improve his pupils' ability to read quickly and accurately. Discarded textbooks, which have been given up in the school, can be kept and cut up into suitable lengths of a few pages, with questions to test comprehension typed and pasted on to them. Whenever the teacher has ten minutes to spare, a set can be distributed to the class and a time limit set for reading and for answering the questions; as writing is not being tested the questions should only require "Yes" or "No" answers, or the ticking of correct statements, or the writing of numbers.

Another exercise may be to set the class to read for a minute and to mark the point reached with a dot in pencil. The winner in the race and the runners-up are then stood in front of the class and questioned—preferably by the losers—on their comprehension of the piece. Another exercise is to set the class to consult passages in books, or the dismembered pieces of textbook just mentioned, to find the answers to questions and stand up when they have found them. In another the teacher writes a passage from a book on the blackboard with some words missing; the class have to find the passage in the book and write down the missing words.

Mental arithmetic problems, simple detective stories or other problems to be solved, can be typed on squares of cardboard; these can be given out to each member of the class and exchanged for others as soon as the answers have been noted; the one who deals with the largest number of cards correctly is the winner.

At an early stage, actions in mime in obedience to flash cards can be a fruitful occasion for hilarity and for friendly competition in the last five minutes of many a lesson, e.g.,

> Drink some water.
> Hop like a rabbit.
> Ring a bell.
> Thread a needle.
> Get stung by a bee, etc.

Cards with exact instructions on them to be carried out quickly can be distributed, for instance: "Go out into the garden and collect a narrow pointed leaf and a round smooth stone," or a much more complicated list of instructions involving observation in the town can be given for homework. A teacher should assemble a large arsenal of such exercises for use at every stage of the course. If they are constantly slipped in when there is five or ten minutes to go to the end of the lesson, very little time will be taken from the routine lessons and there will always be a genuine feeling of urgency and cheerfulness in the doing of them. The teacher will be very thankful for readiness in reading when he wants his pupils to find and quickly prepare background material to textual study, if they have made punctual and steady improvement in speed and accuracy. They will have enjoyed what seemed at the time like play.

PART TWO

LITERATURE

The Study of Prose Literature

Up to this point we have been chiefly concerning ourselves with bringing the pupil's skill in reading up to the standard at which he can read and enjoy newspapers and books in a foreign language. We may now ask ourselves whether there is a place for prose literature in an economical language course. First, we must be modest enough to admit that by literature we mean writing better than most of us can write in a text-book. If we mean whatever writing is excellent in its sphere and include the classics of science such as Darwin's, Faraday's and T. H. Huxley's writings we shall see that we impoverish the course and its emotional and intellectual appeal by leaving it out.

If we attach any importance to the value of mental set as an aid to learning, we must see that writing which appeals by reason of its charm and excellence, its splendour of thought and pattern and the musical rhythm of its sentences, has a very important part to play in the total effect which the language makes on the pupil. If we deprive it of its prestige we deprive it of its chance to survive except in odd corners as a curiosity.

At the end of the course the language must be a possession which the student values and delights in for its own sake as well as for the power and adaptability for use that may be latent in it. In the short view its appeal to him will depend on the delight it gives him. The literature is part of a language, not a supplement to it.

A. INTRODUCING PROSE TEXTS

In watching many lessons on prose texts—"Open the book at page 57, and read, you"—in increasing dissatisfaction with the process of bringing classes myself into contact with prose literature—stumbling, cumbersome reading that estranged rather than brought near—I began to reject some years ago the way of teaching by ploughing through the piece line by line. I felt that the major barrier to enjoyment and understanding was the slowness of the progress from difficulty to difficulty, from obscure word to idiomatic turn of phrase. It seemed as if a cactus hedge of difficulty and dullness was allowed by the teacher to grow in front of the piece which was to have been enjoyed; by the time the end of the piece was reached the beginning had either been forgotten or the conclusion was no longer a surprise or worth reading. If this was the result of tackling worthwhile prose literature, so that it ceased to be worthwhile in the process, surely we had better abandon the attempt and stick to textbookese. This was the way to make the learner hate what he was told he should like.

And yet I had been given as the first rule when I began to learn how to teach a foreign language: "You must always introduce the chief words and sentence patterns of a prose text before you let the pupil read it." It had always seemed too difficult, a counsel of perfection, and I had questioned whether the rule was applicable once genuine literature was to be read. Yet again this was the way to teach fresh language at the beginner's stage. Could there be some real advantage in introducing the words which were unknown to the pupil but had to be known if the piece was to be fully grasped before we started to read it? It would at least mean that we could use them in different ways, perhaps in another setting, perhaps in the same setting but not bound to the actual theme of the piece, so that the reading could be quick and fresh, the climax not postponed by innumerable explanations. Could we cut down the number of explanations drastically? Were we bound to submit to the boredom of these laborious and toneless readings round the class?

At first I may have spent too long on the introduction of unknown words and phrases, but gradually I came to see that explanations which took us away from a natural discussion of the main theme of the piece were best dropped, and instead it was quicker, more economical and easier simply to let the words drift in and use them in various ways that made their use familiar, but left an exact definition, perhaps, to a later stage. I have found that it is usually better not to forestall the impact of the piece by outlining the story or argument, but to begin with any experience anyone in the class, or I myself, may have of similar or comparable circumstances, and make as much use as possible of the vocabulary which has to be introduced in developing this theme. Sometimes a landscape can be sketched on the blackboard or modelled in sand. Any characters can be shown and moved about physically on this, and perhaps their actions can be dramatized by the pupils, more as passive lay figures to carry the various identities than as actors.

Introducing Vocabulary and Setting on a Model Landscape

I have outlined in an earlier chapter the effect on a backward class of the making of a representation in sand of the desert setting for Kinglake's description in *Eothen* of the crossing of the desert. Getting them to help me in the making of the desert, modelling the hills and valleys and the flat plains out of sand, making the dwarf shrubs out of green tissue paper, and cutting the Arabs and camels out of cardboard, not only gave me an opportunity to make the necessary vocabulary familiar—the desert landscape and Arabs being not only seen, while this was being done, but felt and moulded—it also directed their attention on to the subject-matter of the piece, and fixed their full concentration on it from the beginning. They were given a favourable mental set that helped them materially in entering into the situation described, and increased the speed and efficiency of absorption and learning. The words grew in their minds like natural growths.

It is probable that their identification with the situation shown in the sand-table would not have been so rapid or so complete if they had simply watched the landscape being prepared for them, and even less so if it had been laid out ready for them before they came into the room. The sharing in the process of preparation, co-operating with other learners, and joining in this useful work with the teacher instead of passively observing his work from outside it, the identifying of themselves with his efforts to help them, aligned them on his side and gave them an impetus in the right direction. This attitude-building, and the aligning of the mind and personality of the learner with the teacher in the common task, plays a very important part in easing the work of both teacher and pupil, in bringing the piece within the mental reach of the pupils.

Establishing the Setting of the Piece in the Mind

A description of a scene such as the description of Egdon Heath at the beginning of *The Return of the Native* is difficult to grasp unless one has seen such a scene or has an imagination which is easily roused by words to see in the mind's eye images of what the writer wishes to convey; this is partly a matter of practice. To grasp the relationship of the various hills and houses one must read the opening chapters very attentively. This might not seem to be important for its own sake, but attentive reading of the opening chapters puts the reader in the right mood and atmosphere for the experience of the rest of the book, and helps the reader to submit himself to the intentions and spell of the author.

Making up a model of the landscape on the sand-table requires careful interpretation and attention to detail on the part of those who make it; but, more than that, the words are recognized and given meaning by the work of the fingers. The following of the description and the recognition of the words and sentences are then very simple for everyone else. Language which is altogether unfamiliar and even complicated is easy to identify and learn if the attention and interest are completely absorbed in the situation it explains; the significance of each item is instantaneously clear through the situation being clear.

No dislocations of the mind such as translation involves are then necessary, but situation and words are one.

This work is not so much an introductory presentation of the piece as a presentation or parade of the language which has to be known and used in reading and discussion of it. It is similar to the parade of horses in the paddock for recognition, and to see how they move, before a race. The discussion need not be uninteresting, and the piece to be studied can be left untouched so that its full flavour can be enjoyed fresh when it is read through.

The reading of a piece which everyone in the class knows is to be tackled should not be needlessly postponed by a prolonged introductory presentation. On the other hand, there is nothing to be gained by starting the reading before enough words are known for the reading to be quick and meaningful. We take away from the reading stage everything which interferes with understanding, everything which slows down the pace of reading, but those words which are best understood in their contexts in the piece can be left unused and unexplained to be guessed at, or merely noticed in the background, as the piece is read through.

B. READING PROSE TEXTS

When he judges that the class knows enough of the vocabulary and is familiar enough with the setting or theme of the piece to understand at least the gist of it, the teacher reads the piece over once, fairly quickly. If he has based his introduction on blackboard drawing or a sand-table landscape, he may be able to read the piece over and rely on the scene brought to his pupils' minds in this way to interpret what he reads and hold their eyes while he reads. He may point to objects mentioned as he reads about them. For the first reading their books are better shut, so that they can concentrate fully on what he reads as he reads it.

The teacher may have decided that the piece contains too many new words for him to introduce them all conveniently in his preparation; if so, he can make a list of the most important, the most generally useful ones, and introduce them first. The less important ones he may divide up to bring into prominence successively, a few at a time, at each reading. In this way each reading may have new interest and there will never be too many new words at any one time for the pupil to grasp.

I have found that reading the piece over aloud several times, with a break here and there to illustrate the use of a new word and to repeat it several times over to make its sound familiar, is the best way to help my pupils to understand the piece and know it well; sometimes I pause for words to be filled in by the class, perhaps pointing to a detail in a picture to suggest the word. After several readings we open our books and individuals are asked to read aloud, a sentence each, quickly, with no pauses between sentences. After the first reading, each reader can read two sentences, after the second, three, and so on.

If the period comes to an end before the class have read it aloud they can be asked to read it over several times silently at home before coming to the next lesson. It can also be suggested that they ask questions at home about the topic, so that they have some ideas for discussion when the time comes.

If the piece has been chosen by the teacher as suitable for his class at the stage they have reached because it involves the learning of new material but does not contain too many difficulties to the point of being discouraging, there may not be any words at all—not even unimportant ones—which have been left unintroduced when the piece is read through for the first time; but in the last year of work, when preparing for public examinations, it is often impossible to choose pieces precisely graded to the capacities of particular classes.

In reading sentences of unusual construction, one can substitute, in the first one or two readings, an equivalent sentence of simpler construction; as soon as one sees from the reactions of the pupils that they have understood the sentence, one goes back to the reading of the sentence as it is in the text, possibly reading both—one after the other—if it is particularly difficult, as a transition. I always make it a rule to follow every simplification, abridgement, or gloss with a return to the original words of the text, because all these aids are designed, not to bring the ideas of the piece within reach of the class in a simplified form, or to provide the class with a cheap substitute, but to take them to the original. It is not to bring the text down to their level but to raise them up to the level of the text.

C. STUDYING A TEXT: STAGE III—DISCUSSION

The third stage consists primarily of discussion but may include rereading of the piece. The teacher may then increase his pupils' understanding of the niceties of language, noting the correct use of words, subtlety in the interpretation of words, the superiority of one word to another, in a particular use and context. He may perceive evidences of tone and intention, sometimes from the style of writing, sometimes from the use of one word rather than another. This is the stage at which real study of the text takes place; it is the stage at which discussion and exploration of the text is interesting, at which interest in the skill and personality of the author begins to justify some further research by a group of the class. It is the stage when the teacher can talk about the social and historical background of the piece, if he thinks it desirable. This background information has more value and significance after the piece has become familiar to the class; the interest aroused by the piece gives the subject a place and a relevance in the minds of the pupils and arouses interest in the personality of the author.

THE ROLE OF CO-OPERATIVE WORK IN THE STUDY OF TEXTS

A. THE INITIATION OF GROUP WORK

A good deal of the work of presenting texts, and especially the presenting of information and background which can carry the necessary vocabulary and sentence patterns for understanding them—besides opening up the subjects to the interest of the class—can be delegated to groups. While this sort of work is new the teacher may present the first few pieces himself and then say: "Now, supposing we were to ask a group to prepare the class for reading these pieces, what would we tell them to do?" The class would then look for the words which had not been met before and make a list of them, they would discuss how many of the class had heard of the subject before, and if a certain amount of geographical knowledge was required how much they could expect to be already known. On the blackboard they would work out a set of instructions for each piece, and invite groups to prepare dialogues or questions suitable for a preparatory session. These could be tried out on the class at a later lesson and criticized.

With this experience behind them groups can be invited to volunteer for the presentation of other pieces, either being left to work out the material for themselves or being given assignments—possibly on work-cards—by the teacher. Each group can then have the experience of facing difficulty and unravelling possibly tortuous sentences, but no one individual or group has too much of it; the other pieces in the rest of the book are taken care of by other groups. They prepare dialogues and simple dramatizations that lead into the text, with or without a sand-table landscape; they may lead into these with short two- or three-minute talks—perhaps more than one of them—to give description or background, they may begin with questions to bring out or discover the knowledge of the class. Scripts can be prepared in which new words are used six or seven times each. The whole process may be performed to the teacher before it is tried on the class.

Criticism, by the rest of the class and the teacher, of its effectiveness as a means of preparing the class to read and understand the piece and its subject, will draw attention to the essentials of what is required. The class may be expected to find out that the actual reading of the piece should not be made duller than necessary by being summarized beforehand or unduly postponed. They can be brought to see what is required; that they need as much knowledge of the language and subject of the piece as they would have in the middle of a book in their own language. They can be helped to see that the preparation should be:

(1) Linguistic
(2) Factual

and that it should be only as long and as elaborate as it needs to be to do its job effectively. If a group presents a piece badly other groups may be invited to try to deal with the same piece better.

B. CULTIVATION OF RESPONSIBILITY IN THE GROUP

During the first few attempts at presenting prose texts co-operatively the teacher will probably have to direct operations and be prepared to carry on at any moment, but if he selects a group containing the ablest and most enterprising boys for the pioneering work—possibly redistributing them as leaders of other groups afterwards—he should soon be able to keep his active intervention to the rehearsals, and resign the leadership in front of the class to the leader of the group. If each group can provide two or three leading personalities, it may present each of the first two or three pieces under a different leader. This is desirable from the point of view of the members of the group, but as they are performing a service for the form as a whole, the efficiency of this service must be the over-riding consideration; keeping the same leader for each of the two or three pieces presented may help to ensure this. Similarly, although the responsibility for the presentation of a piece will be with the group, the teacher will be always ready to intervene and save them from disaster, or merely to report in a louder, clear voice what otherwise might be inaudible. This sort of intervention should be designed to cover up faults, as far as possible, and give the group encouragement but not rob them of responsibility and initiative; to give the groups the feeling that they have a valuable and powerful ally, not an overwhelming and overawing—and possibly scornful —rival.

C. THE USE OF THE GROUP TO LEAD DISCUSSION AND PROVIDE SPECIAL KNOWLEDGE

The early reading of the piece is probably best done by and under the direction of the teacher; the group stands aside, prepared to supply information when it is asked for. It can split up and take over the supervision of readings from the piece by other groups, at a later stage. They can also take over from the teacher the work of helping the odd backward boy or girl to get extra practice in reading the piece or of going over the meanings of difficult passages.

After the piece has been read through sufficiently often for it to be familiar to everybody, the group may take over leadership of the discussion of the piece and the points of interest that arise out of it. If there is time, the success of the discussion may be increased by the group working out with the teacher in advance the main lines of discussion. If the teacher notices that more pupils would like to express opinions on the piece than there is time for, he may divide the class into groups and split up the presentation group among them to lead further discussion. In this way every member of the group is given an opportunity to lead the discussion of another group or act as an expert consultant to the group. This gives experience in responsibility, and incentive to aspire to it, but also spreads the special knowledge of the group widely through the class.

CONCLUSION

Helping the pupil from the elementary use of the language, with a limited vocabulary and simple constructions, to the understanding of reading material written for native speakers of the language, is not easy; the teacher gives himself a greater chance of success if he delegates what responsibility he can to the members of his class. The responsibility for learning the language is essentially theirs, even if the teacher seems to carry it on their behalf. To pass it on to them in the last years of their course is an important element in the process of preparing them for independent use of the language after they have left school.

The essentials of the way of working are the careful preparation of the class for reading the piece by discussion, led, either by the teacher, or by a group from the class; this discussion lays foundations for the piece in the knowledge of the class and leads up to introductory material—narrative, dialogue, drama or discussion—which will ensure that all the most important vocabulary and the main ideas of the piece are familiar before they are read.

No important words apart from those best grasped from their use in the piece, should be met for the first time in reading the piece through; the reading of the piece should, on no account, be a succession of explanations of words. It should be quick and well understood because the words will not only be understood but fairly familiar. If the teacher studies every text anew with an open mind every time he teaches it his presentation and reading will be fresh. There must be spontaneity in teaching and reading and a new approach, as if he were reading the piece for the first time, however often he may have taught it. This calls for great concentration but he can get a fresh view of the piece by seeing it through the eyes of the group that presents it.

The discussion of the piece and the ideas arising from it can carry the class when there is a background of common consciousness of the piece and its main tenor. The discussion, if it is wisely directed, can also bring out the meaning of whatever was not precisely understood before. It does not follow that because some words may not be clearly understood at the first reading, and because we may be content with the pupils' getting the general drift of the piece at first, that there should

I I

The Teaching of Poetry

A. THE VALUE OF TEACHING POETRY IN A FOREIGN LANGUAGE COURSE

The fashion for tidy language syllabuses, with carefully graded structures and vocabulary, has made some teachers question the wisdom of retaining poetry in an economical course. They say that all merely ornamental, unessential material must go, and suggest that poetry can be justified on sentimental and traditional grounds only. They speak of vagueness, unusual word order, poetic diction, three or four words where one would do, and sentimentality. It is impossible to deny that these words apply to a great deal of the poetry which is used for elementary language teaching at present, and if that were the only material available no sensible person would disagree with this verdict. Even those who might wish to dispute this view of poetry and insist on its retention must take these objections seriously enough to let some of the old favourites of the classroom go, and justify the inclusion of what they feel they can defend for its terseness, urgency, natural speech rhythms and strikingly memorable phrases. This is quite possible if we look for material among traditional songs and rhymes that have stood the criticism of generations, and reject everything which is diffuse, sentimental and trivial.

1. The Aesthetic and Intuitive Sides of the Personality

In conducting a school course we are responsible for the all-round development of the whole personality; we must provide something for all types of mind and ability, not just the intellect and the predominantly intellectual person. Not only are there plenty of people who are not intellectual, but even the predominantly intellectual person has other sides to his personality which need opportunity for development. We can take the medieval classification of personality into sanguine, choleric, melancholic and phlegmatic, or the similar classification by Jung of thinking, feeling, sensation and intuition—with introverted and extroverted modifications of each—to remind ourselves of the need for our teaching to take into account not only individual differences but differences of type. Academic courses and methods of dealing with experience do not suit every type of mind and personality. Not everyone reacts exclusively in one way; though in many people one type of reaction predominates, most of us react in a complex blend of several, or perhaps all, of the four types of Jung's classification, while an overt or conscious extrovert shows balancing introversive behaviour in his unconscious or intuitive life, and vice versa.

Jung has devoted a book to the subject, which cannot be summarized here,[1] but we can remember that poetry makes its appeal in a very special way to the aesthetic and intuitive sides of the personality. Poetry makes a particularly strong appeal to the introverted personality, giving shape and integration to his fantasy. In the form of declamation it also gives a vehicle of expression to the extrovert. Dr. Herbert Read[2] has used Jung's categories very interestingly to compare children's painting and establish classifications which can help the teacher to diagnose the personality traits of his pupils.

Although the scientist is usually thought of as peculiarly an intellectual type of person, the kind of thinking he requires for original discoveries in science is more like the creative thinking of the painter and the poet than the categorizing,

---

[1] C. G. Jung, *Psychological Types*, Routledge and Kegan Paul.
[2] H. Read, *Education through Art*, Faber.

logical, tidying-up type of thinking of the same scientist, or another, who fits what has been discovered into the scheme of scientific knowledge. Even the future scientist, therefore, is the better for a training in the aesthetic and intuitive types of thinking that are encountered in the experience of poetry. A purely factual, analytical course of study has been recognized to be an impoverished and sterile form of education, in that crafts and painting have been given a more and more prominent part to play in education in recent years. The study of poetry gives a further opportunity for those elements of the personality to develop which may remain undeveloped in a narrowly intellectual curriculum; it can help us to integrate them into the process of development of all-round, mature people.

There seems to be a special value in poetry in a foreign language in opening up the fantasy and giving release to inhibited and excessively introverted types. This may be because the inhibitions and reticences have been acquired in association with the home and the mother tongue in early childhood. In a second language one seems to be unobserved by one's own family. Perhaps, too, there is the appeal of putting on fancy dress in declaiming poetry in a foreign language. Aristotle considered that to achieve catharsis through dramatic poetry there must be detachment, and pointed out the value of the chorus in achieving this detachment. Possibly poetry in a foreign language is given this detachment by its being further removed from the reader's or declaimer's centres of consciousness than it would be in the home language, and the reader or hearer is thereby helped to achieve catharsis. I am told by my Indian friends that where, as in some Indian languages, there are tabus and inhibitions in the home society and literature, the learning of poetry in English gives special satisfaction and release, expression for what must otherwise remain unexpressed, and gives corresponding joy. This, they say, is part of the explanation of the charm of English literature for Indians.

2. *We can Confront Reality and Human Problems Directly and Economically*

The poet writes a poem to express objectively, and achieve catharsis through, a strongly felt emotion aroused by and given meaning through some experience or suffering. If he does not feel strongly about the experience, he is unlikely to write a poem, or at any rate the poem—if written for the sake of writing a poem rather than to crystallize out an attitude to an experience—will not, according to this view, be a very compelling or vital one. The poem is similar to the pearl created in the oyster-shell as a result of an irritation or disturbance, but it is not only a creation in its own right; it normally embodies an objective picture or reproduction of the event or disturbance which gave rise to it, presented in such a way that the reader can experience the event and the emotion connected with it and thereby achieve catharsis by facing the poet's predicament, with him, through the imagination. The emotion in a good poem is normally heightened and the experience made vivid and memorable with the help of striking imagery, rhythm, rhyme and devices of pattern and arrangement, condensation and contrast, which make it possible to include a great deal more information and imaginatively realized experience in a few lines than could normally be crammed into as many pages of a prose narrative.

Thus the learner can confront reality through a poem with an immediacy hardly possible through any other medium. If we think of ballads such as *The Demon Lover* or *Lord Randall*, for example, we realize that to present equally powerful dramas so vividly, with so many overtones and undertones, volumes would hardly suffice. In such poems we find reality, but we are also able to transcend it and see beyond the outer skin of reality which is all our eyes can usually grasp in an account of similar goings-on in a newspaper. This is not strange; we must remember that in their day the ballads catered for popular entertainment, education and aesthetic satisfaction in the way the cinema and jazz song hit do now;

most ballads kept their popularity three or four hundred times as long as the most popular film or song hit of today does, namely, several hundred years. They never grew stale, and probably never will grow stale, because they embody permanent values and emotions attached to typical or symbolic actions that are involved in the very nature of being human.

3. *Poetry is a Method of Facing Life with Heightened Emotion*

Uneasiness in the presence of poetry may be due to the fact that poetry moves in a different dimension from that of prose. We can compare prose to walking, moving from one place to another on the surface of the earth, getting the world's daily work done; poetry may be compared then to dancing, rising above the surface of the earth, perceiving its relations, getting a fuller view of its reality.

Because the emotions are often crowded out or banished from school, the product of school, the teacher and many of his pupils, even before the desiccating process is finished, may feel uncomfortable at bringing emotion into the classroom. This is a vicious circle; if there is no place in the school curriculum for the sound development of emotional life, nor occasion for the development of a balanced and mature attitude to questions in which the emotions are involved, the product of the school will not show emotional maturity, nor will he be able to induce a healthy handling or cultivation of the emotions in others. He seems not to notice the emotional poverty of much popular entertainment. Emotional disturbances are on the increase, especially in countries where education is widespread. Is this coupled with the disappearance from the consciousness of the average man of the myths and popular culture—folk songs and tales, the Bible, the *Pilgrim's Progress*, etc.—of his forefathers? With them has gone the emotional training or alignment they helped him to achieve. All this increases the danger involved in passing generation after generation of children through the schools as if there were no emotions and no passions to be canalized and made use of—to be given healthy directions to grow in.

If he hopes to see, at the end of his work, an educated, mature person, the educator must be quite clear in his mind that he is helping a person to develop who may not expect to be supported by the pressure of society to the degree that his forefathers were. Many rules of behaviour, and especially those connected with the emotions, have been subjected to questioning ever since Rousseau, Diderot and Voltaire started to take the attitude of questioning and protest implicit in the Protestant Reformation further than the bounds of religion, towards the evolution of what Paul Tillich, in his *Protestant Era*, has called the autonomous man. The liberalism and free-thinking which have been a logical and even necessary result of this permanently questioning attitude of modern man to his situation, his beliefs and his social structure have produced personalities which, if they are not attached by a firm faith to God, religion, or one of the substitute religions, tend to be solitary and full of anxiety. This has been shown in the evident success of those movements such as Communism, Fascism and National Socialism, that have provided ties for the emotional life of man. If the emotional outlets provided by these substitute religions seem to have a demonic character, it is all the more serious a warning to us that the emotional side of the personality, if left undeveloped or suppressed, does not remain neutral or harmless but can develop cancerously or demonically when at last given an outlet.

If we bring our pupils continuously and systematically to a vital and fully conscious experience of the best poetry that is within their reach, we are giving them a means of emotional expression, and of emotional and aesthetic perception, in that state of heightened awareness that is generated by rhythm and pattern in sound. The formal pattern of the poetry seems to help to give us a frame and a discipline for our emotions; it is almost as if we were treading them out with our pupils together in an imaginative dance. This perhaps helps to explain the attraction and satisfaction of singing in chorus or declaiming verse in chorus. To dance, as it were, thus formally and tragically—or gaily—before a significant and moving account of a human situation gives us the digestive solution in which the experience can be dissolved and absorbed into our total consciousness, that is to say, perceived with more of our consciousness than we are conscious of. To get on the feet and dance the poetry actually is to realize through the body what the mind otherwise achieves directly in the poetry; this is probably one of the best approaches to poetry for children, but as I have no personal experience in this field I can only state that what I have seen of the work of others has impressed me.

Certainly poetry and dance, which were once considered to be intimately connected and are even now practised in alliance in some parts of the world, especially India, seem to help one another and benefit by the restoration of the association in school. The teacher ignores the association if he lets his teaching of poetry become pedestrian, though remembering it need not mean that it becomes florid. To read poetry as though one were reading the fat-stock prices on the radio seems to me, as it seemed to Dylan Thomas, ludicrous; it is to ignore the fact that poetry moves in a different dimension from that of prose. It seems to me, too, that to distinguish between poetry and verse is a mistake. The elements of rhythm and pattern, rhyme and the artifice of rhetoric that belong to poetry distinguish all verse so immeasurably from prose in form, as well as in intention and spirit, that the only useful distinction is between prose and poetry; even here the boundary may be vague, where prose which is poetic and emotional in intention and character approaches the exaltation of poetry.

4. *Poetry is more Memorable than Prose*

It can be no accident that the earliest literature known to us and the folk literature of ballads and popular epics are in verse. The formal arrangement of the rhyme and rhythm—the pattern—make it easier to memorize and to hold in the memory than unpatterned prose. For the same reason, for centuries all drama was in verse, and Shakespeare's and Goethe's utterances in verse on life and its problems are remembered when the words of most philosophers are not. I myself, and many with me, had a great many banal facts about Latin grammar and other indigestible knowledge predigested for me in the form of rhymes that occasionally approach poetry in their innocent pavanning:

> And masculine is found to be
> Hadria the Adriatic sea.

I thought, and still think, that I was escaping from Latin grammar when I was spending my time with them, as a London business man might escape to Brighton for the week-end, and does escape even if he has a few files with him, especially if he keeps them in his suitcase, like lavender to sweeten his intentions. I have remembered the rhymes long after I have forgotten everything else in Latin grammar. If I had learnt any Latin poetry by heart I should remember that, though I have forgotten most of the Latin I learnt at school. I have heard of a book in America that aims to make the opening bars of all the major symphonies of the concert repertory memorable by fitting them with rhyming doggerel. This is so successful that once he has been through the book a sensitive music-lover can never again go to a concert without the fear that one or other of these grotesque verses will leer at him out of the opening bars and lollop after him through the rest of the work; something like this—

> Rumty, tumty, now we're starting
> This will tell you we're mozarting.

Many teachers forget how very much more memorable verse is than prose. Indeed, the definition of poetry cited by W. H. Auden and John Garrett in the introduction to the anthology they prepared for use in schools, *The Poet's Tongue*, is "memorable speech". If verse, or patterned speech, is more memorable than prose, it affects the mind more strongly and attaches itself to us more firmly—sometimes more firmly than we want—it is obvious, then, that we save time and effort by using the device of pattern and rhyme in learning, just as we help ourselves to remember the constellation of Orion by seeing it as a significant pattern.

5. *The Rhythm of Poetry as an Aid to Natural Speech Rhythms*

A rhyme, song or poem, especially if we like the rhythm and sound of it, tends to stick in our minds; we enjoy repeating it or singing it, and it keeps coming into our minds spontaneously. Classes enjoy repeating rhymes and songs in chorus; they may sing the same song every day for a considerable time. A small repertory of songs will give us something to sing after every lesson. In doing so we are obliged to keep the rhythm, so that the unstressed syllables must be hurried over and the stressed syllables uttered with noticeable force. The frequent repetition of the sentences with the swing and rhythm demanded by a poem or song practises the mind and the muscles to work smoothly and skilfully together in the patterns and sonorities of the language; this smooth, instinctive skill is what we usually mean by fluency. There is no other way in which we can get the normal, unexceptionally motivated or compelled, student to repeat so many sentences involving the normal mouth movements and rhythm of the language, without weariness or rebellion.

6. *Repetition of Poetry stores Pattern Sentences in the Mind*

The central problem of language teaching is that of passing representative significant sentences often enough through the mind, when it is in a favourably receptive condition, for them to settle there and become part of the mind's instinctive behaviour. This can be done effectively in two ways: either by the creation or exploitation of situations that really and necessarily recur, and which call for the use of the patterns day after day until they are learnt, or else by their being simply repeated in an attractive and compelling way that engages the mind and spreads out a favourable mental background for them to settle in. When pupil and teacher are tired of one method of absorption, they move on to the other; patterns already learnt through use can be fixed through the repetition of rhymes and songs.

The armoury of pattern sentences which a mind builds up, if it is fed on songs and continually helped to live in them and stretch its language muscles in them, is a very resilient and readily available collection of language units. Sentence patterns learnt in this way are learnt without effort and almost unconsciously; before the pupil is aware that he is doing anything but letting off his high spirits or playing a kind of game, they are firmly embedded in his mind and begin to emerge into his consciousness at unexpected moments. With a very little guidance, or none at all, they begin to enter his speech and writing as viable units of expression. Of course, the teacher will begin with the simpler and more manageable rhymes, and keep, as far as possible, within the range of vocabulary and interests of his pupils, but he will expect a good deal of vocabulary and strangeness of sentiment to be swallowed whole and only looked at critically when the poem has become familiar enough to be held firmly in the mind.

To leave poetry out of a language course is therefore to renounce an extremely effective and labour-saving method of absorbing useful language. It is also to abandon opportunities to humanize and warm what otherwise may be a very dry and chilly traffic in words and information. It is to renounce the hope of delivering us from the pedestrian writing—if not platitudes—of the textbook writer. It is to neglect an important and powerful aid in establishing in the pupil's mind a favourable mental set. It is to stop short of what might be most rewarding in the pupil's experience of the language.

B. POETRY TO BE PRESENTED THROUGH SPEECH

Poetry, like all other language material, must be introduced orally with the books shut, and nothing to distract the attention from—or compete with—the poem through the eye. The same reasons as urge us to present all language material through speech, to the ear first, apply to poetry just as strongly. Poetry is still speech, memorable and eloquent speech, patterned and enticing speech, powerful and insidious speech, incantatory and spell-binding speech, perhaps, but still primarily speech and sound, rather than patterns on paper. There are six additional reasons for presenting poetry through speech and letting its first impact be on the ear, leaving the eye free to see the imagery and not be tied down by trying to decipher print.

1. *Speech is the Traditional Vehicle for Poetry*

Folk poetry has always been passed on by word of mouth; in many countries, still, folk poets travel round from village to village reciting their own and traditional poetry. Homer is supposed to have done it, and there is very little doubt that all early literature took the form of verse which was declaimed. Everyone who has attended a play by Shakespeare and tried to read the same play alone knows how very much more powerful an impression the verse makes on him, and how much easier it is to understand, when he hears it spoken by competent actors than when he has to achieve everything himself through the eyes and his unaided imagination. Delight in listening to poetry seems to be inborn in us. We may lose it by atrophy, but children have usually not yet lost it. Whether or not they lose it may even ultimately depend on us.

2. *Rhyme and Assonance, Alliteration and Rhythm, appeal primarily to the Ear*

Only in recent times has poetry come to be written with the expectation that it will be exclusively read from the page silently; even the most sophisticated eye-poetry has been written on the assumption that the sounds will be imagined in the mind, too, as it is read. As long as a student is uncertain of the pronunciation, rhythm and intonation of a poem, he is quite unable to appreciate or enjoy it; he is without the essential basis of perception of the sound; he certainly cannot be expected to read it fast enough to himself to get a proper impression of the sound in his mind. He needs to hear it read by someone competent to read it fluently and easily if he is to hear the marked rhymes and the rhythmic patterning. We give anyone whose grasp of the language is not yet very sure the most immediately attractive side of a poem if we present him with the sounds first and let their charm draw him into sympathy with the poem.

For the same reason the first introduction to a new poem, or especially a new poet, is best made through the ear, even to someone who knows the language well. I myself found it quite impossible to appreciate or even make contact with the poems of Dylan Thomas until I heard his own readings of them on gramophone records. This was partly because his reading made the meaning clearer to the mind through the ear than my eyes could make it without help, and also because the stream of the reading, pressing inexorably on, made it impossible for me to worry about words or sentences that I could not understand. But it was primarily because I was helped to hear the poems as enchanting patterns of sounds; they were declaimed in a rich, expressive voice that made the best of them as sound and helped me to shelve the question of their meaning. This gave me the initial interest I needed to take more trouble with them and distil out of them, at last, some satisfaction and even a little significance.

3. *Poetry is Easier to understand when Read Aloud by a Good Reader*

When we listen to a poem being read aloud, we pass over whatever is not immediately comprehensible, simply because the mind has no time to arrange it in order, like a hand of cards there is no time to fan out before it is whisked away, and the impression is blotted out by the following words. But we grasp what we can, and the very fleetingness of the impressions causes us to grip tight on what we do catch. This gives a scattered series of focused impressions—some fainter than others—like the visible scraps of a large fresco that has begun to appear from under a covering of whitewash that is slowly flaking off, but unevenly, in patches. If we concentrate very hard on what we can grasp, the patches seem to fuse to indicate a complete and related picture which begins to take shape in the mind and becomes more complete as more of the whitewash peels off; in the same way the opaque areas of the poem gradually become, first translucent, and then transparent, as we concentrate more and more light on them.

When we begin by listening, our ear selects what it can immediately perceive—the familiar forms patterns in the mind—and discards the rest. When we begin by reading, we can see the whole poem in front of us at a glance and nothing can be discarded without an effort of dissociation which the eye is not so well qualified to make as the ear; in this case we normally begin our attack on the poem by worrying and puzzling over what is unfamiliar. This may result in our getting disheartened at the outset and abandoning our attempt to come to terms with the poem. Or else we may find ourselves forced to work so hard to elucidate the meaning that the poem has become stale long before we can confront it as a unified pattern of sound and interest. If this happens, we have—unless some hint of the charm in it bursts on us out of the fog early—no further incentive to try and experience it as sound at all; it is already a puzzle we have solved. We may be content with that; most people are, and poetry never becomes poetry for them.

Read aloud by a fluent and understanding reader who has studied the poem and made up his mind on an interpretation, who helps the listeners to live in the poem by the persuasiveness and eloquence of his reading, who chooses between possible alternative·readings of lines and shows his choice in his intonation, who fortifies his reading with the expression of his face and his gestures, a poem can take·shape in the mind of the listener immediately: this shape will become clearer and more precise with repeated rereadings. If the teacher begins teaching poems in this way, after being used to teaching them by explaining them word by word, he finds that most of the explanations he used to give, or might have given, become superfluous.

4. *The Enthusiasm of the Teacher can be communicated through his Voice*

The printed page, and the teacher's busy midwifery round it, cannot be relied on to produce enthusiasm. The teacher's attempts to explain why a poem is beautiful, or profound, or significant, or morally improving, seldom hit the mark with a reluctant and slightly fogged class, especially if they have not yet formed an impression of the poem, favourable or the contrary. This is not to suggest that the teacher's voice should throb with emotion as he reads it—though this is preferable to his reading it as if he were reading a summary in prose of a government white paper—but a natural and honest enthusiasm should ring out in his voice and sparkle in his eye as he reads. This is important because poetry is enthusiasm. A poet writes no poem—or no successful or moving poem—unless he is enthusiastic about at least his own vision or realization of the subject. Without enthusiasm of some kind there can be no poetry. It is true that the poem may ultimately communicate this heightened feeling of relationship which we call enthusiasm, but the learner is very much helped if he can catch some of it from the tone of voice and the eloquence of his teacher, at the outset.

If the teacher wants to bring out a particular feature in the poem he does so best by reading it and asking the class to listen for something that he thinks they can catch which will bring out the point he wants to deal with; for instance, a change in the pattern of the rhyme scheme, or the rhythm, or the style of writing, that marks a break in the attitude of the poet; or he may simply ask: "How many horses did the man have?" or "What did the briar grow out of?" and leave them to listen for the answer. His eloquent and ringing declamation of the verses, repeated perhaps several times to make it possible for the class to catch what they are to look for, can impress the beauty of sound in the poem indelibly on the minds of the listeners.

Finally, the truest and most significant homage we can pay to a poet's excellence is to read his verses with due care and attention. Unlike the riding of a bicycle, poetry reading does not call for total sobriety, yet the dilation of the nostrils and the labour of the breathing should not be too marked; the intoxication should not exceed what can be induced by the poem itself. The reader should allow himself to be moved by what is intrinsic in the poem, but not by accidental associations or by the sanctity of the theme. Enthusiasm for the subject the poet is writing about is not the same as, and should not guarantee, enthusiasm for the poem as a poem.

5. *The Attention of the Students can be concentrated on the Reading and on the General Effect of the Poem*

If the pupil is allowed to have his book open while the teacher is reading and try to follow with his eye, he will be distracted from whole-hearted and absolute concentration on what is being read. The very fact that the book is open in front of him seems to relieve him from the necessity of absolute concentration, because then the teacher's voice is not the last and only resort; the printed word in front of the eye is a second line of defence that can easily be retreated to, and if nothing important seems to depend on accurate and attentive listening, the effort is unlikely to be made. If we read the poem aloud or recite it, we leave the pupils no other possibility to deal with it but to listen and concentrate all their attention on listening, to strain after it and pursue it, whatever the difficulty. If the pattern of sound is attractive and is often repeated, this concentration will not be an excessive strain, but each fragment of meaning or consciously registered impression will be reward for effort, and incentive to more and intenser concentration.

Quite apart from all these considerations, most pupils are unable to follow with their eyes the words of a poem at the same speed as the teacher can read. Anyone who has watched the eyes of a class following in the book while the teacher reads a new poem aloud to them will have seen that the eyes are all at different points on the page. Any teacher can test this with a class by asking the class to follow with their eyes while he reads an unfamiliar poem aloud to them, and mark with a pencil dot the point they have reached when he stops reading. If he can get them to remember any particular words, sentences or lines that slowed their reading down, he will find that one was held up by puzzling over a word in the first few lines, another found an unusual arrangement of words half-way down the page, and others may have found simply that they could not read so fast without skipping, that in skipping they lost the thread, and in struggling to find it again got left behind.

The quickest and least wasteful way to knowledge of the poem is achieved by the pupil rapidly getting a general idea of the poem, its sound and meaning, without irrelevancies, a preliminary grasp that will prepare the mind for a detailed understanding afterwards. For this the pupil must be trained to concentrate intensively on the teacher's voice and on the general effect of the poem, not allowing himself to be distracted by difficult or unusual words or phrases, or curious spellings. This will have the great advantage of giving the pupil general training in acute and concentrated, in purposeful, listening.

6. *The Pupil will come to his own Silent Reading of the Poem already familiar with the Sounds of it*

If the pupil has heard the poem clearly, rhythmically and impressively read often enough, he will come to his own silent reading of it with the sounds of the poem so ringing in his ears that his reading is hardly more than a recalling of what he has heard. This ensures that the poem runs nimbly through his mind with the correct rhythm and sounds, as an accompaniment to the printed or written representation on paper, while he is running his eye over it for the first time. It will be like the co-ordinating of the sound-track of a film to its action. Reading in a foreign language should, in the early stages, be the reading of familiar sentence patterns and words; even in the advanced stages, reading of the entirely strange should be kept for a small corner of the reading work. Many of those who claim to be quite impervious to poetry may not have had enough opportunity in their youth to hear good poetry read aloud or recited, so that it has never become for them significant sound or the imagination of sound. It has remained, for them, marks on paper.

C. METHODS OF PRESENTATION

Delight in poetry is natural to children. If they fail to take delight in it, it is almost certainly our fault; before they reach adolescence they are living in a stage of development which makes the poetic attitude to life the right one for them. Some of them may lose this attitude as they pass through adolescence into early adult life, but most of them could preserve enough of it to be the basis of a more balanced outlook on life and a healthier all-round development if the training in poetical perception were continued throughout the educational process and even after it. All those who are able to go through life with a keen and developed appreciation of poetry could be helped to keep this approach—their feeling for it as sound—fresh and continually developing if they had formed the habit of reading it aloud and declaiming it whenever possible. This would help to keep the sophisticated taste in poetry more in line with the unsophisticated taste; that is, the connoisseur and the general reader would come together in expecting to enjoy it more keenly and expose themselves to it more profitably by hearing it read aloud or recited.

On the other hand we must recognize that many people who

R

find poetry a bore today find it so because it was presented to them at school as a fancy substitute for something other than poetry; that is, as a story, as a logical argument, as an improving fable, as a lesson, as a picturesque description, that was rendered by the teacher into prose which came to seem to be its proper condition. If the prose summary is equated to the poem, the pupil is justified in saying to himself: "This is simple; this is dull; this is the poem. The poet would have done better to have written it this way; we should have seen at a glance that it wasn't worth bothering about and would have saved ourselves time and trouble." The experience of poetry as a special way of thinking, an attitude to reality, a means of approaching the essence of human behaviour, is missed.

We may make three simple rules:

1. Too much explanation is a mistake.
2. Verbal peculiarities should be passed over.
3. Good art can be allowed to make its own impact.

As art speaks directly to the emotions and the subconscious mind as well as to the conscious mind, we can let the sounds of poetry do their own work. This will lead us to adopt the general procedure outlined in the chapter on the teaching of texts, in which we take care that language and background are made familiar, before the text is approached directly, in a discussion. Or they may simply be taught by the teacher leading up to the subject of the poem, establishing the most important imagery of the poem with the help of drawing on the blackboard or ready-made pictures. The aim must be to put the pupil in possession of the essential imagery and language of the poem in such a way that the first reading of the complete poem by the teacher is a significant experience for him.

There is no need for him to understand every detail or to have an equivalent experience to the experience the teacher may have when he reads it for the first time. The poem can be appreciated and understood at different levels; we must be patient and may be quite satisfied if our pupils appreciate it at their level even when we have finished with it.

They can be expected to appreciate it at our level when they have read as much as we have and lived as long and seen as much of life. It is a mistake to try and squeeze the last drop of meaning from a poem; we do best to let it make its impression gradually, over the course of several lessons, so that more of it reveals itself at each reading. In reading the poem for the first time the teacher may mark the rhythm and the line endings and rhymes rather strongly, for these are what the pupil can perceive and cling on to first, and they give form to the poem in his mind while it is still rather nebulous otherwise. Later readings will become nearer and nearer to normal poetry reading until the poem is quite familiar.

I. THE THREE RULES OF PRESENTATION

It may be useful to explain in a little more detail what is implied by the rule just given that:

(1) *Too much Explanation is a Mistake*

No word should be explained which reveals its own meaning in the context of the poem. No word which adds nothing important to the pupil's grasp of the essential significance of the poem as a whole should be explained in advance or have attention drawn to it during the teaching of the poem. Institutions and customs referred to in the poem which contribute nothing specific to an understanding of that particular poem should be left unexplained, or left to be significant in their application to this poem only.

An example will make this and the first point clearer. After teaching the poem *Gipsy Laddie* I was once taken to task by a training-college lecturer for having neglected my duty in not having explained the word *squire* adequately. I replied that I had said that a squire was a rich man who had a large house, usually just outside a village which was often his property, and he owned land. The lecturer said that this was inadequate;

I ought to have explained the origin of the squirearchy in medieval chivalry and the role he played in relation to the knight. I repudiated such a notion firmly, pointing out that a knowledge of all this would add nothing at all to the pupil's understanding or appreciation of the poem; worse, it would distract him, by its irrelevance, from his concentration on the poem. After this experience I reviewed my whole manner of presenting that poem, and saw that my explanation of the word *squire* was quite unnecessary, because all the essential information for the pupil to look for is given in the poem itself. Now, when I teach that poem I put a boy by the blackboard to write down each piece of information as it comes out of the poem:

(1) A man.
(2) He has a servant.
(3) He has at least two horses.
(4) He can ride all night, so he must be strong.
(5) He has plenty of money, etc.

Examples of the kind of word which need not be taught, but just an equivalent given, if necessary—either in English or the home language—are the words *jocund* in Wordsworth's *Daffodils*, or *scullion* in Yeats' *The Hawk*. These words are not common enough to justify their being brought into the pupil's active vocabulary, yet, by being repeated often in the pupil's repetition of the poem, they will be learnt in their context there. Thus the teacher is relieved of any responsibility towards unusual words, except in so far as they contribute to the meaning of the poem and have to be given value as counters in the pupil's understanding.

(2) *Verbal Peculiarities may be Passed Over*

Such forms as *hath*, *doth*, *yon* or *thou* and *thee*, or the spelling of *chant* as *chaunt* in *The Solitary Reaper* can either be ignored altogether, or, if the members of the class ask about them, they can simply be said to be variants of the normal word and left at that. Everyone knows dialect or obsolete variants of words in common use in his own language which can, if necessary, be referred to. Words such as *behold* or *yon* can be shown simply by pointing as we say them. If their function, if not their meaning, is clear, they will not delay perception of the poem; discussion of them as words can be left until the poem has been learnt, when time spent on them will not muffle or delay the full impact of the poem. In *The Demon Lover* the words "and gurly grew the sea" can have the same treatment, the tone of voice indicating grim harshness and menace.

(3) *Art can be allowed to make its own Impact*

In recognizing that most good art makes its own impact directly on the emotions and the subconscious mind, we may be content with seeing that the pupil has the key to what lies in the poem, but we do not necessarily turn it in the lock for him. He must learn to face and deal with poetry himself, so it is always better to err on the side of explaining too little than too much. For instance, a chorus such as that of the ballad *Gipsy Laddie*,

> Rattle-tum a gipsum, gipsum
> Rattle-tum a gipsum Davy,

has a most important part to play as a sort of drone or accompaniment to the poem. It suggests to me the dancing of the gipsies, as a sort of ironical counterpoint and commentary in unreasonable and unreasoning incoherence at the back of the drama, but it does not state this directly, and it would be a mistake to say that it does. The most we might do is to ask individuals in the class what it suggested to them and pool our impressions, rejecting those that seem unjustified but using it as an opportunity to direct the attention of the class to the part which can be played by pure sound in a poem.

When we present poetry therefore it should be allowed to make, as far as possible, its own impact; the penetration of the words into the mind should be quick and sure. Yet even in our own language we never grasp all the implications and seldom even the whole surface meaning of an important poem at the first reading. The teacher must be patient and suitably modest. It is enough if he puts the pupil in contact with the poem in such a way that it captures his attention and arouses some delight, enough to entice him into further and closer contact with it. If he is satisfied that the pupil can do the rest of the work that remains to be done, the teacher need do no more; but the appreciation and understanding of poetry, and all-round experience of the poetic penetration into reality depends on an extremely alert and accurately focused perception of words. This means that the teacher must sharpen his tools for his pupils before he has to call upon them to use them on the poem; he uses the words and the sentence patterns of the poem on clearly perceived objects, or on experience that he brings to the class, either directly or at second hand through the imagination, until he finds that enough are understood for the poem to be followed when he reads it. He will only do as much of this work as is necessary; he will not bore his class with repetition and emphasis of what they already know well.

II. READING THE POEM

When he judges that the tools will do their work effectively he turns them on to the poem itself by reading it right through once; then he reads it verse by verse, bringing out, focusing and establishing the meaning of the successive sentences in the mind rather than explaining. Here is an example for a third-year English class:

> It was late in the night when the squire came home.
>
> —What is late in the night? and, if no one answers—
> At what time do you go to bed, A?
> I go to bed at half-past nine or ten.
> At what time do you go to bed, B?
> I go to bed about ten o'clock.

Right, then we may say that eleven or twelve is late, can't we? If you go to bed at eleven or twelve, you go to bed late.

C, at what time then do you think the squire came home?

—I suppose he came home about eleven or twelve o'clock.

It was late in the night when the squire came home, enquiring for his lady.—Who was he asking for, D?

If D is unable to answer, we repeat the couplet, asking everyone to listen very carefully.

It was late in the night when the squire came home
Enquiring for his lady.

What question did the squire ask?
—He asked where his lady was.
And who answered the question? Listen carefully:

It was late in the night when the squire came home
Enquiring for his lady,
The servant made a sure reply

—The servant answered,
And what did the servant answer? Listen again:

It was late in the night when the squire came home
Enquiring for his lady
The servant made a sure reply:
She's gone with the Gipsum Davy.

What did the servant answer, E?
He answered that she'd gone with the Gipsum Davy.

The teacher then repeats the verse and may ask the same or simpler questions, addressing other members of the class. He may ask if the squire came home alone; whether anyone was waiting for him, and if so, who; whether his wife was waiting for him to come home, and so on. He may then ask one member of the form to take the role of the squire—asking him perhaps to write out the word *squire* in bold letters to point to on the blackboard or to hold up or attach to himself as a label—and another to be the servant. Another can be the milk-white steed, and can be questioned about his speed, or others can be asked if he is speedier or faster than the black one. This must be understood to be merely a convenient way of establishing the identity of the people in the ballad, not necessarily a dramatization, though that may follow. No time should be lost on unnecessary questions.

1. *Further Reading*

When the whole poem has been presented in this way it may be read over by the teacher again two or three times; as he does so he may pause to give the pupils opportunity to fill in words and phrases, perhaps the rhyming words at the end of the lines and other key words. In time, members of the class may be able to repeat alternate lines, singly or in chorus, and finally whole verses. Now is the time for the books to be opened, or the poem to be written on the blackboard, to be read and then copied out by the class, if it is not in their textbooks. If it is in their textbooks, it is best to open them just before the end of the first lesson on it, when it has become fairly familiar to the ear. The teacher may then read it through aloud once or twice more, according to its difficulty, and leave his pupils to read it through three or four times, silently, at home. It may then be repeated in a later lesson, perhaps after a short interval of a few days; the pupils may read it aloud several times, singly and in chorus; perhaps only five or ten minutes will be spent in subsequent lessons, until it is really very familiar indeed. Finally, it may be practised for speaking dramatically in chorus, or it may be dramatized.

2. *Discussion and Expression*

Then the third stage, equivalent to the discussion stage of dealing with prose texts, may begin. This may well start out from discussion of parallel incidents within the knowledge or experience of members of the class. After a little discussion the teacher may ask the class to write a short composition on the lines of the poem, as shown in the chapter on Composition. When, for example, we ask them to do this for Wordsworth's poem about the daffodils, "I wandered lonely as a cloud", the degree to which their own experiences are truly parallel will tell us how far they have understood the poem. If, for instance, the word *bliss* cannot properly be used in connection with the pupil's experience, it can be shown not to be genuinely parallel, although perhaps in some ways similar.

Once the poem has been taught it can be constantly referred to. The poems learnt in a language course may epitomize and stand for the human predicament, and provide insight into human conduct and thought, so that they can serve as examples and easily citable and portable specimens of human behaviour and attitudes.

Conclusion

To sum up the process of teaching a poem, we see three main stages, as in the teaching of prose texts:

1. *Preparation*, consisting in equipping the pupil for a quick grasp of the main outline of the poem from the first reading of it, by familiarizing the most important words and expressions and ensuring that the ideas involved are not beyond his reach.

2. *Presentation* and reading, including a great deal of re-reading, and calling for intense concentration on the words of the poem, any paraphrase or summary being followed by a return to the actual words of the poem. This reading must be relatively quick, the first reading not being attempted until there is reasonable certainty that most of the class will be able to follow the essentials of the poem and establish in their minds a correct general impression of its significance and scope. Books should not be opened until the poem has been made thoroughly familiar to the ear and there is likely to be no danger of conflict between what is imagined in the ear as it is read and the printed word.

3. *The Discussion Stage*, which should be based on a thorough knowledge of the text of the poem, and be designed

to lead to a deeper all-round perception of the poem and the ideas it embodies, and to expression.

After all this work has been completed, the poem may be considered as learnt, and the teacher may leave most of the rest of the work on it to the pupil. He can economize effort and time, however, by making use of the furniture which the pupil's mind has, so that the poems learnt are continually referred to and repeated, as illustrations of discussion and further reading. In this way they are really incorporated into the habit of thought of the pupil and make an important contribution to his growth; they help to give form and conciseness to his expression.

D. THE CHOICE OF POETRY

No care and skill in the presentation of poetic material can help us if the poems we choose are trivial or tasteless. Equally, they should not be bad, or dishonestly written, sentimental or cheap. The choice of the best and most memorable poems that can be made use of to accompany the language course is supremely important. We should never choose a poem only because it is easy; though the majority of the poems to be found in many textbooks seem to have been chosen on that account alone.

On the other hand, complexity of thought or abstraction, or excessive strangeness of idea, should obviously be avoided. The teacher may have to give up teaching some of his own favourites, or at least he may have to reserve them until the course has been finished, and his own enthusiasm and exuberance can carry his pupils over the difficulties; or they can just be enjoyed for their sound. Whatever is excellent in its own way, whatever is sincere, whatever tries within its limits, however narrow they be, to convey a genuine emotion in an honest and unsentimental way, may be suitable. It is not quite natural for a genuine poet with an academic education to write very simply, though, like Blake, he may write what seems simple on the surface. For this reason we do best to look for suitable poetry for the early stages of a language course among folk poetry, folk-songs and rhymes. Nursery rhymes, if they are childish or have childish associations, may not be suitable for older children to learn, even in a foreign language. But not all nursery rhymes are intrinsically childish; many have begun their existence as topical or political satire, and have only been consigned to the nursery when the point and topicality of the satire have been forgotten and lost.

> Ride a cock horse
> To Banbury Cross
> To see a fine lady on a white horse
> With rings on her fingers
> And bells on her toes
> She shall have music
> Wherever she goes.

Or:

> I had a little nut-tree
> Nothing would it bear
> But a silver nutmeg
> And a golden pear;
> The King of Spain's daughter
> Came to visit me,
> And all for the sake
> Of my little nut-tree.

This is fantasy; it is not intrinsically childish, but we give it to children because we know that they like fantasy.

Simple Folk-songs and Rhymes

In any case, we are on safer ground when we use normal folk-songs and counting and other repetitive rhymes, including sea shanties—the work songs formerly used by sailors to make their work tolerable before machinery began to do the hard work for them. Such rhymes and songs are usually simple, with plenty of repetition and expressed in normal

English; they have been sung by generations of grown-up people to lighten the monotony of journeys or repetitive work, and there is nothing childish about them. Grown-up people can sing them still with delight:

> One man went to mow
> Went to mow a meadow;
> One man and his dog
> Went to mow a meadow.
>
> Two men went to mow
> Went to mow a meadow;
> Two men, one man and his dog
> Went to mow a meadow.

This has a simple tune which is easily learnt, even by unmusical people; it achieves a humorous effect by means of its limitless and ridiculous repetitions. Another song of this kind helps us, incidentally, to teach a form of the conditional sentence, so that, when we come to it in the book, it is already familiar and we have saved ourselves and our pupils a lot of trouble:

> Ten green bottles hanging on the wall,
> Ten green bottles hanging on the wall;
> If one green bottle should accidentally fall,
> There'd be nine green bottles hanging on the wall.

This, too, is very quickly learnt because of its repetitions, and, for some reason, people of all ages are willing to go on repeating it frequently for long periods of time.

A sea shanty which is always popular and can easily be taught is "What shall we do with the Drunken Sailor?" While the teacher is familiarizing it, he can be content with the class singing only the chorus, joining in punctually as he finishes each verse; in this way they learn it by hearing the verses again and again, concentrating on them so as to be able to join in at the right moment:

What shall we do with the drunken sailor,
What shall we do with the drunken sailor,
What shall we do with the drunken sailor,
　　Early in the morning?

(*Chorus*) Hooray, and up she rises,
　　　　Hooray, and up she rises,
　　　　Hooray, and up she rises,
　　　　Early in the morning.

The great advantage of daily repetition of this kind of
rhyme is that it forces the pupil to adopt the natural rhythm of
English speech with its regular beat of stressed syllables, unstressed syllables up to almost any number being precisely but
rapidly articulated between the stresses.

There are many more such simple songs, with strong
rhythm, easy choruses and plenty of repetition that can be
taught in the first year or two of learning English. They will
help very much towards fluency and give an essential introduction to rhythmic speech. Reading them and reciting them
regularly are the best preparation for the reading and enjoyment of poetry, and they lead eventually into undoubted
poetry. The teacher should choose what seems to him to be
within the reach of the particular class he is teaching. If he
finds that a particular song or poem does not appeal to the
class, he should drop it and try something else; he should
never insist on his own taste being accepted. Once he has
established a reputation with a class, however, for giving them
what they grow to like, he may be able to say: "I should like
you to be patient and give this poem a trial, as I like it, and
used to like it when I was your age. I think you will like it
when you know it better, but if you don't, we can leave it
alone and not repeat it." If he finds this happening too often,
he should revise his estimate of what the class can take and
perhaps give them something simpler and less demanding.
I have found affected triviality or tastelessness worse enemies
to deal with than difficulty; children will accept a good deal of

difficulty or even absolute incomprehensibility if there are attractions in the sound, rhythm or imagery that compensate for some intellectual bafflement. I never enquired too closely what phrases such as "buckle my shoe" meant, or what a "tuffet" was when I was a child; I enjoyed the rhymes for their sound and took them on trust.

More Poetical Folk-songs

The gap between simple rhymes and what most people mean when they speak of poetry can easily and suitably be bridged by such folk-songs and ballads as *Early One Morning, Lord Randall, Gipsie Laddie* or the *Raggle Taggle Gipsies, Lord Lovell, Green Grow the Rushes O, The Twelve Days of Christmas, The Lover's Tasks, Billy Boy*—in any one of its three well-known versions—*Where are you going to, my Pretty Maid? The Seeds of Love, Green Broom,* and the *Willow Song,* either in Shakespeare's version as adapted for Desdemona in *Othello* or in the original folk-song version. All these are simple, all are true poetry, some of them very moving, yet they are often neglected by the writer of textbooks for teaching English in a foreign language.

At a higher level of difficulty, and also poetic intensity, but still simple in expression, we have such ballads as *The Demon Lover,* or carols, as *The Holly and the Ivy, I sing of a Maiden, This Endris Night* and *The First Nowell.* With these we can couple the simpler poems of Blake, Shakespeare's songs and Wordsworth's better simple poetry—

> O Rose thou art sick,
> The invisible worm
> That flies in the night
> In the howling storm,
>
> Has found out thy bed
> Of crimson joy,
> And its dark secret love
> Does thy life destroy—

and we shall find that we have brought our pupils to the heart of poetry and the poetic way of thinking, almost without noticing the gradation from simple boisterous rhymes and jingles; the training on them will be seen to have been an essential introduction to the perception of poetry and fluent reading of it.